REGARD FOR THE OTHER

Regard for the Other

AUTOTHANATOGRAPHY IN ROUSSEAU, DE QUINCEY, BAUDELAIRE, AND WILDE

E. S. BURT

FORDHAM UNIVERSITY PRESS

New York   2009

Copyright © 2009 Fordham University Press

Library of Congress Cataloging-in-Publication Data

Burt, E. S.
Regard for the other : autothanatography in Rousseau, De
Quincey, Baudelaire, and Wilde / E.S. Burt.—1st ed.
p.   cm.
Includes bibliographical references and index.
ISBN 978–0-8232–3090–7 (cloth : alk. paper)—
ISBN 978–0-8232–3091–4 (pbk. : alk. paper)
1. Authors—Biography—History and criticism.
2. Autobiography.   3. Other (Philosophy) in literature.
4. Self in literature.   5. Identity (Psychology) in
literature.   6. Death in literature.   7. Baudelaire, Charles,
1821–1867—Criticism and interpretation.   8. Rousseau,
Jean-Jacques, 1712–1778—Criticism and interpretation.
9. De Quincey, Thomas, 1785–1859—Criticism and
interpretation.   10. Wilde, Oscar, 1854–1900—Criticism
and interpretation.   I. Title.
PN452.B87 2009
809'.93592—dc22
2009008224

Printed in the United States of America
11   10   09   5 4 3 2 1
First edition

CONTENTS

AE   *Autrement qu'être ou au-delà de l'essence*
AP   *Artificial Paradises*
C   *Correspondance*
CL   *Complete Letters*
DP   *De Profundis*
EC   *The Epistemology of the Closet*
GD   *The Gift of Death*
HAH   *Humanisme de l'autre homme*
OC   *Oeuvres complètes* (Baudelaire or Rousseau)
OE   *The Confessions of an English Opium-Eater*
PDG   *The Picture of Dorian Gray*

In this book I have used the customary *italic* to indicate emphasis. Where the word or passage requiring emphasis appeared within material that was already in italic for another reason, ***bold italic*** indicates emphasis.

ACKNOWLEDGMENTS

Because this book had two widely separated periods of gestation, with one piece dating from an early monograph on Rousseauian autobiography that never saw light of day, I am overdue with thanks to some of those friends and colleagues who generously read, commented on, encouraged, or otherwise contributed to the writing of some part of this book. I have of each contributor a distinct and grateful memory: Tim Bahti, David Carroll, Cynthia Chase, Jonathan Culler, Suzanne Gearhart, Neil Hertz, Peggy Kamuf, Richard Klein, J. Hillis Miller, Kevin Newmark, Barbara Spackman, Janie Vanpée, and Andrzej Warminski. A Morse Fellowship from Yale University supported the writing of the early chapter; a grant from the School of Humanities at the University of California, Irvine supported the writing of the rest. Early versions of several essays in the volume have previously appeared in print: "Developments in Character: 'The Children's Punishment' and 'The Broken Comb'" *Yale French Studies*, No. 69 (1985); "Regard for the Other: Embarrassment in the *Quatrième promenade*," *L'Esprit créateur*, vol. XXXIX, no. 4 (winter) 1999; "The Shape before the Mirror: Autobiography and the Dandy in Baudelaire," which appeared under the title "A Cadaver in Clothes: Autobiography and the Dandy," *Romanic Review*, 96, no. 1 (winter 2005); "Hospitality in Autobiography: Levinas *chez* De Quincey," *English Literary History*, 71 (winter 2005). I gratefully acknowledge permission to use this material.

This book has benefited greatly from the support of my family—John and Terry, Emily and Larry, Sarah and Mario, Walter and Claire, Nathan and Lynda, Emily, Craig, David, and Mary Annah—and most of all, that of my patient son, Nathanael, whose gentle irony helped remind me of priorities whenever my obsession with a few long-dead writers threatened to get in the way of an important soccer game or tennis match.

Too many on the mental list of those to whom I owe gratitude are no longer here to be thanked: To them, to all the dear dead, I dedicate this book.

Regard for the Other

A Clutch of Brothers:
Alterity and Autothanatography

I shall therefore confess both what I know of myself and what I do not
know. For even what I know about myself I only know because your
light shines upon me: and what I do not know about myself I shall
continue not to know until I see you face to face and *my dusk is noonday.*

AUGUSTINE, *Confessions* X, 5

Between us, I have always believed . . . that the absence of filiation
will have been our chance. A bet placed on an infinite, which is to say
a voided, genealogy, in the end the condition for loving one another.

JACQUES DERRIDA, *La Carte postale*

In the numerous studies that have been devoted to autobiography in the
past 30 years, surprisingly few take on directly the question of the other.
The reason for the surprise is simple enough: One can hardly envision the
self without the other against which it is defined or an autobiography that
does not involve the other both in its narrative and as the one to whom
the "I" addresses itself in its act of confessing. In representing itself, the I
must not only represent the others encountered in life, but must also address that representation to another. What is more, such representations
are confided to an indeterminate third thing: a text, which is to say, to an
autobiographical writing both fictional and documentary in nature.[1] There
is thus, if not exactly a third other, at any rate a third alterity to contend
with whose effects the autobiographer has to calculate. Why, then, has
there been so little direct critical attention to the problem?

   A look at the term in a dictionary suggests one reason why it is difficult
to center a study on the other in autobiography. There is a paradoxical
logic to the concept that makes it all but impossible to make it a proper
object of study. By the other, says the *Oxford English Dictionary* (OED), we
mean "that one of two which is remaining after one is taken, defined, or
specified." The other is its remainder, what is left after the operation of
determining. But when, having seized one through determination and left

the other, we then return to seize the other remaining, that other is imme-diately determined and becomes the one to a new other left undetermined. The other is always the other for a particular I, and as such, is no longer undetermined, no longer quite so other. It becomes the other for the sub-ject: its object. We have learned from Levinas, among others, to suspect the subject for its reductive violence against the other. As the undeter-mined, the other as such always recedes from representation.

Ought we then simply to forget about it, to give up the attempt to seize the other that must recede by virtue of our attempt? Politically oriented studies of autobiography have made us very aware of the stakes of such neglect. The operation by which the one is seized and the other left as a remainder involves political consequences for the "others" left out of the representational field. We cannot conceive of an ethics that does not pay attention to the I's responsibility for the other or a psychology that sets aside an experience of others necessary for, if also wounding to, the sub-ject's narcissistic self-sufficiency. For this is the other part of the paradox: The self cannot entirely leave behind the other, either, but finds itself tied to it as its other, even after its separation through determination. Given our object of the autobiographical text, therefore, we are bound to interest ourselves in alterity. To study the self, independent of any relations to it, would be to forget about the scar left when it is separated from that other in the process of self-constitution. And it is showing the self with its scars, suggests Jean-Jacques Rousseau in one preliminary sketch of the *Confes-sions*, that distinguishes the truth from the studied half-truth.[2] Truthful autobiography leaves at the least traces of its leaving out the other. Critical studies of the I in autobiography have thus always had to suppose an other against which the I is determined. There can have been no studies of auto-biography that did not consider the subject's regard for the other, both its concern for the determinate others it brings into its representational field, and with regard to an undetermined other it holds as a secret, leaves out in constituting itself as subject.

Given then that there are already many studies of autobiography, all of which must in this hypothesis have considered the other in their discussion of the I, why write another one? The answer to that question requires that this book be situated with respect to earlier criticism in the field, to show where despite the swelling number of works about autobiography in the past 40 years, there is a perceptible inadequacy in the accounts provided of alterity that can justify this study.

Georges Gusdorf was the first to discuss autobiography in the generic terms that would come to dominate the critical scene through the 1970s.

Linking its rise to the rise of the bourgeois subject, Gusdorf understood the genre to bring together in an unholy union the discourse of knowledge and the persuasive rhetoric of self-justification in the service of the subject in the mirror, the I responding to the "Know thyself" of the Delphic oracle. The limits of the genre in Gusdorf's account were the limits of subjective self-knowledge, for everything touched upon in autobiography—including the others represented—gets immediately absorbed into the language of the subject, who proves unable to represent them as anything but the objects of its love, jealousy, or admiration: others for a subject that are already determined, subsumed by its self-representation.[3]

Philippe Lejeune saw in the performative a means to limit the runaway subjectivism uncovered by Gusdorf and to settle the hovering of all first-person narratives between autobiographical document and fiction by grounding them in a signed pact. For Lejeune, to write an autobiography is to pactify as responsible subject with another outside the field of representation: a reader. The autobiographer makes a pledge to which she is bound, staking her identity on telling such historically verifiable facts as are critical to understanding, making use of only such fictional or persuasive devices as lie within the narrow limits defined by the pact. In exchange, the reader can read suspiciously, on the lookout for transgressions proving an excessive or inadequate persuasiveness, but has also to read in good faith. That means, she can question whether the I has met the individual terms of the contract, but cannot call into question the I's word in setting up the verbal contract between them, which implies among other things the project to tell the truth about the crucial facts of her experience. Although the autobiography may fail in some local ways—painting the I's unconscious system of defenses rather than its self-conscious knowledge, for instance—the contract itself, the promise of the promise to represent experience, holds. The primacy of the subject's experience is admitted, and the question is simply how to recount it. The other in the case Lejeune describes is the reader as a possible subject with whom the subject enters into verbal commerce as with another rational creature competent in the language. Responsibility in this case derives from the nature of dialogue itself. The responsibility to tell the truth, like the responsibility to stay within the bounds of reasonable interpretation, is what one owes the other to whom one speaks. This was a solution for limiting the reach of the autobiographical hybridity noted by Gusdorf and Gérard Genette that was quite elegant in its simplicity and one that brought out the necessity of considering the other in terms of discourse and address, and not only—as per Gusdorf—as an object within discourse.

Unfortunately, the evidence for the pact proved tenuous at best. It was not simply that there were many recognizably autobiographical texts about which Lejeune had to be silent given his insistence, entirely consistent with his premises, that autobiography must make a narrative account of experience.[4] More seriously, the evidence for binding pacts was never forthcoming. Lejeune could cite few clear instances of autobiographical pledges. Where he could find them, he did not consider that a reading would also have to be made of their status as pacts, given that any attempt by a writer to determine the meaning of the discourse within the covers of a book is, of course, subject to the same indeterminacy as the discourse itself. The stakes are high in autobiography—nothing less than the identity of the I and the certainty of its experience—but the pact cannot necessarily resolve a dispute over them because as text, it would also be indeterminate. Lejeune's attempt to dodge the problem by thinking of the proper name on the title page as a binding signature could not work.

In short, Lejeune's pact was fatally flawed, as Paul de Man quite directly, and Derrida more indirectly, showed.[5] De Man settled the generic dispute by identifying autobiographical writing as an open-ended configuration between author and reader common to all texts, what he called an "alignment between the two subjects involved in the process of reading in which they determine each other by mutual reflexive substitution."[6] What makes for the open-endedness is the fact that the substitution of one subject for another fails to account for the actual nature of the relationship, which is that of a reader to a text. For de Man, the interest of the problematic does not lie in the fact that it allows identities to be formed and generic boundaries to be set up but rather precisely that, "it demonstrates in a striking way the impossibility of closure and of totalization."[7] Autobiography permits but is not exhausted by specular determination, and that means it turns outward to call into question a host of common sense assumptions, such as our idea that experience precedes its writing or that autobiography is about self-knowledge and not, say, a treatise on politics, ethics, or religion. In describing autobiography as a figure of reading, de Man says that the relation of subject to the other is not that of listener to speaker in a dialogue, but rather that of a reader or author to a text.

With de Man's "Autobiography as De-Facement" and Derrida's "Law of Genre," the era of genre studies of autobiography had effectively come to an end, but not before having spawned a new critical tendency in identity studies, which borrowed some of the findings of poststructuralism without entirely abandoning the Lejeunian postulate of autobiography as a policeable, delimited genre for securing identity. These studies noticed that a large number of "others" marginalized with respect to mainstream discourse—third persons victimized by being left out of the space of the I-you dialogue—had seized upon autobiography as a means to appropriate the power of the logos for themselves. This led the critical discussion toward the potential for autobiographical discourse—however broadly or narrowly defined—to serve as a strategy of identity production, as a means for oppressed peoples to find a platform from which to speak. The resulting feminist, identity, and postcolonial studies of the 1980s and 1990s tended to celebrate autobiography as enabling marginalized subjects to become constituted along identitarian lines. They claimed that, in the autobiographical text, a being determined as other grabs the power of language and legitimates itself as subject through its act of self-representation. Seizing the autobiographer's position as subject of discourse, or so goes the argument, allows a host of excluded others to work out a more pluralistic identity in which they might be included. From that position, having acceded to subjecthood themselves, they might then secure a place in the representational field for others in the oppressed minority. A fundamental sense of optimism about political gains and the spread of freedom underlies much of such work, based on the idea, well-expressed in Françoise Lionnet's ground-breaking *Autobiographical Voices* where it is called "somewhat utopian," that writing one's autobiography can be "an enabling force in the creation of a plural self, one that thrives on ambiguity and multiplicity, on affirmation of differences, not on polarized and polarizing notions of identity, culture, race, or gender."[8]

This was a very productive vein for autobiography studies. It opened a virtually endless stream of studies of such marginal identities as they attempted to make their way out of the position of excluded other into the mainstream; it allowed the discussion of the formal innovations by which their difference was expressed; it further encouraged the expansion of the canon to consider hitherto obscure or unpublished forays into the genre; it led to a confessional vein in criticism.[9] In some of these studies, in anti-essentialist discussions of identity as "in formation," for instance, we find resurfacing the open-endedness identified by de Man with autobiography. However, generally speaking, the destabilizing move of considering identity as constructed does not seem to have been followed by any questioning of the primacy of experience or of the assumption that autobiography is intersubjective discourse, never mind of the assumption that the movement of history is toward progressive emancipation.

In considering this vein of criticism, I could not help noticing that, in celebrating the victory of newly fledged subjects entering into discourse, identity studies end by celebrating the hegemony of the subject, along Lejeune's fundamental assumption that autobiography is discursive in nature. However many the differences between these new subjects and the old, they seemed finally only conforming differences: that is to say, differences among those already admitted by discourse into possible subjectivity. A particular identity might be in process, but where that process leads is not allowed to become problematical. In short, identity studies appeared paradoxically more pressed to relieve the other of its opaque indeterminacy than to ask whether it is enough to think of the other as a determinate victim or set of victims left out of the dialogue space, whether alterity might stand for a greater and more powerful resistance to determination, a resistance to incorporation into the intersubjective field of dialogue itself. The question of whether the subject's responsibility might extend to an alterity that has not already been prequalified by a contract as a potential subject capable of entering into exchange is never allowed to come up. From the perspective of pragmatic politics, recuperating the other as a new subject is a commendable move, which aims to open paths to power for disadvantaged groups. However, it is critical as well—is indeed a matter of the survival of subjectivity—that we consider the full range of possible negotiations the subject makes with an alterity exceeding it. One has, for instance, to account for what Emmanuel Levinas and Derrida call the "wholly other" or the "absolutely other," or de Man's "other" as text.

In the view adopted by this study, autobiographical writing—because it is a text, because it testifies in and to the absence of the I—has the potential to witness for alterity unrecoverable by the subject as its other. Such writing would no longer exactly be autobiography, but rather *autothanatographical writing*: the writing of the death of the subject. Among the advantages of pursuing an understanding of this sort is the fact that it opens the limits of our notions of subjectivity to consider the I as it faces its radical loss of self-identity. When alterity strikes to make the discursive subject "I" into a grammatical subject—as happens midway through Rimbaud's famous sentence, "I is an other," for instance—a discourse about experience becomes a discourse about the structure and conditions of experience. In considering the conditions of possibility and impossibility of experience, the work is then called to ask after other possible sets of transactions with those conditions; and, finding subjectivity imperiled and its survival uncertain, to look abroad and invent with those conditions.

It is this question of autobiography as about the I's failed attempts to determine alterity, about its grappling with its death, that seems to have been greeted often by silence or only partial understanding in the field of autobiography studies, which has had little to say about the energetic and decisive anticipations of fiction.[10] The simple reason is that most studies assume that events, whether occurring as brute experiences or as the reflexive turn onto experience, occur before and outside of writing, with writing serving to record them. But perhaps the event—as the passing of one regime of meaning for subjects and the presentation of a new one—is what the autothanatographical account seeks to bring about. It would allow us to seize the subject as it deploys its strategies, explores escape routes, stocks up means for survival, and (its death arriving anyway) gets an afterlife. One implication would be that the writer finds ways to multiply such chances through its exploration of the alterity testified to by language. Another would be that what we call an "event" would be textual in nature and would entail the nonsynthetic convergence of two distinct patterns in the autobiographical text, one of which can be thought of as autobiographical, retrospective life writing in Lejeune's sense of the term, and the other as autothanatographical.[11]

A brief example taken from the epigraph to this introduction can help define more clearly the stakes of considering the writing of one's death. Augustine says in his *Confessions* that he must "confess both what I know of myself and also what I do not know." In this statement, it is evident that Augustine makes himself responsible for doing something impossible. How can one confess what one does not know? And yet, it is equally evident that to say what one does not know (which we might appropriately call "my own death" because my death—the mode and moment of my passing—is what most I do not know) has to be the most important thing for Augustine, as he tries to describe the Christian relationship with the absolutely other and makes up the I's accounts in solitude with God. Saying what he does not know is saying what only God knows, what is and must remain secret to him as knowing subject but is open to the wholly other. Augustine wants to testify for his conscience, for God in him, for the one who knows his secret as he does not and will not before Judgment Day, when, "I see you face to face and my dusk is as noonday."[12] It seems impossible for him to say this, and yet necessary. But, looked at from the point of view of the *Confessions* as a text, it is perhaps the only thing that Augustine can confess. In writing, Augustine writes a text that speaks to his death. His words may be thought as saying what he knows as subject; but as writing, they also testify to what only God knows, to his absence as subject. It is willy-nilly the case that Augustine's words speak of his death. But because he has anticipated that in committing to saying what he does not know, the death blow from writing gives Augustine a chance not only to explain himself in advance to God, but also to explain to others the new experience of interiority that has come into view as a result of his recognition—what his conversion is about, in fact—that written language can testify for him in that sense. They speak to another idea of responsibility and to an extension of the notion of human responsibility. For Augustine has not only to respond to a new call from God to confess what he does not know, but has also to respond to others for his publication of that new responsibility.

The book thus has several rationales for pushing the discussion of the other in autobiography toward a consideration of an alterity outside the subject's categories, all of which address its open-endedness and its specificity as written text.

The first motive is quite simply to provide a fuller account of autobiography, which requires that we consider the emergence of an alterity that refuses subsumption by the specular model. In keeping with this move, I have sought out autobiographical texts that showed a resistance to totalization, either because they were entirely non-narrative or involved interrupted narratives.

A second motive is to critique the celebratory notion of autobiography, common to many autobiographers as well as to critics, as a means for becoming a subject. My idea was to show that by determining the other as another potential subject, one stays within the ready-made framework that the logos gives us for acting as mastering subjects to colonize the world, having given up on empire in name only. There is a very real sense in which autobiography can be understood as little more than a legal form of the sort that tends to show up in the files of the Department of Motor Vehicles or a hospital: a form that captures the details of our difference as insignificant with respect to the more important move of assigning us an identity and a place in a whole system of already-finished identities, citizens filed away for reference. Baudelaire, for instance, is quite clear that the merits and vices of the people of a given epoch are invariably attributable to the preceding reign, so that the current "prince" is always ruling over subjects formed after the model of a dead or deposed predecessor.[13] To critique autobiography as identity-maker is to show identity and the process of identification as open to disruption, and to look for pockets of play or precarious freedom within the confines of the ready-made subject and its categories.

A third rationale arises from the understanding that the process of identification is and must remain unfinished. The point of writing autobiography is not to extend the reach of the same old subjecthood to more subjects, but to consider its potential for extending the understanding of subjectivity itself past radical discontinuities, to see not only identities but identity itself as still in formation and still in question, to take the measure of the part of the adventure of subjectivity that is over as well as the part that still lies ahead. In short, it was the potential of autobiography to surprise, to improvise with death so as to present us with new forms of survival and experience that interested me. The concern was to discuss places where an alterity stimulates the subject to attempt to assimilate the unassimilable, to take in an exteriority foreign to it, and where it finds itself having to answer for its attempt.

The studies in the first half of the book treat the process of identification and its disruption. The strategies the I develops for reducing alterity to that of another potential subject are considered along with the results of its encounter with an alterity too great for it to appropriate. That alterity has, of course, to be testified to in language; however, it does not come in a language I know and recognize, but always as the secret, enigmatic, incomprehensible language of the other, even when it appears in my own.[14] In this half of the book, the chapters consider the disruption of the subject's genealogical narratives and the interruption of its commerce with others construed as possible subjects like it. The focus is on places where the I gets intimations, as if from within recountable experience, of an alterity exceeding its capacity to reduce or appropriate it in narratives of experience. In chapters concerned with memory and the sentiment of injustice, with embarrassment and with Dandyism, the interruption of autobiography as process of identification is under investigation. The chief accent is on the disruption of narrative and the subject's process of identification. Because the major effect of disrupting its life narrative is to break the tie between experience and representation, and thus to trouble the idea of autobiography as first and foremost a representation of the I's experience of the world, the essays in this part will deal chiefly with the effects of those disruptions on its epistemology.

It is not enough to consider things from the standpoint of the failure of the subject to achieve a stable identity in autobiography. The intrusion of what is left out of the subject's experience, an unrecognizable alterity or a threatening exteriority that cannot be interiorized in a representation but that the autobiographer is nonetheless called upon to represent, provides the subject in crisis with its chances for and risks to survival. In the second part of the book, I have sought to look at the subject as it improvises its future. Here, it is in the context of Levinasian discussions of the subject in crisis and of Derridean considerations of the impossible, the conditions of experience, the secret without a content, and so on that I consider the subject as it strategizes with its death. In this second part, the focus is on the co-presence in the text of competing models of the I and its textual other. In one model, the model for successful autobiography, the I testifies for its transactions with the other in terms of the logos, as to another subject. In the second, the I testifies in its autothanatography rather to what it does not know, to its death and survival, to its relation to the wholly other, and to the conditions of its possibility and impossibility. Chapters on hospitality, eating, and the drug experience, the secret and responsibility consider the ways each work lays out the stakes of the models for the I, and articulate their points of intersection. The concern is to show that the thrust of autothanatography is the invention of a testimony of "what I do not know," and the exploration of subjectivity's survival through the interior landscapes the I discovers as a result of its attention to the other left out. Opening as they do into the "beyond" of the subject, these essays are naturally concerned with the ethico-religico-political dimensions of the autobiographical text. For it is toward such questions that the autobiographer gestures in considering the conditions for experience and the subject's debts and obligations to alterity in all its forms.

A word is in order on the selection of texts. As in any study that does not claim to be exhaustive, the choice of texts is somewhat arbitrary, the more so for being in a field where any text with a readable title page, as one critic puts it, has a claim to being called autobiographical.[15] But the selection is not entirely random. It was natural, given my interest in the subject's death and problematic survival, that I should seek out texts that have rused well enough with death to have proven staying power. It was likewise natural that I would look for texts that fell together as in dialogue with one another over the forms for expressing and for querying what counts as a subject's experience or engaged one another over the ethico-political questions of their moment. The persistent mutual concerns of Thomas De Quincey, Charles Baudelaire, and Oscar Wilde are evident even in a detail like their echoing titles: *Suspiria de Profundis*, "De Profundis Clamavi," *De Profundis*. Moreover, Modernist texts, with their keen awareness of the way that fictional models shape possible experience, were particularly attractive places to consider the death of the subject. Emma Bovary's living out of clichéd fictional patterns and Baudelaire's searching out in memory of the forgotten experience of shock, are two halves of the same phenomenon, and they suggest the centrality of *thanatos* in modernist autobiographies, among which—somewhat counter to the prevailing tendency to read him as a Romantic—I place De Quincey's *Confessions*, and to a certain extent, even Rousseau's autobiographical writings. They seemed as well to be concerned with the issue of survival. De Man tells us in "Lyric and Modernity" that the term "modernity" designates "the problematical possibility of all literature's existing in the present, of being considered, or read, from a point of view that claims to share with it its own sense of a temporal present."[16] If we consider that phrase in the context of autobiography, it suggests the possibility of reading the latter's fictional side not in terms of the techniques or pathos of a long-dead writer, but as the source for our continuing interest in autobiography. The autobiographical texts of the literary historical period known as Modernism would not be the only place, under this definition, for considering fiction as sharing our sense of a present as survival, but they might well serve as good metonyms.

The decision to bring together writings from two linguistic communities started from the observation that the authors in question were all more than usually preoccupied with their counterparts in France or Great Britain. Thus, the well-publicized disagreement between Rousseau and David Hume over sensibility is reflected by De Quincey's pronouncement against spurious French sensibility and his ironic preference for English decency in his own *Confessions*. More even than various instances of outright borrowing—one thinks of the particle that the son of the English wool merchant Quincey added to his name, in imitation of the French—I found the problem of translation, bilingualism, and the relations between languages to be central. The bringing of the other's language into one's own is critical particularly for Baudelaire, who set his translation of De Quincey's English *Confessions* in the middle of his treatise on artificial paradises; but also for Wilde, who wrote his play *Salomé* in French and fell out with his translator and lover Lord Alfred Douglas over the translation; and to a degree for De Quincey, whose interlarding of his text with bits and pieces in foreign tongues is well known. The texts chosen are by no means the only ones that would have something to contribute to the questions I have asked then. But they are all concerned in a central way with an imperative to address, beyond the "Know thyself" of the oracle, Augustine's "confess what you do not know."

The position of Rousseau in a study generally eschewing genealogical narratives requires more extensive comment. Rousseau has been identified as the father of modern, secular autobiography, so it is quite to be expected for an account of autobiography concerned with narrative to give pride of place to his work. Given my overriding preoccupation with an autothanatographical thrust to autobiography, however, Rousseau is less clearly the natural starting point. Baudelaire, whose melancholic posture is well known, whom Sartre even accused of wanting to paint himself in his death mask, would seem more important, as the fact that he translated De Quincey and was himself a key figure for Wilde would underscore. And indeed, in general, I have conceived Baudelaire's Modernist work as the glue holding together the parts of the book.

My main justification for devoting so much time to Rousseau comes in fact from Baudelaire. For while Baudelaire was sharply critical of Rousseau for his sentimentality and his glorification of the self, he nonetheless espied in Rousseau a neglected double whom he picked up, dusted off, and set at the center of his own project, among other places as the first comer, the nameless wanderer in the streets of Paris who figures centrally in the *Petits poèmes en prose*.[17] In my view, Baudelaire's choice of the Rousseau of the *Rêveries*, the survivor making up his last accounts, is a decision for the autothanatographer over the successful spinner of the seductive narrative of the *Confessions* that for many critics sets up Rousseau as the father of the autobiographical lineage. Baudelaire seems to have found a failed genealogy in Rousseau, and to have laid out his accounts with Rousseau in terms of a responsibility thriving in the absence of the father and the fatherly example. He found Rousseau to be exemplary where he was inimitable, where he fell outside his lineage in claiming his irreplaceable death. To put it in terms of the family romance, Rousseau was rather an early *frère ennemi* than a father figure for Baudelaire, and accounts with him were to be managed not in filial terms but rather in terms of fraternal struggles and fraternal debts. Rereading Rousseau thus appeared to me a sort of necessity. But it could not be, or not be only, the Rousseau so convincingly portrayed by Jean Starobinski in *La Transparence et l'obstacle* or in "Le progrès de l'interprète," where Rousseau is seized as a cogito, and a dialectical story is told of his developing consciousness, in "the dispersal of his tendencies and the unity of his intentions."[18] It had to be the Rousseau read, as Baudelaire read him, through the lens provided by *Rêveries* where he is the survivor of a catastrophe that set him apart from his fellows.

Even in the *Confessions*, there is just such another Rousseau to contend with. I do not mean that statement to be understood from the first metaphorically, as part of a claim, grounded or not, that I have discovered another aspect to Rousseau's work. I mean it quite literally. Rousseau had a brother, François, who ran away around 1722, and according to Rousseau's brief account in the *Confessions*, was never heard from again.[19] The separation from that brother dramatizes the issues that arise when one of two is seized through an I determining itself as subject and leaving the other behind as the undetermined. For that is exactly what has happened with the *frères* Rousseau: One of them has become Rousseau for himself as for us, the one born in 1712, with a string of important texts to his name and a death in 1778 to be remembered; and the other has wandered off into the unknown. There are epistemological questions associated with this other who represents the unknown. There are also ethical and juridical questions. In writing his *Confessions*, as I shall show, Rousseau does not only write his own life but acts as if obliged to account for his brother's absence and for having, younger brother though he is, supplanted the elder son. He accounts for the inheritance left in trust for the unprovably dead brother, an inheritance that has a different status than the one that came to him through legal channels upon his majority. He has furthermore to give his brother the burial of which he has been robbed by fortune, and while doing so, to come up against his own death. The story of Rousseau and his brother thus has a last dimension, shading off as it does into the story of a writer confronting his text, the analogical other or double that is his written image. A discussion of the scene can show why Rousseau is a good place to start while helping introduce further the topic and methods of our study.

Here is the lone scene where François gets more than a mention in the *Confessions*:

> I had a brother seven years older than myself. He was learning my father's profession. The extreme affection that they had for me meant he was a little neglected, which I consider very wrong. His education suffered from this neglect and he had fallen into the habits of a libertine, even before he had reached the age of truly being one. He was apprenticed to another master, from whom he ran away, just as he had from the paternal house. I hardly saw him; indeed, I can scarcely say that I knew him, but I did not cease to love him tenderly, and he loved me, as much as a rascal [*un poliçon*] can love anything. I remember that once when my father was punishing him severely and angrily, I threw myself impetuously between them [*je me jettai impétueusement entre deux*], embracing him closely. I covered him thus with my body, receiving the blows that were meant for him, and I held on so obstinately in this position that my father spared him, either disarmed by my cries and tears, or in order not to hurt me more than him. Finally my brother turned so bad that he ran off and disappeared entirely. We heard some time later that he was in Germany. He did not write even once [*Il n'écrivit pas une seule fois*]. We no longer heard news from him after that. So it was that I have remained an only son [*voila comment je suis demeuré fils unique*] (*QC* I, 9–10).

François appears in a curious position, literally covered by his brother Jean-Jacques, who throws himself between father and son, embraces his brother from behind and receives on his own back the blows with which Isaac meant to correct the conduct of his wayward elder son.[20] Who knows what might have happened had those blows been delivered? Perhaps had François received them, they would have made all the difference in his education; or perhaps they would simply have catapulted the lost brother off that much earlier into the larger world from which he will never return. In either case, whether Jean-Jacques has saved his brother or robbed him of the benefits of a paternal education, the scene itself appears emblematic of what Jean-Jacques might be doing throughout his life: taking, besides the few blows that were destined for him, the overindulged and much loved favorite of the father, those that might have been aimed at his neglected, truant brother.

Considered in terms of the historical events presented, the story is about love, or more precisely, as is to be expected from Rousseau, about the natural passion of pity. The I, the chief actor in the story, emblematically and sympathetically projects himself under a double relationship to the other around the problem of likeness. Jean-Jacques is related to François as just another Rousseau boy to be beaten, a second son with a literal body like that of the elder son. But he is also the latter's fictional double, his representative, who, covering for him and gathering blows in his place, gives evidence of an imaginative ability to invent doubles that is absent in the brother. This trend continues throughout the narrative. After a hopeful start, Jean-Jacques's early career follows his brother's trajectory; like him but after him, a rascal or *polisson* (François, [*OC* I, 9]; Jean-Jacques, [*OC* I, 40]), our Rousseau is apprenticed to a trade (François to a clockmaker, following his father; Jean-Jacques, after a disappointing start as a law copyist, to an engraver), runs away in adolescence (François at 17; Jean-Jacques one year earlier), leaves Protestant Geneva to make his way into a Catholic region (François to Fribourg; Jean-Jacques to Annecy) and is lost as a result of the father's neglect (*OC* I, 9; 55). Both travel at one point or another, under assumed names.[21] As we follow the protagonist Jean-Jacques, we are watching actions and occurrences that plausibly resemble those of the brother in whose footsteps Jean-Jacques seems to be traveling. It is almost as if the indulged younger brother had sabotaged any hopes placed in him in order to be able to give news of what François might have confronted, where he might have gone, what done, what thought and felt, what become. Jean-Jacques represents himself, and also his brother, for whose life we would otherwise have only the barest of documents to attest. With respect to the lost boy, Jean-Jacques's story has the status of a fiction, of what might have been. His celebrated ability to imagine himself in the guise of a hero of a romance or a picaresque novel is the image within the story of the fundamental imaginative projection of himself as the fictional supplement of his brother. The little episode shows him throwing himself impetuously onto his brother, between father and son, as just such a substitute for the brother—"I threw myself impetuously between them [*entre deux*]"—and in doing so, throwing himself into the fray as a fictional character endowed with the vivid imaginative world that François, even had he survived, would have lacked unless he had testified for himself. Jean-Jacques, in short, makes himself into a brother plus one by throwing himself lovingly onto his brother's back, as a double who attests both for himself as a man like any other for what he knows in his own experience, and for the unknown that can only be conjectured about, for what his lost brother's life might have been.

In this first reading of the I who differentiates himself from, while attaching himself to, his brother, as fictional supplement to his literal existence, the attention is all on the two boys' embrace. Jean-Jacques answers for his brother, takes blows for him, out of love and pity.[22] The impetuousness with which Jean-Jacques makes himself into the fictional double of his literal brother is suggestive of the force of Rousseau's decision for autobiography, in which contradictory principles of verisimilitude and verification, fiction and history vie for supremacy. Almost as far back as the I can remember, he is already predisposed to twinning, speaking for the literal brother left out when the ideal self comes into existence, and justifying the projection of the ideal self into the limelight on the grounds of the deficiencies of experience ("I hardly saw him; indeed, I can barely say that I knew him") which require supplementation to attest for the other's missing inner life. The story is told as a matter of knowledge, to show his passions in operation as Jean-Jacques remembers them, but also to say what can only be conjectured, what might have happened to the other Rousseau.

As we know from Derrida, however, the substitute does not just stand in for, it also supplants.[23] What, from the perspective of the boys in isolation is an act of self-sacrifice, must appear to the gaze of the father an act of usurpation. A second reading of the scene has to consider the fact that the child not only takes the brother's place but also owes it to answer to the father as to why he has done so. When Jean-Jacques interposes himself between father and brother, he anticipates his brother's final disappearance. He hides the brother from the blows of the father, but also from his father's gaze (the "blows" of the eye [*coups d'oeil*])[24] and love. Jean-Jacques stands in the limelight, as recipient of all the father's affection and anger: He is guilty of becoming the only son, or as Rousseau puts it (my emphasis), "*remain(ing)* the only son" [*voila comment je suis demeuré fils unique*]— confirming that François was all along the upstart brother, a mere pretender to the love of the father, never a serious contender for the role of his representative.

What comes forward here in the scene read as one of supplanting the brother are the relations between son and father, and more especially, between father and the favored son: the one who, having chosen to represent the elder brother to the father, ends up as the teller of the family story, and thus as his father's representative. Why is Jean-Jacques chosen to represent the father? On the one hand, he is chosen by default because in thrusting himself forward to bask in the warmth of his father's eye, he blocks out the other and becomes the only one remaining to tell the story. He has supplanted the brother, and, a new Cain, in justice he owes an account for François's disappearance from his father's sight. Isaac Rousseau had two sons, and now one only, who is summoned to account for the loss of the first one. Jean-Jacques takes no blows for his brother. He has earned his blows since, acting as if to take them *for* his brother, he has actually taken them *from* him, by taking his place as his representative. The I, alone with his father (and after the disappearance of the father, alone with his conscience) is judged by a father who wants to be equitable, to give each of his boys his fair share of the beating. Whereas François has gotten blows for his "disappearances," Jean-Jacques receives his for taking his brother's place. As Rousseau supposes, the father may have ceased his blows out of fairness, "in order not to hurt me more than him," neither more nor less. The father's severity in punishing the supplanter is a sign that, for Rousseau, "speaking for" another subject is usurpation and is contrary to justice. In Rousseau's view, we are subscribing to an injustice when we say that the autobiographer speaks for others like her. At best, the representative can only provide a conjecture as to what the other might have said, while occupying the stage so that the other cannot do his own saying.

On the other hand, Jean-Jacques is also the father's best, his chosen, representative; he is his one and only, his unique son, and he prefers him even before François disappears. That is because Jean-Jacques, as remaining son, is the one who stands for the others invisible to the father, and reminds him all unwittingly of other lost Rousseaus. We know already that the boy's birth has killed his mother, and every time Isaac looks at him, he remembers his dead wife. In this scene, Jean-Jacques does not remind of the dead brother because he looks like him or because he was his murderer. Jean-Jacques, struck by his father at the moment that he covers his brother and reduces by one the brace of Rousseau brothers, does something remarkable: He weeps and cries. Probably he is crying because the beating hurts. Nevertheless, for the father, the spectacle of the one brother weeping over the other has a meaning that as actor the boy may ignore: He weeps as if in mourning ahead of time for the lost boy he is displacing. His tears signal a reflective inner life, and they anticipate on François's departure as the only scene of mourning, the only funeral honors, the brother excluded from the gaze of the father will ever have received. By the beating, Jean-Jacques is punished for his past usurpation of François and perhaps, too, for his replacement of the latter's life story by his own. But by his tears and cries, he answers in advance of any knowledge of what is to take place, for François's ultimate disappearance.[25]

The tears are interesting because they speak to the I's interiority, and more especially, to his interiorization of the lost brother. The sheltering embrace already represents the interiorization, but Jean-Jacques's tears do something more than express his being as feeling subject: They witness in excess of the boy's present meaning. They reveal the I as a subject self-constituted through the annihilating taking in of the lost brother and the taking over of the latter's single most important characteristic: namely, his characteristic of invisibility, of disappearance from sight and even from report. François is the "inside" world of Jean-Jacques himself, the world we know about only through the intermediary of the word. If the narrator posits that the father has stopped the beating, "perhaps disarmed by my cries and tears," it is because the father has indeed been disarmed. For by his annihilating interiorization of the other, as expressed in his tears and cries, the boy fathers himself, comes into existence as a subject with a conscience, speaking a language that testifies to everyone, including to himself, about his invisible interiority. All that is to be heard from François is the sound of his brother's weeping, as the sound that signals the death of the boy and his brother's nascent interior life. Levinas expresses this situation very precisely in *Alterity and Transcendence*:

> To have to answer for one's right to be, not in relation to the abstraction of some anonymous law, some legal entity, but in fear for the other. My being-in-the-world or my 'place in the sun,' my home—have they not been the usurpation of places belonging to others already oppressed by me or starved, expelled to a Third World: rejecting, excluding, exiling, despoiling, killing.[26]

The scene from the *Confessions* shows Jean-Jacques as a split representative. He has murdered the brother who was to inherit from the father; he is also the son favored in the father's decisive election because he "answer(s) for (his) right to be . . . in fear for the other." His is a case calling for justice, and the blows cease to rain down on him only when the father judges the younger son has received as many blows as his truant brother; but he also stands for the father's mercy, and the blows cease because all unknowing Jean-Jacques has reminded the father, in his mourning for the lost brother through whom they both father and son inherit from the mother, of the lost wife. He is chosen by the father because he has interiorized a split, always himself and more or less than himself: Guilty in his father's eyes for his brother's disappearance, even as he affirms his own right to be by that displacement, he is also his brother's first and only mourner, and the reminder to the father of the natural passions of pity, mercy, love. Jean-Jacques testifies to his brother's coming death, even as he hastens it.

In this reading, Rousseau writes autobiography as the best way to get at a split in the I in his accounts with the father in terms of mercy and justice. The narrating I has to tell the story because, as subject, he has usurped the place of the other and owes an accounting for that act to the father. But, as the remaining son whose side of the story will prevail, he is also called to justify the father's preference through his interiorization and mourning. As the only son left and as the son who fathers himself, he represents the father: his justice, his impartiality; his love for his sons, his clemency.

Read in this second way, the scene is about the constitution in autobiography of a responsible subject summoned to account for his acts with respect to others like him to a higher court, punished for having acted to exclude the other in establishing his own right to be. Yet the scene is also an I taking on a responsibility that exceeds his knowledge. The I has a secret he does not know: He has become his brother's keeper. To the father, he is an unknowing representative of absence and mourning through his tears and his turned-away face. He represents a split between meaning and action, and as such, can represent a responsibility, answer for an answering for that is structured differently than the one where a knowing, complacent subject answers for an other. It is the inadequacy between what he means and what he does that makes him a representative of his father's mercy and love. When little Jean-Jacques answers for the other, it is not to say what the other would say, but rather to say his mourning of the other he has annihilated. A responsibility that entails accounting for a meaning of the deed unknown by its doer, accounting for the gap between a deed and its meaning, exceeds the concept of the responsibility of a knowing subject, of equitability as justice. That responsibility is one that elicits the father's clemency and opens outward toward a notion of a meaning to my actions invisible to me but not to the other who sees me. In this second reading, the episode ceases to concern itself with the narrow story of the individual empirical subject and concerns itself instead with the theoretical question of what is the subject, taken in its double relation to the other of self-constituting mourning and triumphant usurpation, in justice and ethics.

The episode provides a third representation of the relations between the I and the brother that is depicted neither by the direct embrace of the brothers nor by the mediation of the logos that passes through the relation of the I to the father as representative of the absolutely other, whose "look sees me without my seeing him see me."[27] This third representation concerns the inheritance left in trust for the brothers by the dead mother, a trust of which the father is to touch the interest until the boys reach their majority. The mother left a house that was turned into money, and, as we know from the opening pages of the *Confessions*, she also left a library of novels and histories from which Jean-Jacques learned to read. That library gave the boy access to his maternal tongue. It is particularly through this symbolic capital of written words testifying to her solicitude in her absence that the passage in the *Confessions* approaches the problem of the maternal inheritance with respect to the two boys. That is evidenced by a colorless but revealing phrase about François: "he didn't write even once" [*il n'écrivit pas une seule fois*]. By the time he pens the *Confessions*, Jean-Jacques, as is well known, has written much and often. His writings have gone home to Geneva where they have been received well and badly, with accolades in the case of the two *Discours*, the *Lettre à la Providence*, the *Lettre à D'Alembert* as the works of a favorite son, censoriously by some in the case of *La Nouvelle Héloïse*, burned in the case of *Emile* and the *Contrat social*, with Rousseau placed under notice that he would be arrested if he followed them. Through his writing on pity and justice, Jean-Jacques has fallen even further afoul of the law than François, who was locked up for his escapades,[28] or than Isaac, who was threatened with prison for his violence against a fellow citizen. His writings have also traveled around Europe, as if in search of the model brother, the man still loving truth and justice—*Le François*, as he is called in *Les Dialogues*—who might at last give Jean-Jacques the reading he deserves.

So there is opened a third set of accounts between the brother who disappeared without writing, François and the well-known writer Jean-Jacques Rousseau, over the capital left in trust for the boys and what to make of it. These accounts are not simple ones. Anything may have happened to keep François from sending news, including death but also a host of other accidents. His letters might have gone astray. They might have been deliberately and maliciously deflected in their course. They might have failed to reach their destination because both Jean-Jacques and his father left Geneva soon after François. There is an extra set of chances, good and bad, to be connected with writing; and with the statement, perhaps a statement of nonreception by the grieving boy still awaiting a letter from his brother, perhaps a gloating insertion by the successful rival brother, that François did not write home even once. Our sense that there is an authorial intervention is not mistaken, for as we shall see in a moment, Rousseau plays actively with the chances given by writing, which are also, for him, chances to reach a brother whose address and destiny he ignores. The accounts here are not just between Jean-Jacques and François, or between Isaac and his only son, but—with Jean-Jacques still throwing himself *entre deux* in the brief line—the accounts between a writer and a nonwriter over the page between them.

The accounts of writing are, as one would expect, testamentary and funereal. Jean-Jacques's line, like that of a new Antigone, seeks to bury his brother, writing his epitaph as the Rousseau who didn't write home once. In a sense, it is another attempt, now by the writing Rousseau, to cover François; it betrays perhaps some urgency due to the fear of contamination from an unburied corpse. Yet it also reminds of François, tries to protect him from the oblivion that would otherwise be his. It remembers him as the Rousseau boy who never did touch the inheritance left by the dead mother. How does Rousseau's text interpose both to shelter his brother and, true to form, to shut him out from his chances with fortune and from such reputation? What is the relation of the I to the brother as revealed by this line, and in what sense can we see here a decisive, properly historical, choice on Rousseau's part?

One way to get an answer is to consult the second important text in which Rousseau remembers his brother, the legal document suggestively entitled "Mémoire pour répéter l'héritage de mon frère" by means of which Rousseau hoped to obtain a legal declaration of François's death, so as to entitle him and his father, the lost brother's two heirs, to claim the inheritance of Suzanne Bernard.[29] The "Mémoire" is a much longer document than the brief passage from the *Confessions*. It details such facts as are known, follows them up with the reasons available for supposing François to be dead in the absence of any real proof, and ends by explaining the reasons his heirs have for requesting a prompt judgment. The text thus makes some of the gestures we have found in the *Confessions*: We see Rousseau asking for justice, for what is his by right, and throwing himself on the mercy of the court; we see him pleading the case of self-interest and also the case of the father; we watch him mourning his brother. But there are a few crucial differences between the "Mémoire" and the *Confessions*, which show where Jean-Jacques is making decisive interventions in writing his autobiography. They give us another vision of the brother: neither the brother whom Jean-Jacques loved as another himself, nor yet the bested rival for his father's affection.

The first thing that we notice in comparing the texts is that Rousseau has taken some chances with his material by which he parries or tallies profits from the blows of fortune. One such decision entails the use of the proper name. In the "Mémoire," François Rousseau is named first, as the elder of the two brothers left by "Suzanne Bernard, my mother."[30] It was his luck to be the first-born; in contrast, Jean-Jacques's name is not even mentioned in the "Mémoire," which in the copy we have of it, is moreover unsigned. Another, related decision concerns the traces left of François's passage. According to the "Mémoire," the runaway left no tracks after a certain point. The disappearance of any trace is one reason Rousseau gives for conjecturing that François probably took a pseudonym. Besides, his brother was last heard of traveling in a foreign country where François, whose name is a homonym of the eighteenth-century spelling of the word for "French," was perhaps "unable to make himself understood" (*OC* I, 1215) The mediation of the spoken word would then have become impossible, and no news could travel back from the effectively gagged brother. What is more, says Jean-Jacques, François disappeared in a Catholic part of Germany; and in Catholic countries; if one dies outside the arms of the Church, one gets no funeral honors, and one's name is not written down anywhere. One loses one's legal existence and one's legal death, which is wrapped up in documents like church registers where proper names are inscribed. In Jean-Jacques's opinion, it would be useless to look for François for he has left no trace in the phenomenal world of his passing through it. If anyone has seen him, they cannot have remembered him because in putting aside his own name, François has not left anything by which to recognize and recall him.[31] If he has died, he has left no legal trace of it. In short, he has left no traces of his existence or his death at all. In every sense of the term, he has not written, and so his name has been lost as if he were dead even before death. And yet, because he has not left any traces, he cannot properly receive his death or be buried either.[32] That is why Rousseau and his father need the court's clemency. They need the court to step in to decree François's death on the basis of what Rousseau calls a "moral certainty" (*OC* I, 1215), emerging from a lack of the traces that would have constituted "authentic proof" (*OC* I, 1215).

Note the decisive choices that Rousseau makes with respect to the same elements in his brief story in the *Confessions*. He doesn't wait for the right chronological moment in the narrative to note the disappearance of François or the loss of his name; he makes him sink into oblivion ahead of time, without any explanation, simply by not naming him: "I had a brother," he says. He anticipates on François's disappearance and doesn't call him anything. He doesn't even really recall him, if one considers that revealing picture of brother covering brother, which really features Jean-Jacques more than the faceless François. It's as though Rousseau were saying, forget about François as I have already almost done, so much so that I don't even remember his name or his face. Again, Jean-Jacques steps in to gather all his brother's fortunes, good and bad, by leaving remainders early and often, and by choosing to write from the position of the usurper, *entre deux*, through a fiction. The result is that the patronymic Rousseau will be carried forward by the younger son.

So this is a first decision, a decision to neglect François all over again, to make him disappear so as not to be able to be recalled by anyone who does not go "outside" this text, into the archives, to find his name. It goes along with another decision, equally violent. The "Mémoire" cites as one of the reasons for believing François to be dead that after one year of frequent letter-writing and news, all communication ceased: "while we often received letters and news from him during the first year, he suddenly stopped sending any, and in 19 years we have heard nothing more of him" (*OC* I, 1215). The cessation of writing was taken as a sign that things had probably gone badly for François in the petition. But in the fiction of the *Confessions*, François did not write even once. His brother Jean-Jacques has deprived him of his pen. He also takes away what François's letters would have meant: a reputation for family affection like that of the other Rousseaus, all of whom are notable for having a big share of the passions (marital love, parental love, fraternal love, patriotism);[33] a name he might have earned as an adventurer, one year or so more of existence before his final disappearance; a share with his brother in remaining through the remainder. As if Jean-Jacques had not been favored enough over his brother, in writing the *Confessions*, he applies himself to taking away even the latter's name, his reputation, his meager lifespan, the few traces he left. Writing that his brother did not write, Rousseau takes his brother into himself and stands forth as the exemplary: indeed, the sole descendant of Suzanne Bernard and Isaac Rousseau.

By taking the pen away from his brother as one who also writes, Rousseau takes away from him the possibility both of the life and death related to survivorship. François never has a chance in Rousseau's account. The only thing he ever does is disappear, in one way or another. Even in the text where he is being remembered, it is as one who cannot be recalled because he has no name to be called by. What an indictment against Jean-Jacques, that he should have taken such licenses with the material, and erased what little definition the poor boy ever had. The violence exerted against the other when Rousseau wrests name and pen from his brother is even greater than that exercised in taking over the latter's beating or basking in the gleam of the father's eye given that the very memory of François is at stake.

And yet, the same two gestures are working to finish the portrait of François in a way. They let us glimpse his secret, a secret ignored by himself and by everyone except his remembering brother Jean-Jacques: the secret of his life and death, of his most fundamental and coherent gestures and choices, including the choice of his death as that of one who will not have written and, having left no traces can neither be said to have lived nor to have died either. According to Jean-Jacques's epitaph, his brother does not, cannot, witness for himself; his defining action, amidst all the disappearing acts that are determined by other forces, by habit or instinct, by usurpation, is the choice he makes not to write home even once, the choice to disappear without leaving a name behind and without returning to touch his mother's inheritance.[34] Rousseau may not have given us the facts, but in a sense he re-presents his brother to our view endowed with a moral meaning, as the brother witnessed for by his brother in his essential posture. It may be an offense against justice to speak for a living brother who could speak for himself; it is an act of love to testify for a mute one, to give him his own irreplaceable death. Rousseau bestows on his brother great evocative power, as the one who has to be remembered although he is the nameless, faceless, traceless other lying outside of all transactions. We can see him as an avatar for Baudelaire's first comer, for De Quincey's pariah, for Wilde's mute other, for the absolutely other outside of all contracts, denied a home by history, by law, by choice, by chance, and yet claiming from his writing brother his equal share in the mother's inheritance. This is as much as to say that there is something of François motivating Rousseau's state of nature, that state of equality which never existed, which is only a fiction, but of which we must have some idea in order to understand where we are, our determinate institutions and laws, and what we have lost or left out as they have developed, that state we have to remember to understand our rights and see where we are to go.

As writer who has taken the pen, Rousseau metes out to François his very specific choice of a death, which is the choice of a shadowy other who can never quite live or die, never quite be declared dead, because to be declared dead, one has to have a name to call and recall. François utterly disappears as phenomenal being, so he is not living. But he has lost his name before dying, so he is not ascertainably dead either. François has a third sort of indeterminate existence, as neither living nor dead. It is worth noticing that as Rousseau seeks to give his brother his death, that brother seems to have taken on the characteristics of a text, as if the problem of Rousseau and his brother were the problem of a writer and the textual analog that is his self-portrait. Indeed, the scene seems an allegory for the writer's struggle with the page and the pen, with Rousseauian autobiography the place *entre deux* where the accounts between father and disappeared elder son are to be carried on.

François's choice of death, and Rousseau's choice to give him his death, have another side, however, which can be related to this allegory. François can have disappeared so many times only because he kept on turning up again unexpectedly, like the proverbial bad penny. It is difficult to see how he could return: No one can announce his coming, can either call or recall him, because as nameless one, he leaves no traces of his own. But by the same token, because he has not been properly buried with a tombstone that has his name written on it, he is not really forgettable, either. Jean-Jacques has been complicit to some extent with the authorities here. Just as he had stolen the father's love and blows and even François's writing and name from him beforehand, and he has now helped make it impossible for François to be buried. François will keep on haunting the *Confessions* like a guilty conscience, like one who has been refused a tomb, who can neither live nor die, who stands outside all legal and phenomenal determinations. François is a pariah figure, a wandering other, and we might almost see Rousseau's smothering covering of him as one unsuccessful attempt among many to protect himself and his relation as the determinate remaining son inheriting through the father from the undead François and his deadly surprise returns.

We could do so at any rate were it not for the *ex nihilo* emergence of Jean-Jacques as the sole remaining son at the end of the scene: "***voila*** comment je suis demeuré fils unique." He's not the remaining son simply as a result of François's defection or his father's preference. Rather, he has made a decisive move for remaining that marks even the present. That decision is a decision not to anticipate his brother's death through premature mourning, but to anticipate his own death. He is unique, exceptional, in his early decision to supplant his brother in death. There is no doubt that he anticipates death as part of a strategy of survival. But his decision also has the result of allowing the brother to effect his returns.

For the haunting of the *Confessions* by the brother is not simply a possibility foretold by the text. The very "lie" that Rousseau writes about François, the fiction that he did not write, provides an example. Rousseau says: "*il n'écrivit pas une seule fois,*" which we have taken to mean, in the context of the scene as scene of mourning, "he didn't write a single time." But what the pen of the only son left to the father (the only authorized Rousseau) writes, contains a message "from" the other brother, who never left traces of his "own," but who has the ability, as indeterminate other, as text inheriting from the mother, to mean otherwise and to deliver unauthorized, "libertine," unfathered messages. There is nothing to prohibit us from reading the line as meaning "he didn't write just once, a single time," and thus as an assertion that François wrote and will have kept on writing often. The text says this; it renders to the brother a hundredfold the possibility of returning through the pen of his brother, of sending letters, delivering by-blows in the very text where Jean-Jacques (the preferred, "legitimate" son of his father) is laboring to take even the blows of fortune from his brother. The unauthorized message is the message of Jean-Jacques's death as the death of one from whose hands the pen falls at the moment of writing because writing is reduplication, repetition.[35] Jean-Jacques cannot "speak for" his brother, but his brother can speak for himself as excluded remainder through the apparently unified body of Jean-Jacques's "own" confessional text. The responsibility that Rousseau has taken on himself here, the responsibility to welcome the brother's intrusions into his life story, is a responsibility outside the one that the father and the paternal structures of the text authorize. It's a responsibility to answer for the brother in a text that allegorizes the death of the father and the father's representative, to be hospitable even to what denies subjectivity. It's a responsibility to let the other in even at the price of his own death and the end of the paternal line.[36]

Rousseau's text entertains a message from a brother hostile to the father as to genealogy, a blow to the narrative structure, which assumes François's disappearances and appearances already had to have taken place for Rousseau to write about them and which is thus discountenanced by the

returns of François in Rousseau's text. François's epitaph as written by
Jean-Jacques seems to sum him up so as to allow Jean-Jacques to close out
the ethico-juridical accounts with the brother and to emerge as a fresh-
minted only son. But Jean-Jacques's words form patterns outside the legal-
ities he has set up in establishing himself as the representative of the father.
These patterns are not a matter of an allegorization by the observing
father, who sees a meaning that the I does not, and elects it preferentially.
They are patterns owed to the iterability of writing, to the peculiar economy of the French language: The new development in the allegory is not
necessarily a matter of someone else seeing what I do not see; it may be a
matter of happenstance. Chance strikes a blow against the subject as
usurper of the elder brother's position. From one perspective, Jean-
Jacques tells of his having already taken on his brother's fate, and that
story is a tale of events provoked by the human passions of love and pity,
guilt and betrayal, mourning and fear. From another perspective, the story
is a vehicle through which the living brother takes the place of the dead
brother to prepare that brother's return. The nameless brother strikes
through the brother who has embraced him, and embracing him, displaced
him in the father's favor, at the father and the father's law.

We can speak of a textual event here, in which a new regime of signification is emerging, together with a new responsibility. Two incongruent
logics converge without synthesis: On the one hand, the text points to the
death of the speaking I, to self-writing as autothanatography and a vehicle
for the return of the dispossessed brother, and to the text as dismember-
ment; on the other hand, a new sort of subjectivity emerges here, in the
notion that Jean-Jacques has to answer for his usurpation by writing himself into the other's place as excluded other.

What de Man called the materiality of writing provides testimony of an
alterity outside the self and its usurpations.[37] That alterity cannot ultimately be appropriated by the subject as another human subject like it, or
even as the absolutely other who, like some transcendent father, sees and
knows what the I does not know. Writing gives the I the chance to invent
an exorbitant fiction of fraternal struggle and love. In terms of the ethico-
juridical question of responsibility, it is evident that Rousseau's text answers to and for the other in terms of a responsibility that not only exceeds
the empirical subject and its categories, but exceeds even the recuperative
moves made possible by the I, as consciousness representative of the
father.

Rousseau is a split figure in this last reading of the episode. On the one
side, he's made himself the only remaining Rousseau by his attachment to

the mark; and as such will scoop the whole of the Rousseau family inheritance in the father's name, as his representative. On the other side, Jean-Jacques disputes the paternal right to the whole, and makes his French testify over and over for the nameless, neglected, and forgotten brother. Whenever, as Rousseau says, holding tight to his pen, "the pen falls from my hands" (*OC* I, 34), we can be sure that there is a situation like the one we are describing, in which the loss of mastery and the death of the self as totalizing representation signal an indeterminacy greater than the I can appropriate, testimony which constitutes for the I a chance to interpose in fear of and for an alterity outside all determination.

Rousseau's scene of two brothers signing and countersigning one another's letters is an example of the rationale that leads our writers to consider the problem for ethics and justice of a writing that does not obey paternal law. Rousseau's accounts with the other go beyond his brother (the other Rousseau, *François*); beyond the other consciousness that is his reader moved by pity or interested in justice (*Le François*) to encompass the inhuman alterity of the French language, the maternal inheritance he shares with his brother (*le français*), which is where he gets testimony of an alterity outside determination, and which constitutes for him at once the risks and the possibility of a future.

The third set of accounts I have been discussing entails the encounter of the I with its death, the practice of autothanatography. These accounts are opened in Rousseau's fiction between brothers, who live and die within various authority structures and participate in the process of self-constitution. Every subject inserts itself in the place of a brother and internalizes the indeterminacy of a lost other, in the split we saw between Rousseau's imagined and his real existence, or between the meaning of his case for justice and for pity. But in writing a new indeterminacy emerges; the I has thus also to be considered in terms of its relation to an undetermined, a nameless other, outside given conditions and structures. It is only from that perspective that there is a potential for something to happen that has not already happened, that Rousseau can interiorize the risks and possibilities implicit in the confrontation with the homeless other and elaborate them into a new notion of responsibility and of subjectivity.

Autothanatographical writing allows the other to return with all its good fortunes and misfortunes, and it enables the I, in its life-oriented direction, through its anticipation of those fortunes, to explore and exploit them. Autobiographical writing is apparently concerned exclusively with the subject; paradoxically, however, it is as autothanatography, where the

other outside of all previous determinations regularly puts in an appearance, and the I does its accounts with "who" wrote "what" in the absence
of a subject, that autobiographical writing deploys a future. The reason
for studying such scenes is at least double: On the one hand, the authority
of our preferred social, political, and ethical representations of the other
are in question, seen as confining and reductive, allowing in only certain
others, solicited by but unable to decide about rascals like François, whose
appearances and disappearances take place outside the legal structures set
up to govern them; on the other hand, they are scenes where exorbitant
fictions, like Rousseau's fiction of the state of nature, find their conditions
for production. In short, Rousseau's story of the surviving brother suggests
there is ample justification for our inclusion of him amongst the Modernists to be treated.

   If one doesn't pay attention to the text as witnessing to the subject's
death, one neglects that it proposes new, extramural transactions instead
of simply reporting on past ones. The essays that follow are driven by the
urgent sense that, in the midst of the current critical dialogue on cultural
diversity, on nationalisms and transnationalisms, we have ever and again
to look at texts that have done more than simply make use of already extant
modes for reporting on the I's love for, exclusion of, or dispossession by
the other. It is, rather, the possibility of collecting and calculating in
advance with what exceeds the subject—and in doing so, of making the
subject responsible to and for what lies outside knowledge as its conditions—that there is potential to consider autobiography as providing surprises, something more than the confirmation of previous models. In what
follows, I will focus on places where the I's converse with specularly conceived others gives way to a regard for the other as such, and, through its
death, draws a line within the text between what is past and done with and
where something is happening that still has a future.

   In taking up alterity in this way, I have had to seek out examples in
autobiographical discourse of the subject in crisis. I have not looked chiefly
for crisis experiences recounted, where an I confesses what took place
while leaving the notion of experience itself intact. Instead, I have sought
crises evident in its testimony suggesting that what it has hitherto called
"experience" may be at stake. Thus I have not necessarily gone to the
well-known death scenes—say, Rousseau's brush with death in the *Second
promenade*—but rather to less-frequented places in the text where a language, in becoming enigmatic, reveals itself as the language of the other.
In a word, I have looked not simply for the life signs of the subject, as
Lejeune nicely puts it in the title to a recent book, but for its death signs.[38]

For it is there that the I's chances, its good fortune and its misfortunes, are available. It is there that the cornered subject, in endeavoring to respond for its death, for its irresponsibility, proposes exorbitant fictions to compensate for having acted as a subject to colonize all others as all others for it. These exorbitant fictions, what Rousseau calls "moral fictions," help reconfigure basic political ideas as to human rights and obligations. But they are also the places where faultlines emerge in its calculations for cheating death. They are worth reading, as they are where the autobiographer, in pushing the regard for the other to the limit, gets the chance to surprise us with an unknown, and so perhaps, for good and for evil, with a future for subjectivity.

I

Autobiography Interrupted

CHAPTER I

Developments in Character: "The Children's Punishment" and "The Broken Comb"

> I write the life of a man who is no longer, but whom I once knew
> well . . . That man is myself.
>
> JEAN-JACQUES ROUSSEAU, *Ébauches des Confessions*

"Reading" is a term that, through overuse, can easily become confused with interpretation. In fact, there is a crucial difference: Reading involves the undoing of interpretative figures; because it is not an operation opposed to the understanding but rather a precondition for it, it allows us to question whether the synthetic moves of the understanding can close off a text. It leads away from meaning to such problems as the text's constitution and meaning generation. Unlike interpretation, which implies a development over the course of a narrative toward a single figure reconciling all its diverse moments, reading states the logic of figures and the logic of narratives to be divergent. Divergence implies that an autobiographical text, for example, does not simply serve to bring meaning to the unorganized events of a subject's experience as well as self-recognition to author and reader, but serves the further function of making those events available to a reader allegorically, as exemplary of the manner in which all narratives are constructed.[1] We could even define as autobiographical the text produced by the confrontation of consciousness with effects of ordering excessive to the capacity of totalizing figures to regulate them. Such confrontations dramatize the potential for the subject's writing of its life in autobiography to become an autothanatography, the writing of its death, and to present through allegory meaning unavailable to the subject.

Rousseau's *Confessions*, which provides a particularly rich source for the study of narrative figures and strategies, will allow us to pursue the distinction between interpretation and reading and to determine some of the stakes involved.

I've started from the hypothesis that understanding the difference between a linguistic term (like reading) and a term with a rich philosophical past (like interpretation or hermeneutics) can help further our inquiry into the differences between autobiography and autothanatography, which also ride on how the text's alterity is to be considered with respect to the self-conscious subject. But the difficulty of the enterprise is perhaps already apparent in the terms just used to define the project: for what are we doing in understanding the difference between reading and interpretation but moving onto the terrain of interpretation, casting the linguistic term of reading we are trying to define in terms of a philosophical conception of a difference between how a thing appears to us (a text is a signifying object that is like a consciousness) and how it might really be in itself (a differential system unlike a consciousness)?

For Andrzej Warminski, an alert reader of German philosophy as well as of Derrida and de Man, the problem is indeed one that implicates the interpreter. When we ask a theoretical question like, "What is reading?" says Warminski in the preface to *Readings in Interpretation*, we are making use of the most powerful methods of philosophical interpretation to differentiate reading from interpretation by considering them in their opposition to one another. This deployment of interpretative method is necessary. A first approach to reading as differing from understanding must be to try out the steps of interpretative method upon it if only to learn that the approach is finally a defensive strategy that reduces all difference to opposition. Warminski consequently takes on the absurd and contradictory, yet necessary, task of setting out in "three easy steps" what leads him to assert with authority that "the path of reading is not reducible to a method."[2] Where the progressive steps of interpretative method falter and stop, as Warminski describes it, a step out of step, outside the sequence of steps, a third (dance?) step, has to be taken to set forth the actual relation of reader to text. The supplemental step is exorbitant to the dialectical and hermeneutical logics of interpretation, in which difference is defined as opposition. It entails a break with narrative construed as a dialectical progression from error (step one) to truth (step two) or as *aletheia* where a hidden meaning is retrospectively revealed.

The step to reading has still to be taken, Warminski says, because within the text surfaces an excess or a lack that cannot be accounted for by a rigorous philosophical conception of a negative, any more than it can be discounted as just a moment when an author, like sleepy Homer in the old saw, "nods from time to time." It is "an other, heterogeneous or asymmetrical excess or lack irreducible to the work of the dialectical or ontological negative"[3] (xxxii). Such heterogeneities wrongly appear appropriable by meaning systems through the reduction of difference to opposition.[4]

But in fact, says Warminski, the heterogeneity of the text is an asymmetrical difference that resists understanding because it opens onto the material conditions of meaning. These latter suggest that while reading does not operate like the understanding, it cannot be symmetrically opposed to it either. Reading is a pre-step to interpretation, a step that we have had already to have taken and to have forgotten in order to understand. Therein lies another difficulty: For reason to take the step to reading, it has to take a step out of synch with a progressive notion of time and step-taking because it has to remember a repressed, what we have had to forget about in order to understand something. But, in the process of remembering, we are translating the forgotten thing into consciousness as a determinate content; we are thereby forgetting reading all over again, and the prize recedes again just as it seems in our grasp. Reading is prospective, then, because the heterogeneity that has surfaced is never anything but a placeholder for an always-open, reiterating possibility that the text may disruptively free itself from signification. The step to reading is always a step in lieu of the methodical step that could take in through a single example a field of similar examples. Insofar as it is a step, the step to reading always and again entails the forgetting of reading. And insofar as it is a step in prospect, given the nontotalizable, differential nature of the text, the step to reading recedes as impossible.

In Warminski's view, there is a solution to this double impossibility. Instead of answering the question of the linguistic negative by translating it into a philosophical negative, we have to answer it linguistically, remember it by reinscribing it in a new text, which also takes on the care of the impossible yet necessary step to reading.

Warminski's discussion helps orient our own, first by pointing to memory and forgetting as a *locus classicus* where an out-of-sequence step is indicated. It further tells us that our own procedure must pass through interpretation and indeed never get to the end of it, condemned as we are with Baudelaire's man to keep on "passing through a forest of symbols," as one translation of the line from his famous sonnet "Correspondances" has it. This passage is necessary both in the sense that we invariably suffer the common fate of never getting "outside" interpretation or outside the outside/inside distinction so long as we are delivering—as we must—a meaningful content "in" a given form. It is also necessary in the sense that we must hold to interpreting with as much rigor as possible because it is within interpretative schemes that the inappropriable heterogeneities will show up, and the costs and benefits of remembering or forgetting them be discovered. A rehearsal of familiar narrative schemes, which are the schemes—as Paul Ricoeur comments—necessary for the articulation of personal identity, will provide us both the décor for and the stakes of the disruptions to be considered in Rousseau's memory book.[5]

The problem can be seen dramatized in two episodes from Book I of the *Confessions*, emblematic of a Rousseauian autobiographical sequence: "the children's punishment" and "the broken comb."[6] The first of these episodes concerns the hero's education into the difference between the sexes, and thus casts difference as sexual difference along an oppositional model. The second episode consists in a scene of reading. Let me recall the events for you briefly. In the pastoral paradise of Bossey where the protagonist and his cousin are studying Latin and the catechism with M. Lambercier, the hero discovers he enjoys being spanked. Apropos of the first spanking, the narrator recalls another, less-pleasant punishment, which he recounts to us from the perspective of an apparently disinterested observer: Mlle Lambercier's comb was broken while the child was reading; the child underwent a cross-examination but insisted that he did not break it; all the evidence pointed to his guilt, and he was severely beaten—for willful mischief, for lying, and for stubbornness. The narrator then declares that he did not break the comb.

A Developing Character: Bildungsroman

The chronological narrative naturally imposes the form of a *bildungsroman* on the *Confessions*. We follow the hero as he passes through various learning experiences that appear as exemplary stages in his moral and psychological development. In interpreting the educational progress made by the protagonist, we could understand the two episodes in question as representing two formative experiences linked as a development by consciousness: The first leads naturally to the second, and the second implies the first.

A first spanking, administered by Mlle Lambercier, irrevocably determines the shape of the child's desire: "this child's punishment . . . disposed of my tastes, my desires, my passions, myself for the rest of my life" (*OC* I, 15). Henceforth, the hero will seek his pleasure in the re-creation of a masochistic relation: "to be at the knee of an imperious mistress, to obey her orders, to have forgiveness to ask of her, were very sweet pleasures to me, and the more my imagination inflamed my blood, the more I had the air of a transfixed lover" (*OC* I, 17).

Simultaneously with the education into pleasure occurs the child's introduction into the hitherto-uncharted territory of fault and merit, a pre-ethical world where the morality of good intention reigns, "the sway of benevolence" (*OC* I, 15) as Rousseau calls it. The transition is marked by the introduction of a moral vocabulary of merit, fault, will, conscience, and so on conspicuously absent from the first pages of the *Confessions*. The appearance of intention in conjunction with the awakening of the senses can be explained by the fact that a single interpretative error by the sensuous imagination is responsible for awakening both. The scene is worth quoting because the error is a direct result of the child's first positive encounter with written signs—a spanking is an impression made on a *tabula rasa* of sorts—and shows both the effects on the hero of his attempt to explain the excesses and deficiencies of signs in terms of his old value system, and the effects on the old value system itself:

> As Mlle Lambercier bore the affection of a mother for us she also had a mother's authority, and carried it sometimes so far as to inflict on us the children's punishment when we had *deserved* it [*quand nous l'avions **méritée***]. For quite a long time she held herself to threats, and the threat of a punishment entirely new to me seemed very dreadful; but after it was carried out, I found it less terrible in experience than its expectation had been, and what is even more bizarre was that this punishment made me more affectionate toward the one who had imposed it on me. Indeed, all the truth of that affection and all my natural sweetness were needed to keep me from seeking the return of the same treatment by *deserving* it [*pour m'empêcher de chercher le retour du même traitement en le **méritant***]: for I had found in the ache, in the shame itself, a mingling of sensuality that had left me with more desire than fear of experiencing it again at the same hand. It is true that, since there was no doubt mingled in with it some precocious sexual instinct, the same punishment received from her brother would not have seemed pleasant at all to me. But with a man of his humor, that substitution was scarcely to be feared and if I abstained from *deserving* correction [*si je m'abstenois de **mériter** la correction*], it was solely for fear of angering Mlle

Lambercier, for such is the sway of benevolence in me, even of that one born of the senses, that it has always ruled over them in my heart. (*OC* I, 15; emphasis mine)

Mlle Lambercier has promised the child a punishment, which the child anticipates will be as great as he imagines he deserves, that is, very fearful. But upon execution, the punishment turns out to be smaller than the one expected, the pain less terrible than the anticipation. It is the difference between the punishment promised and the impression actually received that is accorded significance by the child. The difference is marked in two ways. In the first place, his sensual being is awakened by it: He experiences as a positive pleasure the release of anticipatory tension. In the second place, and more importantly for the development of a system of moral values, the difference between a promise and its execution provokes a full-scale reinterpretation by the child of what Mlle Lambercier has to teach him. Hitherto the *moi* has read her feelings of content or discontent from her expression ("I knew nothing so charming as to see everybody content with me . . ."; "nothing troubled me more . . . than to see on Mlle Lambercier's face marks of disquiet and pain" [*OC* I, 14]), and her love and severity have been undifferentiated from her brother's ("When it was necessary however, she was no more lacking in severity than her brother" [*OC* I, 14]). But after the punishment, Mlle Lambercier is a figure upon whom the child concentrates affection ("this punishment made me more affectionate toward the one who had imposed it on me . . . a person whom I loved like a mother, and perhaps even more" [*OC* I, 22]) and wields a specifically female authority, in contrast to the brutal, legalistic forms of masculine authority he will encounter in the next scene. Before the spanking, the child shares in the system of rewards and punishments, of sin and retribution that Mlle Lambercier wishes to confirm in him. But what she does is surprise him with a possibility, hitherto unforeseen, of applying his own private meaning to signs. He discovers language, hitherto assumed to be literal, delivering figural, hidden meaning.

Now the hero's revision of his interpretation of Mlle Lambercier seems to occur by means of a simple reversal of cause and effect, bringing about a consequent reassessment of values: If he didn't receive the punishment (pain) he deserved, did he perhaps deserve the punishment (pleasure) he received? A slippage occurs in the value attributed the action of deserving punishment to which the spanking refers. The different meanings of the word *mériter* in the passage indicate a path the child might have followed as he revised his ideas of Mlle Lambercier's severity and love: In the first instance, "merit" means "retribution for a fault" ("when we deserved it"). In the second, it appears to have been emptied of all ethical value, and to indicate, like the pleasure of seeking pleasure, its own reward ("seek the return of the same treatment by deserving it"). By the third appearance, however, deserving punishment has been ascribed an entirely positive value; in the context, it means to earn a recompense—or, even, to earn a recompense for the virtue of deferring the pleasurable reward by deferring the action that will bring it about ("if I abstained from deserving it").[7]

The child has come up with two convergent hypotheses to cover the failure of the sign to mean what it promised, one of which addresses the issue of a fault in the transmission of meaning by ascribing it to sexual difference, and the other of which assumes an insufficient understanding of the promise on the part of the self. Mlle Lambercier's womanly hand may have slipped in the act of making her meaning clear: The mistake frees the written sign from its conventional meaning, and makes it available to the child for private interpretation. Desire awakens when the overruling interpretative structure is shown to be inadequate to include all meanings of the sign, and becomes determined as the desire for a repetition of that demonstration. At the same time, the protagonist posits that his own understanding of the code might have been insufficient: He learns not to read people's faces for signs of their intentions and comes to suspect that Mlle Lambercier, a watchful and benevolent teacher, might have wished all along to teach him that meaning involves a temporal unfolding. The child discovers the arbitrariness of signs and is given the potential by the freed signifier to defer decision as to what that freedom signifies; this constitutes for him a first appropriation of difference as the possibility of an interiority, a being at home within himself free from the inspection of others.

The imaginative freedom the child enjoys and his paradoxical good conduct—he prefers to imagine passively a masochistic relation rather than to pursue actively any other kind of relation with the opposite sex—as well as his bizarre concatenation of female affection and authority in the figure of the loving dominatrix or teacher, is owed to an interpretative gesture that lands him in an impasse. The hero discovers a sign (the spanking) in excess of the intent to punish, which make his interpretation vacillate over whether signs are arbitrary, appropriable by the stealthy imagination for its own ends, or motivated, signs whose meaning has not yet been revealed.

The substitution of an imaginary relation for a real one accrues positive benefits to the child's conduct and in constitution of his inner life, but arrests the development of his conscience at a preethical stage, and actively interferes with the development of his reason. Indeed, his reason is so impaired that, as Rousseau suggests, the very subject of his greatest curiosity (the difference between the sexes) is the one he will have the least knowledge and the fewest ideas about. Because his only interest in the opposite sex is to transpose women into imaginary scenes as imperious school mistresses, he will have little objective curiosity about them, and will consequently learn the facts of life very late: "until adolescence I had no distinct idea of the union of the sexes" (*OC* I, 16). In a word, the substitution of teleological fictions of desire for the literal world empowers the imagination; blocks the moral faculty at the level of the morality of good intention; and, temporarily at least, paralyses judgment. This lesson is absorbed without trouble in the practical sphere. The literalism of stern Calvinist doctrine has given way to a more benevolent deity who hides meaning in figures, without damage or gain to conduct.

For reasons to be discussed throughout the rest of the chapter, the relation of the second episode to the first is vexed. Despite some difficulties in making it fit the pattern, it has often been read as a continuation of the same topic, with the child discovering that the difference between appearance and reality learned in the first scene leads to misjudgment and manipulation in real-life ethical situations. In the second episode, the child experiences "[the] first sentiment of injustice and violence" (*OC* I, 20). He is spanked, after a trial and a conviction, by an executioner officially appointed, for a crime he claims he did not commit. He discovers that, however unfairly, persons are sometimes attributed responsibility for actions. Too young to know that "appearances condemned [him]" (*OC* I, 19), he himself blames an unjust human agency. "Butcher, butcher, butcher" (*OC* I, 20) he cries, revolting against the impersonal hand of the executioner as if against a sadist. The experience of injustice provokes and justifies unjust indignation, mistrustful vigilance, secrecy, stubbornness, cunning—all the evils the punishment was calculated to correct. It makes the child an expert in using appearances, whose capacity to veil intentions he now appreciates; he learns to hide behind them, to harbor secrets, to conceal his projects. He loses his fear of acting reprehensibly and directs his energies at hiding the traces of his actions, for now he only fears getting caught. "We were less ashamed of doing bad thing, and more fearful of being accused" (*OC* I, 21).

In the account just given, the hero's character undergoes a distinct evolution over the course of the two episodes. In the first, he discovers desire and the private, interior world of the imagination. In the second, he learns to know the world of action and how to manipulate appearances. The second stage comes to correct the child's early substitution of subjective categories for objective ones, without ever entirely eradicating that original desire, which will continue to dominate his relations with the opposite sex and explain his persistent preference for fictions over objective accounts of human history. We recognize in the sequence the beginning of a genetic account of human development, similar in its linearity to the one Condillac's statue follows as it gets progressively more complex ideas, and that could lead toward a dialectical resolution in the fully formed psychological and moral being of an adult after the protagonist learns to renounce completely the errors of his imagination for the rewards of reason. Such an account has as its endpoint the assumption by the I of its place in the world as exemplary sovereign subject, autonomous and responsible for its acts.

Developing a Character: Discursive Unity

But of course, an illusion quickly dispelled by autobiography is the illusion that the chronological narrative, the story of the events, *l'histoire*, is a true representation of a natural progression toward a single, recapitulative figure.[8] For while we follow the development of the protagonist's character over the narrative in our naïve first reading, in fact, the end toward which the development leads is in sight from the very beginning, in the figure of the narrator the hero has become.[9] It is he who tells the story, whose modeling presence shapes the narrative from the beginning. The work remembers and restores already played-out scenes. The *Confessions* can be understood according to a hermeneutical model then. It takes as its horizon the final revelation of an original fold in the narrative: The end, the self developed, has become the beginning, the self being exposed. That fold had to occur for the narrative to be possible, and the narrative itself is the unfolding of the fold as an interpretation. The discrepancy between a literal understanding arrived at in proximity to events, and their later, figurative significance is healed through a progress in the understanding. Hence the reference in Rousseau's preamble to a teleological being, to a future moment of Divine Justice, when the end of all events will be revealed and justified: "Let the trumpet of the Last Judgment sound when it will, I will come this book in hand to present myself before the sovereign judge" (*OC* I, 5). Present at the very least in the choice of events told, the narrator naturally predetermines the meaning of the events that appear to determine him: From the outset, every episode in the narrative represents either a normal moment in the development of the model, or a temporary deviation away from that main path. The autobiographical narrative, in this simplified hermeneutical account, is a teleological fiction. Each episode of the *récit* is understood to be a signifier pointing toward the omnipresence of a shaping self-referential intent. What is gained by a teleological vision is the possibility of exploring a meaning to events unknown at the time of their occurrence but retrospectively available to narrating consciousness. It allows Rousseau to step into his role as writer of a pedagogical treatise and to judge the moments of his own education from the perspective of justice, ethics, and so on. The author of *Emile* reveals the shameful episode of the children's punishment, for instance, on account of "the great lesson" (*OC* I, 14) about early childhood education that can be drawn from it. These accounts all relate to his justification for telling his story to others, as exemplifying in some way the theoretical principles laid down in his other works.

Since the narrative implies a reformed narrator, however, one who is no longer doing but is only recounting, the episodes appearing nearer the end of a narrative sequence will tend to explain why the story is told, serving as conversion moments not covered by the temporal frame of the other episodes. The question then arises as to why, having already set himself up as a pedagogue-narrator in the scene of "the children's punishment," Rousseau should feel obliged to add the episode of the broken comb. Jean Starobinski sees that scene as an addition necessary to explain a secondary motivation for the autobiographical narrative that complicates the motivation of desire.[10] In that episode, says Starobinski, the narrator learns to feel the accusing eye of Protestant Geneva upon him, and with it the press of judgment. From an early accusation and the fear to which it gives birth—"more fearful of being accused" (*OC* I, 21)—comes Rousseau's need to exculpate himself and thus to write the *Confessions*.

Starobinski's discussion of the scene is relatively brief. However, Lejeune has provided a more extended treatment that goes in a similar direction, investigating it as potentially disruptive with respect to Rousseau's desire structure, but concluding that it ultimately reinforces it. We will follow his argument at some length because it provides a good example of a hermeneutic strategy for dealing with disruptive forces in the narrative, besides letting us see the stakes of the scene of injustice for Lejeune's influential notion of the autobiographical pact.[11] For Lejeune, the scene bears features of repression, denial, and partial revelation that at first threaten the compact, but then turn out to have opened an interior space, a sort of unconscious at work shaping the narrative, that restores and expands the model of understanding.

The places where the narrative structure is threatened by an excess or a lack awaken Lejeune's hermeneutic suspicion. In particular, he notes a contradiction in the narrative perspective: Rousseau first presents the case of the broken comb as if from the perspective of a detective who reconstructs the crime and then later adopts the discursive position of a confessing subject. Along with this strategy, Lejeune points to the narrator's extraneous declaration that he did not break the comb: "This adventure happened almost fifty years ago, and I am not afraid today of being punished for the same act. Well, then, I declare in the face of Heaven that I was innocent of it, that I neither broke nor touched the comb, that I didn't approach the ledge [on which the comb lay], and I didn't even dream of doing it" (*OC* I, 19). Lejeune's thought is that the reader would tend to believe Rousseau's innocence without this declaration, whose excessiveness tends on the contrary to suggest that the trauma of being falsely accused and unjustly punished has not been resolved. Rousseau's declaration has thus to be understood as a denegation, according to the Freudian concept of *Verneinung* in which a subject reformulates one of its repressed desires by denial, and in so doing speaks a desire while still maintaining its partial repression. Coupled with the airtight case made against the child by the "objective" narrator, this declaration means that Rousseau did not break the comb but wanted to do so, in the hopes of "deserving" another spanking from Mlle Lambercier.

In such a view, then, the *Confessions* develop as an exposition of the storyteller, in his character as fiction maker. The narrative is teleological rather than causal and emerges, under the impetus of an obscure accusation and an unnamed guilt, from a sack of memories that is being emptied. The compulsion to confess comes from the second episode, but what Rousseau wishes to achieve in emptying the sack is a return to the innocent state represented in the first episode, as it would pertain to the narrator and his *récit*. Just as the general impression the child gives is of good behavior, despite all the delirious erotic scenes he is imagining, so the general impression the narrator wants to give is of having a good intention in revealing all the things done and left undone by of his earlier, deluded self.

For Lejeune, the narrator's aim is to convince after telling his story that he stands fully revealed as a transparent intention to communicate the truth. The model of the *bildungsroman* has been put into place by the first episode. The second episode of the broken comb provides the necessary corrective to the hero's "innocent" fiction-making tendencies within the narrative of developing consciousness by showing the wary reader the narrator's concern with truth-telling. For, as the second episode shifts the focus of interest from hero to storyteller, from *récit* to *discours*, it extends over the narrative precisely the same hypotheses concerning the relation of written signs to intention that the protagonist had discovered in the isolated case of the deserved punishment, but this time within the context of the courtroom. Narrative continuity is the stake in the second episode; the issue is whether the anecdotes reveal a single far-reaching design or whether Rousseau has not indulged in subterfuge and lying in introducing gaps and distracting excesses into the evidence. Although the excesses and lacks in the story at first seem breaks in the compact Rousseau makes to tell the truth about his experience, the entire thrust of Lejeune's proof in "Le Peigne cassé" is to show that in the end, the episode tends toward a unified self even in its inadequacies: Occasional memory lapses or miscalculations in self-presentation are revealing exceptions that give a glimpse of the I's repressed desires, proving the general rule of the autobiographical pact with its pledge to tell the truth about the subject. Unconscious desires and conscious narrative strategies can converge because both reveal the self-identical being guaranteed by the proper name.[12]

The complication Lejeune brings to the hermeneutical model is possible because the act of confessing, what Genette would call "narration," also figures within the *Confessions*. In the act of confessing, Rousseau repeats the fault he wants to expiate, and thereby renews the possibility of misunderstanding since the story is a performative, in excess of the content—his simple good faith—that it reveals. Each confession is therefore potentially damaging to the promise of total self-revelation. Once Rousseau begins excusing himself for confessing, each confession will potentially branch into a supplementary series of confessions, although, from the hermeneutical perspective, it will suffice to explore a single modeling confession to understand the principle.[13] At best, Rousseau can manage to convince his readers by confessing confessions that the performative excesses of each confession are involuntary faults; that he, Rousseau, has been caught up in the machinery of the communication process he is attempting to elucidate. At worst, the excesses will simply generate further misunderstanding. In either case, Lejeune's Rousseau will feel excused because he will have done his best to explain the problem at its source.

The hermeneutical model, the most totalizing account of the confessional narrative possible, has to grapple constantly with misfires in the performances of confessions, but it recuperates those misfires by revealing that they are localized misunderstandings that do not put into question the teleological structure and discursive unity of the whole. Thus Lejeune, following Starobinski's lead, will show how the potential for misunderstanding confessions can be made into the object of the confession, how, "failing the possibility of ever telling the truth of desire, one tells to the end what keeps it from being told."[14] That Rousseau finally understood politico-ethical concepts like justice to be predicted on a mere morality of good intentions would follow from such a model, as would the establishment of his persuasive aim in his autobiographical texts to be the unfolding, by the way of the narrative, of figures of the self, with the self now enlarged to include unconscious or partially conscious motives.

Developing Prints: Reading Characters

But questions arise. Is Rousseau's autobiography as seamless as this model makes it? Is the convergence of pathos and strategy the overall effect achieved? Is the discrepancy between persuasion and conviction dramatized in the episode of the broken comb actually overcome in the figure of the strategic narrator, or does it persist as an open threat to narrative coherence, a persistence that Rousseau wants to elucidate? The fact that the scene is built around a death, the death of the newly awakened sensuality, ("If . . . they had wanted to deaden my depraved senses [*amortir mes sens dépravés*] forever, they could not have gone about it any better" [*OC* I, 19]) is just one indication that the passage might ultimately find an unbridgeable gap between the two orders, and be as occupied with measuring its effects as with overcoming it. If it is thinkable, as Lejeune would have it, that an objective stance might be only a pose, are there any circumstances in which the subjectivism and pathos of the *Confessions* might also prove to be part of a ruse? Critics have long been divided over whether Rousseau's systematic works are self-justifications disguised as philosophy (the view of Starobinski);[15] or whether, for an unsystematic spirit like Rousseau, the autobiographical works are part of a gigantic strategy for revealing the truths of the system (the view first put forward with any consistency by Ernst Cassirer).[16] The decision to privilege the autobiographical works over the systematic works may depend on the axe one has to grind; a more interesting question is, what explains the fact that both of these views appear legitimate but partial readings of Rousseau?[17] If Rousseau provides the answer to that question, we would have to conclude that explanation, rather than self-disculpation, has determined the order and manner of presenting the episodes. For instance, he may have wanted

to show how totalizing figures like the paralyzed lover (*amant transi*) of
the first episode, which collects and expresses opposing narrative forces
in his ecstatic state of suspended animation, are inevitably followed by
fragmentary pieces uncollectible by recapitulative figures. The second episode, which gains its meaning from reference to literal events—the breaking of a comb, the beating of a child, the declaration of innocence—would
follow the first because it expresses the inevitability of such literalizations.
The representation within the confessional narrative of Rousseau's life as
a process of degeneration, in which fragmentary effects of order are increasingly found that resist being subsumed by the imagination into its
categories (what Rousseau in his paranoid mood increasingly identifies as
"plots" against him), would lend credence to such a reading. This kind of
question recenters autobiography, whether conceived as tracing the genetic development of a child's character or as a teleological narrative
bringing out the narrator's act of self-interpretation, on reading and the
impossible narratives of autothanatography.

Is there such a narrative in the *Confessions*? Is there evidence in the
broken comb episode that its uncertainties are not merely local? We will
need to examine more closely what the scene leaves suspended—to enlarge
and print, as it were, certain significant negatives[18]—in order to determine
whether the divergence between persuasion and conviction, verisimilitude,
and truth is not too great to be recuperated even by reference to a repressed desire. I quote the passage in French and English because it is in
the twists of Rousseau's language that those negatives emerge:

> *J'étudiois un jour seul ma leçon dans la chambre contigue à la cuisine. La servante*
> *avoit mis sécher à la plaque les peignes de Mlle Lambercier. Quand elle revint les*
> *prendre, il s'en trouva un dont tout un côté de dents étoit brisé. A qui s'en prendre*
> *de ce dégat? personne autre que moi n'étoit entré dans la chambre. On m'interroge;*
> *je nie d'avoir touché le peigne. M. et Mlle Lambercier se réunissent; m'exhortent,*
> *me pressent, me menacent; je persiste avec opiniâtreté; mais la conviction étoit trop*
> *forte, elle l'emporta sur toutes mes protestations, quoique ce fut la prémiére fois*
> *qu'on m'eut trouvé tant d'audace à mentir. La chose fut prise au serieux; elle*
> *méritoit de l'être. La méchanceté, le mensonge, l'obstination parurent également*
> *dignes de punition: mais pour le coup ce ne fut pas par Mlle Lambercier qu'elle me*
> *fut infligée. On écrivit à mon oncle Bernard; il vint. Mon pauvre Cousin étoit*
> *chargé d'un autre délit non moins grave: nous fumes enveloppés dans la même*
> *execution. Elle fut terrible. Quand, cherchant le reméde dans le mal même, on eut*
> *voulu pour jamais amortir mes sens dépravés, on n'auroit pu mieux s'y prendre.*
> *Aussi me laisserent-ils en repos pour longtems.*
>
> *On ne put m'arracher l'aveu qu'on exigeoit. Repris à plusieurs fois, et mis dans*
> *l'état le plus affreux, je fus inébranlable. J'aurois souffert la mort et j'y étois résolu.*

*Il fallut que la force même cédat au diabolique entêtement d'un enfant; car on
n'appella pas autrement ma constance. Enfin je sortis de cette cruelle épreuve en
piéces, mais triomphant.*

[I was studying my lesson alone one day in the room next to the kitchen.
The servant had put Mlle Lambercier's combs out to dry on the ledge at
the back of the fireplace.[19] When she returned to take them, one was found
to have a whole row of broken teeth. Who was to blame for the damage?
No one other than myself had entered the room. I am interrogated; I deny
having touched the comb. M. and Mlle Lambercier join forces, exhort,
press, threaten me; I obstinately persist; but conviction was too strong and
prevailed over all my protestations, although it was the first time that they
had found me so audacious in lying. The thing was taken seriously; it deserved to be. The ill-nature, deceit and obstinacy seemed equally worthy of
punishment: but for once it was not by Mlle Lambercier that it was in-
flicted. My Uncle Bernard was summoned by letter: he came. My poor
Cousin was charged with another offence no less grave: we were enveloped
in the same execution. It was terrible. If, seeking the remedy in the evil
itself, they had wanted to deaden my depraved senses forever, they could
not have gone about it any better. So it was that for a long time my senses
left me in quiet.

The confession exacted could not be pulled out of me. Though gone at
several times and put into an awful condition, I was inflexible. I would have
suffered death, and was resolved to do so. Force itself had to give in to the
diabolical pig-headedness of a child, for that was what my constancy was
called. At last I emerged from that cruel trial, in pieces, but triumphant].
(*OC* I, 18–9)

The episode of the broken comb can be read as a dramatic representation of two very different kinds, in keeping with the two views of narrative
discussed so far. In the first place, it confronts an autonomous subject (a
moi) and an agent or representative of another subject (the servant) over
the issue of responsibility for an event, the breaking of a comb. The servant, unlike the *moi*, is not an independent entity but merely acts to carry
out the commands of another. The alibi of the child appears to be that he
has been lost in study: his mind on his books, and his senses asleep. But
the Lamberciers find it infinitely more logical—"conviction was too
strong"—that an autonomous subject should have caused the damage than
that a mere servant, a hand animated only in the service of Mlle Lambercier should have done so. Rousseau himself shares this view enough to
have made the Vicar state in the *Profession de foi* that his mind refuses to
assent[20] to the idea that any movement could begin without a cause;

". . . seeing a body in motion, I immediately judge either that it is an animated body, or that motion has been communicated to it. My mind refuses all assent to the idea of unorganized matter moving by itself, or producing any action" (*OC* IV, 575). No suspicion is attached to the servant because she plays the role of unorganized matter, moved under Mlle Lambercier's communicated orders, incapable of inventing or destroying things on her own. Through their shortsighted overlooking of the servant, the Lamberciers are assuming as a fact what is actually a judgment: namely, that the transformation of objects is the result of intentional action; they are determining the breaking of the comb to be one such planned event.

On the other hand, because every episode in the *Confessions* can alternatively be understood as a fiction into which the narrative consciousness has projected itself, the scene can be read as representing, within the autonomous student who provides the décor of the scene (through the imperfect tense, *j'étudiois*) the dramatic moment when a new idea is formed, abstracted, like the teeth from the comb, from several perceptions. Does the child get that new idea from an unaccustomed perception, or does judgment create it by moving things around? The scene is highly Cartesian,[21] and the drama is centered on the possibility of distinguishing the role of perception from that of judgment in the passage to a new idea. In one room, a *moi*, a reason removed from its senses, is studying; in the other room, the kitchen, the senses go about their business of providing fragmentary and isolated perceptions for consciousness to appraise: and between the two, an opening—a ledge—on which the combs are placed. Without the senses, judgment can have no perceptions to compare for resemblances and differences. But without judgment, it seems impossible to get anything like the organized perception of a comb, in which teeth are differentiated from the connecting back of the comb and compared with one another. For the combs to be presented to consciousness as perceptions analyzable into parts, they need to have been "moved" around by consciousness: The senses, however capable of providing two separate perceptions they might be, cannot find resemblances between teeth, or differentiate between teeth and comb. Just so, the Vicar states that judgment, although it appears inactive, actually plays an active role in comparing perceptions which sensation would be incapable of distinguishing or combining:

> By sensation, objects offer themselves to me separately, in isolation, as they are in nature; by comparison, I move them, I transport them, so to speak, I

set them one on top of the other to pronounce on their difference or their resemblance, and generally on all their relationships. . . . I seek in vain in a purely sensitive being that intelligent force that superposes and then pronounces, I do not know how to find it in its nature. That passive being will feel every object separately, or will even feel the object formed of the two, but having no force to fold them back onto one another, it will never compare them, it will not judge. (*OC* IV, 571–2)

As far as the representation of the subject is concerned, then, the active role of judgment in the formation of organized perceptions is being foregrounded. The *moi*'s denial of having literally touched the comb is the equivalent, so far as the representation of the subject's judgment is concerned, of an admission that he has been figuratively moving the combs in order to abstract ideas from them. The narrator assents to the organizing power of judgment over an orderly presentation by the senses. The senses can lay perceptions on the ledge between the rooms, but judgment denies the former any ability to compare or differentiate between the latter.

The two representations—of events and of the subject's judgment— bear a synechdochal relation to one another. The animated being capable of independent action in the representation of events is shown in a close- up view to be ruled by an active force of judgment that gets its ideas by transporting and comparing perceptions. The two representations, despite the contradictions they present as far as the comb is concerned (in one case, the subject is called to account for its participation in a literal crime; in the other case, the broken comb is a metaphor for the invention of ideas by abstracting from perception) and despite the differences in the kinds of evidence provided (opinion provides the basis for thinking the damage deliberate; whereas a lack of evidence to the contrary, the impossibility of discovering whether the senses actually are organized or not, explains the *moi*'s conviction that judgment is as figuratively active as the senses are literally active) both support a consistent reasoning: The child could have broken the comb if he had wanted to, but he didn't because he was study- ing, judging things instead. The notion that autobiography aims at the presentation of the self-willed subject for whom interpretation has come to take the place of action seems supported by the dramatic scene. It is significant as well that the synechdoche linking the two ways of under- standing the scene is consistent with reason. Finding a metaphor for the self in each representation of an action dovetails with logical presentation, where the difference of language is determined to be a strategic choice for revealing a difference between the narrator's past and present attitudes toward experience.

But there are other synechdoches in the episode that substitute parts by way of metonymy rather than by metaphor, by difference rather than by resemblance, and that call into question the convergence of the two interpretative schemes. To get at their operation, we need to enlarge some details further, starting by noting that the reading episode displaces the attention from the subject and his self-consciousness to the status of the memories and their recounting in narrative form. The episode is generally under the aegis of memory, rather than of the imagination, which dominated in the first episode. It is set between Rousseau's claim to be "returning to the first traces of (his) sensible being" (*OC* I, 18) and his ending reflection that he has been engaged in "seizing life again at its beginning" (*OC* I, 21). It causes Rousseau to think about the extent to which the connection of memories into a narrative entails artifice and erasure:

> Nearly thirty years have passed since my departure from Bossey without my having remembered my stay there pleasantly in memories a little connected to one another: but now that I have passed the age of maturity and am declining toward old age, I feel that these same memories are being reborn while others are being erased, and are engraving themselves on my memory with features whose charm and force grow greater each day [*ces mêmes souvenirs renaissent tandis que d'autres s'effacent, et se gravent dans ma mémoire avec des traits dont le charme et la force augmentent de jour en jour*]. (*OC* I, 21)

Here, Rousseau is considering the episode not in terms of the juicier details of desire but in terms of the relation between memories and memory book–making: between memory fragments that return disjointedly and the task—necessary for a writer—of making those fragments into a pleasing narrative. The reflection requires us to ask what evidence we have in the episode of Rousseau's having made a continuous narrative of disconnected pieces. In fact, the episode picks up in a very deliberate way on Rousseau's statement in the preamble that, "if it has happened to me to use an indifferent ornament, it has only ever been to fill an empty space occasioned by my faulty memory; I may have supposed to be true what I knew might have been so, never what I knew to be false" (*OC* I, 5).

In this light, we would have to reconsider the discrepancy already noted between the first and second paragraphs, which can exemplify the problem of parts and whole for us. The first paragraph provides a formally perfect mystery story, complete with beginning (suspect deeds), middle (review of evidence and conviction), and end (execution of criminal responsible). It reviews the substantial evidence, names names, and cites a proliferation of circumstances. This is the paragraph Lejeune found to present events objectively, not as they were lived by the uncomprehending child but as they appeared to the Lamberciers. The second paragraph, on the other hand, enlarges a single scene from the narrative, and repeats the same information over and over: "A child is being brutally beaten." This is the piece Lejeune finds to supply the discourse, the subjective feeling lacking in the narrative, with the narrative voice coming to compel belief in a continuity between child and confessing subject.[22] Proof of innocence as to the breaking of the comb (and his guilty desire to break it)[23] would thus come from both memory parts: On the one hand, the I has no memory of having touched the comb; he has nothing to confess and can give us only the facts to which anyone might have access; on the other hand, he was as well intentioned a youth as the narrator now is, heroic under torture, incapable of deliberate acts of violence or untruths. The narrator's vivid memory of what he felt as an outraged innocent establishes a continuity between the past and the present selves; a single part of the story allows for the restoration of the inner, subjective evidence.

In fact, however, the narrator does not have much to say about what the protagonist thought or felt. Indeed, he states quite categorically that the hero's ideas and feelings are mute, impenetrable mysteries to him— that even imagination does not allow him to establish a continuity between the past self and the present:

> Imagine a child [*un caractère*] timid and easily led . . . who has not even the idea of injustice, and who for the first time undergoes [*éprouve*] one so terrible at the hands of precisely those people he loves and respects the most. What an upset in the ideas! What a disorder in the feelings! What a revolution in his heart, in his brain, in the whole of his little moral and intellectual being! I say, imagine all this if possible; but as for me, I don't feel myself able to disentangle, to follow out, the slightest trace of what was going on inside me then. (*OC* I, 19)

The narrator is reluctant to accord belief to inner evidence or assume continuity between the past feeling and the present one. Indeed, belief is not the main issue for him in proving the boy's innocence. He states without any equivocation that he *knows* he did not break the comb: "Let no one ask me how the damage was done [*comment ce dégat se fit*];[24] I do not know nor can I understand it; what I know very certainly is that I was innocent of it" (*OC* I, 19). The narrator appears to have arrived at his certainty much as we must, by a sifting of the evidence, as if the source of his certainty could only be a text.

A second solution to the mystery of how the writer has linked his memories is possible. This one is more in the spirit of the metonymical principle that presides over the passage, among other places, in the insistence that this episode follows the previous one not because it occurred immediately after it, but by association, as another story on the same topic but different from the first. Here, we will claim, the intervention of fiction does not occur as a conscious, strategic move on the narrator's part so much as a move by memory itself as it seeks to recall things sequentially. In this solution, we will have to invert things and read the second paragraph about the punishment as the more primitive memory, in contrast to the narrative memory of the first paragraph (which we will consider a memory elaborated secondarily) to make for a continuous narrative. Our claim is that the narrative of events can be thought as a plausible frame provided by an inventive memory to set off the memory fragment of the second paragraph that returns unaccompanied by any other circumstances. We could easily understand why the narrator is so certain that the child is not guilty of touching the comb or even of wanting to touch it, if he were raising the possibility that, reading over his account, he had realized he might have made the crime up to fit the remembered scene of punishment.

The claim noted earlier, according to which Rousseau "may have supposed to be true what may have been so, never what I knew to be false" (*OC* I, 5), is germane here. The statement is generally read as Rousseau's performative promise that he has not told any positive lies but has merely embellished his memories. However, it can also be read as the narrator's self-reflective comment stating the conditions of possibility for differentiating positively false memories from merely fictitious ones. As such, it sets Rousseau in the position of a reader judging the memories he has written. For it is indeed possible for memory to have *supposed* to be true what nothing tells us is false, but it requires an act of bad faith to assert as a fact what one *knows* to be otherwise. Such a statement of the conditions of possibility for distinguishing truth from falsehood in memories gives us little to go on in determining in any given case which of Rousseau's specific memories are not suppositions, and raises a number of questions about the status of the *Confessions* as memory-book, which will be concerning us in the remaining pages. Our ordinary notion of storytelling in autobiography—according to which events precede the memory of events and invention works to pull them together into a persuasive narrative—is stood on its head by this kind of statement and by the example we are considering in the broken comb episode. The claim it supports is that the events of the episode do not precede their recording but show up in the effort of re-membering sequentially.

What is the evidence for this solution? Why should we suppose that the memory recounted in the second passage, the memory of a subject under torture, is the origin of the sequence? To begin with, the surprising lack of any referential features in the second paragraph indicates that it might not refer to the same memory as the first paragraph. Not only is no new evidence forthcoming as to what took place, but no names, no mate-rial circumstances, no times or places are cited. In the place of the local-ized, individualized world of Bossey emerges the nonspecific, impersonal "one" of a justice machine, "***On** ne put m'arracher l'aveu qu'**on** exigeoit . . . **on** n'appella pas autrement ma constance.*" Given the abstractness of the fragment, there seems to be no particular reason to think that it is *necessar-ily* contemporaneous with the broken comb story.

There are reasons for thinking that the second paragraph is instead more primitive. For one thing, the paragraph is about an I constituting itself of its fragments [*en piéces mais triomphant*]; discursively speaking, it's a confession about a non-confession, that has nothing to say but the en-during of a long-suffering I. We have gotten down to bedrock, to a first memory of a mute I coming into expression.

The terms of the passage are very suggestive of what allows for this constitution of the I as speaker by way of a recollection of a forgotten scene of suffering. The paragraph brings out the forgotten writerly side of the memory that we had noticed in passing in the episode of the children's punishment, and then set aside in our consideration of the meaning of the sign for consciousness. The I recalls having borne up under blows; it has suffered (*sub-ferre*—"under" plus "to bear") impressions made on its body, as a page would do. Its emergence from the process as I is also recounted in a way that seems allegorical of a writing situation: The I emerges from a test, *une épreuve*, which is also a term for page proof on which traces have been engraved. Rather than understanding the I as a subject constituted over and against an object, the passage understands it as emerging from the remembering of a repressed scene of reading and writing. In other words, the passage remembers the memory trace being engraved on the I as *tabula rasa* in sensation—sensation that had to be sublimated as pleasure by the I in the first episode of the children's punishment in order to tell the story of the developing imagination. The memory is not only of a situation more primitive than the events of the story of the crime told just before it; but, we begin to suspect, it may even be a piece broken off from the episode of the children's punishment. It speaks to the conditions for the I's developing consciousness, which are that he must have forgotten all about the pain of having had a sign imprinted on him in order to get pleasure from the sign's ambivalence, just as the child in the second episode has been forgetting all about having to move things around on a *plaque* (in its more usual French meaning of "tablet on which something is inscribed") in order to understand letters as meaning.

Once we recognize this memory as possibly the more primitive, the elaboration in language of a remembered sensation of pain without a cause, the first paragraph then appears a secondary elaboration, a plausible narrative that provides the circumstances to explain how the memory trace forgotten and broken off by the sublimating imagination in the first episode might have come to be imprinted upon the boy.

Evidence that the first, narrative paragraph might well have been elaborated to explain the missing parts of the second, punishment paragraph is provided by a series of compositional features that point us away from judgment as a problem of understanding intentional acts and appearances to judgment as a problem of deciphering the accidental features of language. The circumstances of the crime appear as potentially generated by an inventive filling in for the lost event: Various figural elements from the second paragraph turn up as the plausible sources for the events "invented" narrative. For example, the cruel methods used to try to extract a confession from the I—"the exacted confession couldn't be pulled out of me [*m'arracher l'aveu*]—is a possible origin for the literally yanked-out teeth of the comb. The fragmentariness of sensation, against the underlying unity of the I's body—"I came out of that cruel trial in pieces, but triumphant"—can be read as the source for the literal comb, still one despite its broken-off teeth. As for the sensation of having been a page on which impressions are made, it finds a host of equivalents: in the letter sent off to Uncle Bernard; the offense itself (a *délit*, with its relation as homonym to *lire*); the punishment in which the children were *enveloppés*, like so many letters; the piece of inscribed metal (again, giving *plaque* its usual sense); the book the child is studying; and finally, the whole series of *mises à l'épreuve* (that is, the tests of a student).

In short, the fault is probably in the memory of the narrative maker. The narrative about the broken comb looks indeed to be one of those indifferent ornaments that the narrator has used "to fill an empty space occasioned by my faulty memory."[25] The evidence for this reading is fundamentally negative: The two passages are connected by proximity and by the signifying code. Here, Rousseau's "charlatanistic transitions"[26] reveal their law: Fragments placed side by side persuade of a continuity of development in the narrative at the very moment they *prove* that in fact there is none.

The synechdoche that lets the memory fragment stand in for the whole does not lead to the convergence of the codes of belief and conviction then. On the one hand, it restores what is lacking from the review of the evidence—persuasion, feeling—by means of a mechanical procedure, placing two memories side by side, so that the order in which they are presented comes to be judged unjustly as a causal order with an author. On the other hand, it reminds that what is lacking from the spanking sequence is the sensation of pain, and suggests as a reason for the synechdoche the representation of that lack as explaining the presence of the scene in the *Confessions*. The scene provides two contradictory arguments: either Lejeune's theory that the child, a subject with lots of high moral feelings enduring over time, wouldn't have broken the comb; or our counterclaim that he couldn't have broken it because in writing down his memories, the author becomes convinced that the narrative was probably made up in the effort to remember things in a sequence. The aporia, which pits the synechdoche as the subject's strategic weapon for reminding of inner feeling against the synechdoche as laying part beside part, cannot be resolved. The persuasion that there is a moral being like the self arises in the face of proof that there is no inner guarantee of continuity with the past, and that consequently, the continuous development of the protagonist and the smooth unfolding of narrative consciousness as it exposes the progress of its ideas are both mirages. Instead, the passage dramatizes the possibility of disruption. Memory is jolted by the possibility that it might not be reworking past material but rather, inventing a story to explain the fragments lying about.

Now, as we have been reading it, there appears to be a sort of guarantee that Rousseau's memory, however faulty it may be in supplying stories of events that never transpired, is nonetheless his memory insofar as it is resident in his body as page on which one spanking was imprinted. By getting access to those memories stored in the body that had to be repressed in order for stories to be elaborated, he can still hope to link his present with his past. When we extend the model suggesting that part of the episode of the broken comb has been invented to both the episodes of the Bossey sequence, we start by anchoring them in a single traumatic event. For what better origin could there be for the sentiment of injustice and violence[27] than the feeling of pain without a cause, a punishment received for which no memory of a reason remains? That would be the situation if the pain of a single spanking had been repressed, then remembered first as the cause of pleasure and delight in imaginative pursuits in the episode of the children's punishment, and then as the causeless pain around which the enigmatic narrative of the broken comb is built. We post-Freudians should not be surprised that the repressed pain of the spanking should take the odd form of an inconclusive narrative about an uncertain crime because the inconclusiveness, the compression and repetition, the literalizing of figures, would be clues that the feeling—the sensation repressed so that Bossey can be sentimentalized in the first episode—is being recalled through a process recognizable as dreamwork. Although the whole Bossey sequence would be misleading in its details— the sentimental paradise did not really exist, and the events of the broken comb episode are as likely to have occurred as what you dreamed last night—still, it would tend to demonstrate that a body on which a sense impression was once made has persisted over time. The memory fragment would restore the whole, the body enduring over time, as the meaning of the episode. In remembering the same spanking twice, Rousseau would still be vindicating the confessional project, but this time from the perspective of an author recognizing, as the narrator does not, that the episode sets limits on the understanding.

But there are some features of the broken comb episode that call into question the continuity provided by the body. Once again, it is a matter of exploring what is missing from the passage rather more than what it says. For, much as a poet will sometimes construct a poem around a missing term, Rousseau seems consistently to have constructed the episode so as to call attention to missing elements.[28] Gone missing is not only the evidence necessary to convict the boy, but also definitively to convict the narrator of having made up the story to account for the bodily sensation remembered. The scene of torture, which, thematically speaking, is all about the sensation of pain, never once says the word that seems central: namely, pain. Suffering is represented only in the conditional, as what the boy would have suffered rather than confessing. Similarly, the torture scene points to missing interiority, but it expresses that by insisting on exiguity ("exacted," "pulled out," "came out," and so on). The scene is about the pain of being causelessly beaten—*une peine sans cause*—but again, that is never stated but is rather indicated by the operation of the impersonal justice machine and the fragmented, heroic, and mute I. If we then look to the narrative passage, however, the missing signifiers do surface, but poetically, in their rhyming equivalents: *la peine* shows up in a near homonym, *le peigne*; the missing interiority or *dans* translates into the missing "dents" of the comb; *une peine sans cause* finds a good homonym in *le peigne cassé*.

The two parts of the episode can be read as originating in an act of memory that makes a double translation of the two sides of a forgotten trace into a voiced signifier and into thematic elements. In this reading, remembering a trace, such as the trace *p-e-i-n-e*, has generated them.

What such a reading does—a reading, because it involves the difference that language makes—is to bring out the extent to which Rousseau's attempts at self-examination must be reinscribed in a language capable of overturning at any moment the meaning-directed stubbornness (*entête-ment*) of its speakers. The episode is about the conditions the narrating I has had to forget to constitute itself, and about the potential for those forgotten conditions to return to interject discontinuities into the narrative. The text provides no assurance that there ever was such an impression as a spanking made on the hero; and consequently; that the episode provides a certain link to Rousseau's past through his bodily memory of being butchered. The blows that fill the early books of the *Confessions* are in more than one place equated with a mechanical action like the blows of the pen, as if it were in and by writing that they were being delivered.[29]

We can't help but feel some unease at the conclusion toward which we are moving, which is that Rousseau is guilty of having made up the two-part sequence around a single trace: first its forgetting (in the scene of the children's punishment), and then its recollection in the fragmented scene of the broken comb. The unease doesn't come only from the fact that our conclusion seems very like the Lamberciers' decision that the boy broke the comb, since it implies a belief in an intentional subject of the parts lying about, and restores—in lieu of the continuity of the author—a continuity supported by language construed as body. The anxiety has also to do with a question as to the exorbitant authorial power and responsibility we thereby invest in Rousseau, as inventor of a narrative meant to illustrate the operation and effect on narrative of remembering the trace. We seem close to concluding for the authority of Rousseau by way of an interpretative key—however twisted it at first seems to be—that allows us to judge the cause responsible for all the wreckage lying about. But Rousseau has told us he doesn't know the cause of the wreckage (*comment ce dégât se fit*). That means we have to wonder whether remembering the trace *p-e-i-n-e* isn't a stand-in for a more general situation. Or, what amounts to the same thing, we have to wonder whether Rousseau isn't as involved with forgetting about writing as with remembering it.

That is certainly one way to read the passage quoted earlier concerning the problem of sequence and memory. Here's what Rousseau says again:

> Almost thirty years have passed since I left Bossey without my having recalled my stay there in any agreeable fashion by memories somewhat connected: but now that I have passed maturity and am declining into old age, I feel that those same memories are being reborn while the others are being erased, and are engraving themselves in my memory with traits whose charm and force augment from day to day [*ces mêmes souvenirs renaissent tandis que d'autres s'effacent, et se gravent dans ma mémoire avec des traits dont le charme et la force augmentent de jour en jour*]; as if, feeling life already escaping, I were seeking to seize it again at its beginnings. (*OC* I, 21)

We've been reading the passage in terms of memory, as concerning the way that the forgotten trace is being recalled and the ensuing narrative sequence being engraved in the memory book of the *Confessions*. The two-part process of memory makes the narrative sequence that Rousseau so enjoys writing. But the passage says something quite different if we understand the last part of the sentence ("and are engraving themselves . . .") to have as its antecedent not the "same memories," but "the others," more proximate in the sentence, the memories that are being wiped out. The point would be that Rousseau is not remembering traces, so much as engraving new traces being forgotten about. What the sentence suggests is that the sequence might be about the way that in remembering things in new stories, one is ever and again forgetting about the traces in which that story is couched, which makes the drama of remembering reading a mere stand-in solution indicating a growing amnesia.[30]

This reflection about the part that remembering things in a narrative has always and again to play in forgetting about the letter, reading and writing is general enough—it covers the whole of the Bossey sequence, itself a synechdoche for the whole of the *Confessions*—to give pause. It sets the question of (forgetting about) reading the trace at the center of the autobiographical text. It's as though Rousseau were measuring a widening gap, saying that each time he is trying to recollect himself, staging the problems posed by reading for narrative, he is actually scattering himself further abroad. The growing divergence means, among other things, that the sequence is not generated by Rousseau's brilliant double translation remembering the single term *p-e-i-n-e*, but by the forgetting of other traces laid down as he tells the two-part sequence, with a consequent shift of textual focus away from a problem of an injustice affecting the individual author in a single spot to the injustice of attributing authority by way of storytelling.

In this spirit, the reader might discover further patterns testifying to this divergence whose meaning is not exhausted by the single pattern mastered by Rousseau. For instance, perhaps the first spanking—the *fessée* that gives the I access to sexual difference in terms of intentional acts, even as it keeps him long in ignorance of woman's actual sexual parts (in vulgar parlance, *le con*)—is laid next to, told with, *con*, another *fessée* so that the law of the production of confessions from remembered bits of language can be revealed. The origin of the entire sequence could be the phrase *confesser confessé*; the first is an apparently meaningful and mastered confession of a self knowing and excusing itself, legitimating the act of confessing by the revelation of his "dirty secret" of having taken pleasure in the freedom of the signifier associated with sexual difference; the other is an unmastered confession whose silences and excesses prove that the sequence is artificial, made up to illustrate the pieces of the imprinting of the word *confesser*, the blows and the erasure of the blows of the pen. The implication would be that textual reflexivity—for a word that represents itself in its two aspects is a text, not a subject—would be at the origin of the *Confessions* in its entirety, with each attempt to account for it only a stand-in solution that remembers what is forgotten by a new inscription that also forgets. This situation is not merely negative, an indication that Rousseau's own memories are not his own—that is, mental images of his past life—but are, as it were, memories of his reading of the letters of the word *confesser*. It is also an episode about getting new ideas through the return of the forgotten letter. Rousseau gets the idea of injustice; he gets a more comprehensive idea of memory as involving the necessary forgetting of the letters to which a mental image is entrusted; he gets an idea about a possible limitations placed on the intentional subject demanded by the Lamberciers; he gets an idea of a responsibility to tell the story of the passage to reading, a responsibility that exceeds the very concept of responsibility, with its supposition of a sovereign subject capable of knowing and telling that story. It is a scene of authorial death but also a scene where exceptional authorial responsibilities are being discovered.

The Bossey sequence can be read either in support of Rousseau's recuperative self, or in support of the text's reflexivity, but it cannot be read as both. For in one version—the version of the understanding—the memory of a repression is the cause of a small interruption of the narrative thread, leading to the constitution of the self as a readable book, by way of a persuasive substitution of part of a totality. But in the other version, restoration of meaningful order is merely a pretense for the retrieving of literality. No subject could understand what all those letters spell given that they spell the end of understanding. The part stands in for the whole by synechdoche because the whole is: part after part after part. The passage asserts a disjunction, a mutual miscomprehension, between the two ways of organizing the episodes of an autobiography, as life narrative, as auto-thanatography. The gap constituting that miscomprehension, the divergence between reading and interpretation, cannot be closed because the effort to throw a bridge across it by an act of understanding is itself the reenactment of the persuasion into the agreeable illusion of narrative, and has as its effect the obliteration of the literality signified.

The step to reading indicated by the broken comb episode indeed requires the step out of sequence and interpretative method we discovered described by Warminski at the beginning of this chapter. Moreover, just as Warminski notes, it is not a one-time step because each time the supplementary step is taken, it can be only a stop-gap measure that, while purporting to have understood the difference that reading would make, has had to translate the trace into signifieds and signifiers and so to fail to read it. For all its impossibilities, however, reading autothanatography is an important task to undertake. It has allowed Rousseau to concern himself with an exorbitant responsibility and with the critique of justice as a system that thinks that confession can supplement for the holes in stories, and wants to force persuasion to converge with the grammar of the evidence. It has identified as the challenge of justice to write its codes in the absence of a convergence between those two logics, visible among other places in the subject placed, as child, as narrator, and as author in this sequence, before the law. The impossibility of accomplishing the step to reading can be no excuse for not making the attempt.

CHAPTER 2

Regard for the Other:
Embarrassment in the *Quatrième promenade*

One difference between shame and embarrassment in Rousseau can be stated quite simply. Shame is a passion productive of discourse. The confessing done under its aegis seems marvelously able to serve as an action of which to be ashamed, and so to provoke more confession. Embarrassment, on the other hand, is tonguetied, an anacoluthon in the grammar of feelings. Where, under influence of timidity, Rousseau manages to blurt something out nonetheless, the effect is not to end the silence but most often to prolong it, rendering the hapless speaker even more incapable of timely speech. The blurted phrase is less than successful at helping along a faltering conversation. No stopgap measure after all, it serves as a conversation stopper.

In "Excuses," de Man has said what there is to be said on the narrative productivity of performatives motivated by shame. De Man shows that the gesture by which Rousseau explains his accusation of Marion—a self-exculpating, other-accusing gesture that heaps more shame on him and reproduces its paradoxical structure every time he returns to right the balance through further narration—is indeed interesting in the fullest sense of the word.[1] Ethics and justice, the two tribunals before which Rousseau always tries his words, are interested by the slanderous, aggressive lie told out of shame over his theft. As for aesthetics, culpability (like remorse) is a parasitical passion, of the sort a beggar-poet might willingly nourish because it helps feed him lines. It is not surprising that a Baudelaire, for instance, should notice the rake-off for artistic production given by shame-driven performatives.[2] For where shame is concerned, signifiers are easily transformed into signifieds of another utterance.[3] Like the ribbon Rousseau accused Marion of stealing, which "can circulate symbolically as a pure signifier and become . . . the articulating hinge in a chain of exchanges" ("Excuses" 283), the free signifiers of shame emerge as cut off from reference (*coupable*), and so as innocent and as guilty (*coupable*) as fiction itself.

However, not everything has been said about embarrassment in Rousseau, nor about the thwarted language—a language incompletely freed from reference and yet dogged by a fictionality inappropriate to the context—that distinguishes the speaker in that predicament. In his analysis of the *Quatrième promenade*, de Man (for instance) has set aside the lie motivated by embarrassment. In answer to a woman's half-teasing question as to whether he had ever had children, Rousseau's response—"I answered that I had never had that happiness" (*OC* I, 1034)—was instantly recognizable as a lie, as he had to have known it would be, if only because he had written at some length about the birth and abandonment of his five children in the *Confessions*. De Man has some good reasons for dismissing this lie, not the least of which is that treating a passion characterized by a lack of ideas and where the self is seen as failing to present itself would take him outside his announced topic of the relationship between cognition and performance in autobiography ("Excuses" 278). Rousseau typically talks of embarrassment in a public situation where he feels called upon to utter and, having no ideas and no terms ready, represents confusedly the single idea possible: the self's inability to present itself adequately in speech, what Rousseau more than once calls "my embarrassment in speaking" (*OC* I, 518) [*mon embarras à parler*]. In the *Neuvième Promenade*, as just one instance, Rousseau claims an increasing blockage:

> I have never had presence of mind nor facility of speech; but since my misfortunes, my tongue and my head have become more and more obstructed [*ma langue et ma tête se sont de plus en plus embarrassées*]. The idea and the proper word both escape me. (*OC* I, 1088)[4]

With neither ideas nor proper terms forthcoming at the moment of blockage, any statements clarifying of embarrassment are necessarily non-contemporaneous with it: "ideas slow to arise, embarrassed and that never are ready until after the fact" (*OC* I, 113) [*des idées lentes à naitre, embarrassées et qui ne se présentent jamais qu'après coup*]. Because it gives rise to so

limited a knowledge, and one confused, untimely and alienated with respect to the situation it claims to know, the embarrassed lie is indeed not
a good place to discuss cognition in Rousseau. The very etymology of the
term, which links it through the Spanish *embarazar* (to hinder, to annoy)
to the Portuguese *baraço* (cord or strap), suggests that unlike the signifier
of the ribbon that circulates so freely and allows for aesthetic play, with
embarrassment signifiers still tether us to reference and its obligations,
and insofar as they obtrude upon our notice as signifiers, it is as interfering
to some extent with the idea of free play.[5]

De Man's dismissal of the embarrassed lie is even more understandable
in view of the limits Rousseau imposes on the reach of embarrassment. In
most of his pronouncements on the topic, the failure to perform can be
set down to the lack of ideas or appropriate terms in a particular speaker
in a particular predicament. Unreadiness of mind afflicts his *empirical* self
caught up in the world, whereas the reflective self is rarely touched by it.
Embarrassment is moreover punctual, tied to a specific moment when a
capable individual, feeling itself on display, momentarily lacks the human
capacity for responsive speech. In the *Confessions*, Rousseau discusses at
length why he has so often been adjudged "if not entirely inept, than at
any rate a boy of little wit, few ideas, almost without acquired knowledge,
in a word, in all respects very limited" (*OC* I, 113). His general unreadiness
of mind taken together with the obligation to speak right away has often
led others to this judgment:

> I find no constraint more terrible than the obligation to speak right away
> and always. I do not know whether this comes from my mortal aversion to
> all subjection, but it is enough for me to be required absolutely to speak for
> me infallibly to speak foolishness [*c'est assez qu'il faille absolument que je parle
> pour que je dise une sotise infailliblement*]. (*OC* I, 115)

To be obliged to speak without delay and always—that is the terrible fix
of the I in conversation. The downside of Benveniste's notion that through
the deictic we become subjects in language is suggested by this dash of
Rousseauian empiricism, where the I does not freely and responsibly assume language but is rather subjected by it to expose its unreadiness.

From this fact that the empirical self momentarily appears stupid to
others in a spectacle, we may ask whether the localized failure does not
stand in for a more general breakdown. If we consider the constatives
Rousseau provides about embarrassment, not simply in terms of the spec-
tacles of verbal ineptitude they describe but also in terms of what they
seem to forestall in the way of a greater disruption, they may be as easily

called premature as belated statements of knowledge. The knowledge of stage fright is a foreclosing maneuver that lets the specters evoked in this predicament—for instance, of language as sheer babbling, of performance as never successfully tying together idea and persuasive force, of a mind never quite contemporaneous with itself—be laid to rest before they are ever allowed to come on the scene, never mind to haunt it. In embarrassment, the self takes onto itself as its own defect, surmountable by a bit more education or usage in the world, what might be a more general predicament, in a defensive move that makes the threat more manageable.

As it happens, the main reason de Man adduces for setting aside Rousseau's lie about his paternity, besides its sterility in terms of cognition, is its defensiveness. He says that the lie is "a less interesting example than the ribbon, because there is nothing enigmatic about a lie which . . . is *only* a defense" ("Excuses" 293, de Man's emphasis). It could have done Rousseau no personal good to deny his well-publicized paternity ("I said what shouldn't have been said and which could serve me in nothing" [*OC* I, 1034]), so at first it seems hard to see what Rousseau could be defending. De Man's point seems to be that Rousseau's lie is not a screen that hides a fact from view, but rather one hiding the more radical implications of his unreadiness of speech from surfacing at this point. Rousseau's lie is defensive because it tames questions of considerable theoretical interest—Is there fatherhood? What is a father?—by translating them into an empirical question (Are you a father?) and then giving it a yes or no response. Rousseau did not lie because he denied his biological paternity, but because in denying, he takes paternity to be a granted fact, and not, as in his more lucid descriptions, a dubious legal fiction with implications for theories of society and morality.[6] Rousseau's lie consists in his having substituted an empirical question for a theoretical one, the domain of "factual truth" [*la vérité des faits*] for "moral truth [*la vérité morale*], a hundred times more respectable than that of facts" (*OC* I, 1031). Embarrassed speech from the point of view of a would-be authoritative I is a sort of apotropaic maneuver, a version of the Medusa defense that reduces the anxiety to a manageable one.

But embarrassment is not a defense only in the sense that it protects the self against a threat. As verbal blockage, it also inhibits the self from embarking on the trajectory of desire; it defends in the French sense of *défendre*: That is, it forbids the self from communicating or carrying out its own latent wishes. That becomes apparent when we consider the role of writing, well known since Starobinski as the route Rousseau takes to circumvent embarrassment. His absence of mind in speaking leads him to choose writing as the stage from which an adequate re-presentation of his reflective self and theories could be attempted. By way of the detours of writing, the I need no longer appear inept and unreflective, coerced by the speed of social converse and his own thwarted wishes into awkward utterances. Instead, through the self's withdrawal, it can time its appearance, and emerge to demonstrate its superior reflective capacities and linguistic mastery. This comes clear in the often-cited comment: "the strategy I have adopted of writing and hiding myself is precisely the one that suited me best. With me present, no one would never have known what I was worth" (*OC* I, 116) [*Le parti que j'ai pris d'écrire et de me cacher est précisément celui qui me convenoit. Moi présent on n'auroit jamais su ce que je valois*]. Because it frees the self from inhibiting stage fright and grants it time to reflect and to strategize, writing allows it to demonstrate its worth.

Paradoxically, however, what writing lets Rousseau expose is not the I's prowess so much as the undoing of the self and of authority. Writing exposes the self to a more thorough-going undoing than embarrassed speech. It can do so because the body of the embarrassed speaker does not step in to limit self-absence to mean the mere ineptitude of an empirical self. In discussing the impossibility of successfully staging Mallarmé's lyrical drama, *Hérodiade*, Peter Szondi makes a similar point with some striking parallels to the Rousseauian situation. The chief action of Mallarmé's drama, says Szondi, is the decomposition of the dramatic character Hérodiade, an action that the physical presence of an actress in a staged production must blatantly contradict. The lyrical drama, Szondi states, cannot be performed; it has to remain a text because only in writing would the drama not give the lie to the decomposition of the metaphors of the self.[7] The body is an embarrassment for Hérodiade for the same reason that we are suggesting it was for Rousseau: because it inhibits the reception of the action—the undoing of the self—by turning it into a determinate undoing, and one focused on one part of the body (the hair, in Hérodiade's case; the stuttering tongue or the stopped-up mouth [*la bouche bouchée*] in Rousseau's). Rousseau says something close to this in the first pages of the *Rêveries*: "My body is no longer anything but an encumbrance [*un embarras*], an obstacle for me, and I disengage myself from it beforehand as much as I can" (*OC* I, 1000). Rousseau's recourse to writing can thus also be explained as a detour taken to surmount the defensive foreclosure of embarrassment, the better to expose the self to the radical discrepancy between meaning and saying that ends in its undoing. Embarrassment is situated at a crossroads: It expresses a partial prohibition on the free expression of desire (*défense de parler*) and serves as a defensive screen hurriedly thrown up to manage a greater threat coming from writing.

In short then, de Man seems justified in neglecting the embarrassed lie as the less-productive road where Rousseau's account of the relation of cognition to performance in autobiographical writing is concerned. Rousseau cannot succeed at presenting himself and what he knows; he can neither express his desire nor proceed with the undoing of the self, so long as embarrassment inhibits the full force of his insights into a disjunction between saying and meaning from being received. Our reading confirms so far that embarrassment is a blockage affecting the speaking self that partially defends it from the threat that it has to face in writing, where the alibi of a punctual, empirically based unreadiness is not available to parry the blow. We might well understand the blush of embarrassment as in keeping with the defensive strategy: The flush that seems to expose the self as inadequate, does so only to cover up the larger threat by providing a visible manifestation reassuringly linked to the self's inner operations at a moment when the self is in doubt. A human face capable of showing emotion at its failure to speak appropriately realigns outside expression and inside feeling. Douglas Cairns has said something similar about the blush: The embarrassed self shows itself temporarily bereft of self-assessing capability; its blush attests to the return of self-reflection and so helps mend the break between meaning and saying.[8]

So far I have argued, in line with de Man, that Rousseau's embarrassed lie about fatherhood defensively replaces a substantive theoretical question with a lesser version of the same question, the latter presumably referentially verifiable. The inevitable conclusion has been that from the perspective of content or knowledge, the embarrassed statement provides little of interest, and its value as a strategy is largely that of a foreclosing defense.[9] Now I would like to make a rather different claim, and argue that Rousseau's embarrassed lie is of more interest if we consider it in terms of an address to the other and ask about its place in the written text. A relation to the other is implied not only by the fact that embarrassment arises in situations of speech but also in another motif that often arises when it is discussed by Rousseau: the motif of doing justice to others in speaking. One has not only to consider whether inhibited speech does justice to the self but also whether it pays a debt owed to the other. One of the implications of this claim is that neither the self-awareness of the speaker nor the content of the speech are the central problem with embarrassed speech; rather, the possibility of justice and the happiness of performatives are implicated in it. To begin exploring these points, I'd like to turn briefly to a passage from the one autobiographical text that Rousseau claims actually to have written under the aegis of embarrassment, the *Dialogues*.

In the introduction to the text, Rousseau explains his problem in terms of doing justice to others:

> In desiring to carry out this plan, I found myself in a singular predicament [*dans un bien singulier embarras*]. It wasn't a matter of finding reasons in favor of my feeling, it was a matter of imagining contrary ones, it was to found the procedures (of others) on some appearance of equitableness where I could see none. (*OC* I, 662)

Embarrassment affects the writer where it is a matter of presenting the reasons that could have prompted others to a course of action. Rousseau is called upon in justice to make this attempt, but all his work to motivate the conduct of others has led only to a disorderly presentation, and brought the characteristic blush of embarrassment to his cheek: "I have often blushed, I admit, at the reasons that I was forced to lend them" (*OC* I, 663).

In the passage from the *Dialogues*, we see in sharp relief some of the features already discussed. An obstacle inhibits the self from performing a verbal task and is as ever traceable to an absence of ideas. The inhibition is defensive: It defends against the possibility, unacceptable to a man Starobinski diagnoses with "delirious self-concern," that the indifference of others is not studied at all but simply unawareness; it also defends against the looming threat of a breakdown in social relations, one of the issues raised by the discussion of the I's obligations to others.[10] Here, too, a blush testifies to the author's good faith. But there is a further feature of importance here. The failed performance is related to a lack in the reasons found to explain the conduct of others. Rousseau reddens in writing when he has to render a fair account of minds *other* than his own. This is a crucial point. In the context of accounting for the self, Rousseau finds himself obliged to render account of others. The autobiographical vein opened with the *Lettres à Malesherbes* and the *Confessions* turns *autre-biographique* at the very moment that—eschewing writing as a strategic detour around embarrassment in the name of self-worth—Rousseau decides to put pressure on the obstacle and to write through what embarrasses him, which is doing justice to the other's reasons. In the *Dialogues*, embarrassment is thus not a just a defense; it is a signal of the writer's coming to face the impossible yet necessary task imposed by a regard for the other. Embarrassment is the feeling that attests to the "thousand obstacles" in the way of a relation with the other as another like oneself (*OC* I, 669).

Now the difficulty Rousseau describes in the preceding passage, what he calls "a very singular predicament" (*un bien singulier embarras*), derives from a discrepancy between two kinds of obligations. The I has to speak as a self-conscious subject rendering a rational account in the name of truth. He must weigh the evidence, say what he perceives and cannot perceive, know and speak his own mind, test his opinions against opposition, write the truth as he finds it. The obligation to speak the truth comes from the logos:

> General and abstract truth is the most precious of all goods. Without it, man is blind; it is the eye of reason. By it, man learns to direct himself, to be what he ought to be, to do what he must do, to head toward his true end. (*OC* I, 1026)

On the other side, the I is acting under an obligation to believe that others have their reasons for acting as they do. He doesn't want, he says, to "outrage a whole generation" (*OC* I, 662) by refusing them their good faith. This obligation is related to the speech act, to the fact that by entering into verbal commerce with one another, interlocutors incur debts to one another, and are, for instance, engaged to carry their part in a conversation: "when, *having* to keep up a discussion . . . I *absolutely have* to speak . . ." (*OC* I, 1033, my emphasis) [*lorsque **ayant à** soutenir un entretien . . . il faut **necessairement** parler . . .*].

We can see these obligations operating together, or—to be more precise, interfering with one another—in Rousseau's statement that he had to establish others' actions "on some appearance of equitableness." Rousseau has to establish that appearance in motivating others' conduct because he has to do them justice, to assume them not willfully cruel, but in error. He has also to show that the conduct was based on what they mistakenly took for equity but turned out instead to be its mere appearance or simulacrum, so as to explain how the error could have occurred.[11]

There is a bind in this for the I. Truth, eye of reason that it may be, can never just appear on the horizon; it has always to be spoken, dispensed to others according to the rules of equity applied by conscience (*OC* I, 1028), in an act of doing justice to the other. As Rousseau sees it, if the man who would be true takes justice and truth as synonyms, it is because for him truth has been absorbed into justice and become a matter of rendering credit:

> The holy truth his heart adores does not consist in indifferent facts and useless names, but in rendering faithfully to each one what is owed in things

which are truly his own [*à rendre fidellement à chacun ce qui lui est dû en choses qui sont véritablement siennes*], in imputing good or bad, in making retributions of honor or blame, praise or disapproval. (*OC* I, 1032)

The claim is not that truth is relative to justice, but that telling it always is. The priority of justice over truth in terms of speech as performative leaves the speaker, at the moment of addressing the other, bereft of reason's counsel, faced with a myriad of questions as to how to honor or blame to the other, incapable of constituting itself judge of appropriate speech yet obliged to address the other. That may be out of social pressure because not to respond to the other's address is a hostile act, either disrespectful of the other or exhibiting oneself in a not quite human aspect. Or it may be for a more essential reason, because the I's very existence as speaker relies on the indeterminate other to whom it speaks. Through its address, the speaking I makes itself a subject and at once gives itself as the replacement for every other potential speaker; it thus has to say first and foremost its debt to and violence toward the other as conditioning its speech. As early as *Totalité et infini*, Levinas declares that the vocative, interpellative function of language, through which the other is called as other, is more fundamental than what is said in it.[12] Embarrassed speech, as a speech that doesn't answer the communicative function but still responds to the other, would bear Levinas out. A speaker's *embarras* consists in appearing to be using a constative language, a language of determinate meaning, when in fact the I's response wants to be antiphony, where responses alternate as in a ritual and where it is the *act* of replying that ultimately counts. In a word, embarrassed speech acknowledges the priority of the call of doing justice to the other over that of saying the truth, even as it remains fettered to determinate referents.

In this sense, embarrassment is a constitutive feature of the speech situation and not simply a failure in empirical performance. Embarrassed speech recognizes better than fluent speech the subject's violence in having silenced the other, in having supplanted all others in becoming the subject of discourse. The I has to acknowledge a debt to the other over and over, and to find itself always unable to constitute itself judge of how best to make acknowledgment since it has always to dispense truth (*dispenser les lumiéres* [*OC* I, 1028]) before being able to think truth (*penser la vérité*). Or, as Rousseau says in the *Rêveries*,

> Its pace (of conversation), more rapid than my ideas and almost always forcing me to speak before thinking, has frequently suggested to me foolish and inappropriate things of which my reason disapproved and which my

heart disavowed as soon as they escaped from my mouth, but which, rush-
ing ahead of my own judgment, could no longer be corrected by its censure.
(*OC* I, 1033)

The *Dialogues* translate this scenario to the scene of writing, where even
time for reflection does not appear to allow Rousseau to find the right fit
between equity and truth.

But there is more to be said of the unknown other the I has to address,
to establish just how unknown and other an other it is. In the *Confessions*,
Rousseau details a few of the unanswerable fears and questions that beset
him when he feels he must speak:

> . . . to speak to the point, one has to think promptly of a thousand things at
> once. The very thought of the number of social rules, of which I am sure
> to forget at least one, is enough to intimidate me. I do not understand even
> how anyone dares speak in company: for at every word one ought to pass
> in review all the people who are there: one ought to know their characters
> and their histories to be sure to say nothing that could offend anyone. In
> that respect those who live in the world have a great advantage; knowing
> better what has to be kept quiet, they are more certain of what they do say;
> even so blunders often escape them. Now consider one who falls from the
> clouds! It is almost impossible for him to speak for a minute with impunity.
> (*OC* I, 115)

How to credit others when one doesn't know them well enough to know
their sensitive spots, their histories or their characters, never mind the
language of the group in which one finds oneself? Only to a superficial
glance is Rousseau's case that of the stranger who doesn't know the first
thing about what is appropriate to a given milieu, and whose plight might
be helped by education and longer familiarity. As the passage makes clear,
his breakdowns are not exactly like the gaffes made by those who, living
in the world, have an acquaintance with it. He is no Rastignac, upstart or
ingénu freshly arrived from the provinces and ignorant of the world's ways.
It seems rather likely that his disruptive speech models their gaffes. For
his speech is that of one who is not of this world at all, one radically
estranged: Says Rousseau, he "falls from the clouds." Because he is foreign
to the world he visits, his ignorance is broader than issues of personality,
intrigue, convention, or a salon's language, and could be better stated as
an ignorance as to the degree of the others' difference from him. Visitor
from the sky, he does not know how to read others' characters: Are they
men with feelings, or are they more literally characters, signs that point
upward to some other source for their meaning? The minds of others

appear so opaque to him, the interior workings of those he meets so mysterious, that in the *Rêveries*, Rousseau is ultimately led to hypothesize that,

> My contemporaries were for me nothing more than automatons [*des êtres méchaniques*] who acted when impelled and whose actions I could calculate only from the laws of movement. Whatever intention, whatever passion, I might have supposed in their souls, would never have explained their conduct with respect to me in a manner that I could have understood. Thus their interior dispositions ceased to be of any importance to me. I no longer saw in them anything but randomly moved masses, destitute of all morality with respect to me. (*OC* I, 1078)

For Rousseau, others are those for whom no guarantee of an inner being, of passions, intentions, and dispositions is or can be forthcoming. The I does not know what those he meets are like. More problematically, he does not know whether he ought to consider them in terms of likeness, as men like him whose expressions reveal their interior self; or of difference, as masks or robots at the bidding of some other being or force.

Austin, in a text called "Other Minds," writes of similar doubts that arise when we try to get to the bottom of a question like, "How do you know he is angry?" For Austin, the answer to the question is ultimately: "By hearing his testimony to that effect." More is at stake for Austin in this question than just whether the man is angry; the more critical question is whether he is a man at all. When we ask how we know a man is angry, we are asking how we know he is a man like us, with an interior life. Fortunately, man speaks, and in speaking about his feelings brings before us an inner world for which we ultimately have only his word. The declaration of anger thus allays a fear deeper than that provoked by mere hostility: the fear that the other might be one of Rousseau's mechanical beings. Austin can then end on an upbeat note: "It seems, rather, that believing in other persons, in authority and testimony, is an essential part of the act of communicating, an act which we all constantly perform."[13]

If the critical ingredient for belief in the other man is that he break silence to testify to his inner life, then Rousseau's acceptance of the mechanical-man idea makes sense inasmuch as the chief act the Rousseau of the *Dialogues* has to account for is the others' keeping of silence, "the profound, universal silence, no less inconceivable than the mystery that it covers . . . this frightening and terrible silence" (*OC* I, 662). Still opaque, however, is why he should have arrived at the theory of this inconceivable, universal, and terrifying silence in the first place. Why, contrary to Austin, whose man is constantly communicating, is Rousseau's other man so mute?

The answer lies in the fact that, whereas for Austin, speech is about communicating a thought to another that the entrance into dialogue assumes to be like one, for Rousseau, the I ultimately always addresses itself to a *silent* and indeterminate other, to the other acknowledged as violated by the I's appropriation of language in speech. One way to acknowledge the silence of the other is to impute to the other intelligence, the capacity of response, and of itself saying I. But that imputing, which takes place in the name of carrying on a conversation, erases the silence and alterity of the other addressed and makes it into an other for the subject, already modeled by that subject.[14] Other, more extraordinary acknowledgments are necessary to honor the silence of attention; reproach the silence of indifference; offer thanks for the silence that, by calling for speech, enables the I to come into existence as speaker; offer an apology for that silence as imposed on the other by the I; blame the silence that does not speak out against injustice; solicit the breaking of a silence that, too long prolonged, becomes heavy with the menace of death. Rousseau is embarrassed by having to lend reasons to others for their silence in the *Dialogues* because to do so is to translate a problem of justice into a problem of truth.

The paradigm for the silent other is ultimately not to be found in social circles, where interlocutors always testify to others who are potential interlocutors. Rather, as the appearance of the supernatural (the visitor from the clouds dropped into a world whose code he ignores) and the transformation of men into robots (signs moved by an absent author) suggest, Rousseau's paradigm comes from the relation of author or reader to a text. The I does not want to address another he has already made into a potential subject but wants to acknowledge the other as muted by the violence of speech. Conversing with another subject futilely turns it away from the other it wants to address by assuming that other is a possible subject just like him. Conversation is embarrassing in the same way the Rousseau's body embarrasses him; it fetters him to thinking in conditional terms what he wants to think about in relation to the absolute. Rousseau's madness in the *Dialogues* consists in recalling the primitive address, the first direction of speech before obstacles make it veer off course.[15] What Austin's insistence on ordinary speech leaves out, in its concern with a testimony convincing of other minds, is an address that is not immediately transformable into an address to another potential subject; he forgets a limit case where ordinary speech does not serve as the paradigm but gets its paradigm from writing as an act of reparation to the other silenced in the speech situation.

Placed in this light, the pathological speech of embarrassment is a matter of sympathy, of the I over-reaching itself to say the silence *of* and its reason *for* the other. The I stammers; its speech is obstructed and inappropriate, its writing chaotic and repetitive. Its verbal performance fails as a performance, but it succeeds in paying homage to the mute other. It is embarrassed for the other, where the preposition "for" has the meaning of "in the place of, in honor of." We might even say, it is embarrassed, encumbered, *with* the other, because the other can be seen as speaking through it in its stammered speech. The sense of being burdened with having to do more than make conversation, with having to pay a debt to the other to whom, as I, he owes his ethical being, leads Rousseau to the question of fiction in the *Quatrième promenade*. It remains for us to sketch out the operation of that regard for the other in the embarrassed lie from that text. Here is the scene:

> Some time ago M. Foulquier persuaded me, against my normal practice, to bring my wife along for a dutch-treat dinner with him and his friend Benoît at Madame Vacassin's, who was a restaurant-keeper; she, along with her two daughters, also dined with us. In the middle of the dinner, the eldest, who was married and pregnant, ventured to ask me brusquely, staring at me all the while, if I had had any children. Blushing up to my eyes, I replied that I had not had this good fortune [*si j'avois eu des enfans. Je répondis en rougissant jusqu'aux yeux que je n'avois pas eu ce bonheur*]. She smiled mischievously while looking at the rest of the group. All that was not very obscure, even for me.
>
> It is first of all clear that this reply is in no way the one I should have wished to make, even if I had intended to deceive; for, given the disposition in which I saw her who addressed the question to me, I was very sure that my negative reply would change nothing in her opinion on this point. They expected this negative reply; they even provoked it so as to enjoy the pleasure of having made me lie. I was not dolt enough not to sense that. Two minutes later, the reply I should have made came to me of itself: "Now that is hardly a discreet question for a young lady to ask a man who has grown old as a bachelor." [*Voila une question peu discrete de la part d'une jeune femme à un homme qui a vieilli garçon.*] By speaking in this way, without lying and without having to blush from any admission, I would have placed the laughers on my side and I would have given her a little lesson which naturally ought to have made her a little less impertinent in questioning me. I did nothing of the sort; I in no way said what should have been said; I said what should not have been said and which could serve me in nothing. Thus it is certain that neither my judgment nor my will dictated my reply, but that it was the mechanical effect of my embarrassment [*l'effet machinal de mon embarras*]. (*OC* I, 1034)

The narrative is set under the aegis of a female tutelary spirit, Dame Vacassin, a *restauratrice*—that is, primitively, a "restorer"—and, by a 1771 neologism, specifically a restaurant keeper. Both the particular occasion— *une maniére de Pic-nic*, a dinner where the guests have all engaged to pay their share of the meal—and the particular guest whose question embarrasses the I, the pregnant eldest daughter of the restaurant owner who also sits down at table—are telling. The I has to pay his share not only in the *fausse monnaie* of fictions for which he has become famous, but also in the genuine, literal coin of the realm. Two of the three types of fellow diners are immediately significant as others to whom Rousseau owes payment: Rousseau has promised to lunch with a M. Foulquier, who has brought his friend M. Benoît along; these are representatives of the social milieu in which Rousseau moves by virtue of his writing, and they presumably expect him to show his stuff as maker of moral fictions, in repayment for his invitation to dine. The restaurant owner and her two daughters have joined them, and to them, presumably the literal truth was owed in exchange for the restoring meal. An appropriate answer to the question as reported by Rousseau—"if I had had children" (*si j'avais eu des enfants*)— would thus touch on both his biological fatherhood and on matters of legal paternity. Rousseau's reported response ("I had never had that happiness" [*je n'avais pas eu ce Bonheur*]) fits neither of these two publics. The more suitable rejoinder he subsequently finds, "Now that is hardly a discreet question for a young lady to ask a man who has passed his life as a bachelor" (*voila une question peu discrete de la part d'une jeune femme à un homme qui a vieilli garçon*) underscores the point. The witty riposte would have reminded the indiscreet questioner from the lower classes of the literal acts that, making men out of boys, make for biological fathers, and the listening intelligentsia of the legal act of marriage that gives a bachelor (in French, *un garçon* is both a boy and a bachelor) the right to the title of paterfamilias. It would have satisfied both groups of interlocutors.

Yet the lie told yields something of interest. In the first place, it provides the example from which Rousseau is able to conclude for the radical irresponsibility of speech: "It is thus certain that neither my judgment nor my will dictated my response and that it was the mechanical effect of my embarrassment" (*OC* I, 1034). The lie is the occasion for Rousseau's elaborating a theory of why paternity, authority, testimony are always open questions although they never can be treated as such where empirical or legal beings are concerned. His speech at its most spontaneous is not dictated by the judgment or the will; it is what de Man calls a "free signifier, metonymically related to the part (it) is made to play in the subsequent system of exchanges and substitutions" ("Excuses" 289). When such free signifiers are instead without any relation to the surrounding text, they can be made to signify the guilt or innocence of free play. As Rousseau says in a similar situation, "only too happy when . . . they (the words) mean nothing at all" (*OC* I, 115).[16] But when the signifier taken as free is instead already caught in the web of signification, as it is in this instance, it opens a gap in the web where metonymy's mechanical operations show through, and we enter, as de Man says, "an entirely different system" ("Excuses" 289).

Here, that system can be identified with the response dictated by the debt to the other, in keeping with Levinas's judgment that it is the *Dire*— the saying, the signifier—rather than the *Dit*—the said, the meaning communicated—that indicates a response to the other as such.[17] It has as one shape the sudden manifestation of a hidden desire. If we look back at the "picnic" we have been examining, perhaps the most startling thing is that the question of paternity seems to come out of the blue, whereas maternity is indicated throughout. The meal is provided by the maternal figure of Dame Vacassin, mother of two daughters, one of them pregnant. Furthermore, it is represented by a third, more shadowy, category of guest, Thérèse Levasseur, the mother of Rousseau's five children all left at the door of the Foundling Hospital, who here makes one of her few appearances in the *Rêveries* as *ma femme*. Thérèse is not only a hidden interlocutor *to* whom he owes something, hidden by virtue of appearing as Rousseau's dependent ("*my* wife"); she is also, as dependent, the guest *for* whom Rousseau is presumably engaged to pay. How is Rousseau to respond to and for her, and to and for all these mothers? One euphemism for pregnant woman in Spanish, *una mujer embarazada*, underlines the point. Surprisingly, Rousseau's response, ridiculous when considered in terms of its other publics, approximates a sort of answer, as for the silent Thérèse. Neither of the forms of question and answer—"*si j'avais eu des enfants . . . je n'avais pas eu ce bonheur*"—make reference to fatherhood. The wording is rather that of a dialogue between two women: the pluperfect tense (*avais eu* and *n'avais pas eu*) is suggestive of parturition (having *had*, that is, borne or perhaps enjoyed, children), which the imperfect tense—*si j'avais des enfants*—would not have been. Rousseau's words impose on nobody so far as his *paternity* is concerned ("It is clear first that this response is not the one I should have made, even had I had the intention of deceiving" [*Il est clair d'abord que cette réponse n'est point celle que j'aurois voulu faire quand même j'aurois eu l'intention d'en imposer. . . .*]). But they superimpose on the scene a surreal image of one woman blushingly admitting to another, under-standably anxious about the coming event, that she has herself never given birth, or at any rate, and more in keeping with Thérèse's actual circum-stances, enjoyed for long the pleasures of having had them.[18]

The point is not that the scene is about mothers rather than about fathers. It is rather that, through the embarrassed speech of the I can be heard the response of the other (the silent and long-suffering Thérèse mourning that she has never had the happiness of having had children? Rousseau's unconscious maternal envy? the cries of the abandoned chil-dren?), identified by Levinas as maternal. The free signifier is indeed im-mediately caught in the web of signification, but it is a signification that does not have to do with the I and those passions to which it self-con-sciously testifies, but with the other as welcoming or hostile maternal fig-ure. The passage indicates the potential for language to host unfathered, parasitical meanings, and as such to pay a sort of tribute, act as a repara-tion, to and for the forgotten other that Thérèse represents.

Now it can be objected that Rousseau's response does not do full justice either to Rousseau or to Thérèse on the matter. The response appears mechanical—Rousseau does not even invent his own sentence, but merely negates that of the questioner, adding only a trite figure substituting "hap-piness" for "children." This is not Rousseau the inventive genius speaking. In that he is utterly failing Thérèse, whom he had after all convinced to give up the children by some taradiddle about being a genius who could not support them, all the while styling himself an exemplary citizen and father of Plato's *The Republic*.[19] Rousseau's response is inadequate, makes a mockery of the I as the "father" of *Emile*, the *Social Contract*, and so on, notion for which Thérèse has made considerable sacrifices. We would have to say that the response as response for the silent other is not success-ful. It puts Rousseau into travesty as an incapable, feminized father, and it still does not let Thérèse have her say. One never can speak for the other; one can only ever testify for oneself, and Rousseau's embarrassed speech at the time serves as a case in point proving his double failure either to achieve the impossible or to perform the possible adequately.

Yet such is Rousseau's folly that he compounds the error and persists on the path of embarrassment even in the *written* text of the *Fourth prome-nade*, as if even reflection could not save him from further verbal tripping. Perhaps his idea was to redeem himself with Thérèse, just as the witty riposte he thought up afterward would have redeemed him with respect to his other interlocutors, by turning the scene of failed interpellation and response into a successful one.[20] Certainly, the story exhibits a few of

Rousseau's narrative gifts, compressing a considerable symbolic potential into a brief anecdote, and providing no fewer than three separate "pay-offs" for the picnic: first in the response that exposed him to ridicule, then in the response that would have turned the tables on the questioner and given her a "little lesson" in discretion, and finally in the greater moral lesson about embarrassment rather than judgment or will as dictating his responses. Nonetheless, all his prowess as a writer notwithstanding, the scene contains several bad social gaffes of the sort that reflection ought presumably to have guarded Rousseau against. These gaffes are especially concentrated on the proper names—the patronymics—and titles of the company. Few are those who can stand to have their names played with, and two of the gaffes in the written text offended one of Rousseau's fellow diners so much that he appears to have insisted on emendations in the text after Rousseau's death. At any rate, the Marquis de Girardin, Rousseau's host at Ermenonville where he wrote the *Rêveries*, made a few changes in the manuscript that appear aimed at smoothing things over. The blunder was this: A certain M. Benoît, who had thought himself enough Rousseau's friend to introduce the latter to a M. Foulquier, was offended first for having his title struck off and then for being relegated to second place as M. Foulquier's friend (*son ami Benoît*). Benoît, which is also a given name in French, has connotations of hypocrisy and foolishness, so the loss of the title made the already slighted M. Benoît into an outright figure of fun.[21] Rousseau then made M. Benoît's friend M. Foulquier into the instigator of everything, the one for whom, against his habit, he has engaged himself for the Dutch treat meal. From a worldly point of view, Rousseau's autho-rial decisions were gauche to the point of being insulting, and Girardin's editorial decisions to scratch out *son ami* and to insert a Monsieur in front of Benoît's name are the offices of a friend to Rousseau who wants to avoid needless injury and to restore a measure of social decorum.

But the blunders that Girardin repairs are odd ones. Beyond the ques-tion of M. Benoît's feelings, Rousseau's blunder spreads the ridicule—hitherto focused on his lie about fatherhood—to the other men present at the picnic, as if each had indeed to pay his share in the general entertain-ment of the women by the discomfiture of the patriarchal system that by way of their names and titles, they represent. Why else push the patro-nymic, the proper name M. Benoît that refers to a given individual and that, as proper name, guarantees the referential function of language, toward its common uses as noun or adjective if not to continue the work of embarrassing fathers begun by Mme Vacassin's pregnant daughter? Once the proper name begins to lose its propriety and starts to serve as a meaningful word in the language, stability of reference is in question along with it. It is as though Rousseau were exposing to ridicule a certain pretension that one can tell the difference between literal and figurative language, pretension underlying the system of class and sexual difference in the scene, which would rely on the stability of reference. The embarrassment is not just at having to respond to others in a way that pays honor to them, but at having to do so in a language that is losing the distinction between literal and figurative and thus the ability to pay the ones and the others in the right coin.

What is more, the choice to make M. Foulquier into the meal's host, so far as Rousseau is concerned, has to have been inspired by a particularly ironic demon. At a dinner where people don't hold rational conversations in which timely lessons can be given but just blurt out indiscreet questions and foolish answers that don't reflect common sense, M. Foulquier's name makes him the perfect king of the feast. It pays its share in the general folly of fathers by saying a madness it doesn't mean: *Foul*quier. Rousseau puts a fool in charge of the day, and the potential for the name to generate meaning even as—name that it is—it is meant merely to refer, is enough to expose to ridicule the notion that meaning is a function of thoughtful speech and not of random accidents. The embarrassing question by the mother-to-be ricochets off its original target of Rousseau's fatherhood to take on, through the names of the other two male figures, the idea of communicative language as grounded in the proper name and of meaning as the investment by a willful, autonomous subject of itself in its speech. Where the proper name is both more than proper, as is the case where a name can produce illegitimate meanings, and less than proper, as is the case where it is in the process of becoming a common noun, who can blame Rousseau for denying paternity?

The point is borne out by some further proof of authorial work on the spelling of another patronymic, this time one borne by a woman and not corrected by Girardin. Dame Vacassin, as it happens, was actually a certain Dame Vaucassin suggestively rebaptized by Rousseau.[22] As altered by Rousseau's pen and in the context of maternity, the name bears audible witness to a vacant breast (*sein vacant*), and thus to the empty signifier as reigning over the meal, not to the plenitude of meaning that the daughter with the fuller belly would have suggested. In calling this member of the party by the title of Dame, Rousseau has taken a term that designated a noble woman in feudal times (as in "the favorite of the Lord and Lady (*Dame*) . . . I was happy" [*OC* I, 45]), and has used it in its later meaning of married woman, to indicate instead a member of the lower classes. *La*

Dame Vacassin is elevated to the role of female spirit reigning over the scene, and her name is as well suited as that of M. Foulquier to a repast where the guests seem required to participate in the embarrassment of communication taking place by way of empty signifiers, in this case, by proper names that produce meaning effects in excess of their function. The hope is that giving meaning production over to the signifier might ultimately allow the repair of the damage caused by linguistic indeterminacy because it would presumably provide a reliable rule for understanding if we could know that meaning was being generated in such a fashion.

In a sense, the written scene seems indeed to have overcome the difficulties of embarrassed speech through its exorbitant play with the signifier. We can see that Rousseau is honoring saying as a potential source of meaning, and thus making up to the other through a praise of a maternal meaning production. As if to pay for *ma femme*, representative of the indeterminate other, patronymics themselves become a source of meaning, with Rousseau responding from his hidden place as writer to show retrospectively that his embarrassed speech, despite or even because of its irresponsibility, participates in a larger linguistic situation of indeterminacy in which the signifier, the saying, can do the speaking. Albeit found through mad methods, meaning is available in the passage, and we can see writing the scene as an attempt on Rousseau's part to pay some guilty homage to the maternal figure of Thérèse, to legitimate retrospectively the illegitimate spawn of the sort the signifying names represent.

It is worth noting that success comes despite the fact that the obstacles in the way of appropriate response have increased given that now it is not only not a mere matter of figuring out the fitting thing to say to the others, nor even a matter of finding a fitting way to pay homage to the other silenced and reduced by speech. Now Rousseau has also had to find a language adequate to express the indeterminacy of saying. Everyone is always in the position of speaking otherwise than as a responsible subject on account of the nature of language, but Rousseau's job is to find a way so to exploit the language as to say that. The vacant breast of the motherly Dame Vacassin is a language made adequate because it says "saying," the empty signifier, as the source of meaning, in the proper name, where paternal power is concentrated.

If we were to end the analysis here, we might well conclude that Rousseau has managed to extricate himself from all difficulty by calculating as writer with linguistic indeterminacy. He appears to have succeeded in paying off all debts: He responds, albeit belatedly in a way that would have satisfied both his friends and the family of restaurant owners; he answers for Thérèse by paying homage to motherhood through the working of a language bearing unauthorized meaning possibilities; he answers for himself by showing his considerable linguistic mastery over the scene. If paying for restoration (*restauration*) is the problem the scene has taken on, we might well conclude that the scene successfully repairs Rousseau's damaged prestige, all the while paying homage to his wife.

However, if we delve a little further into the problem raised by playing with patronymics, the possibility that a single example of indeterminacy might be sufficient to stand for all the others, recedes. For the name of *la Dame Vacassin*, which seems to clinch the argument that the story is about embarrassment as the problem of a name that refers and yet that also signifies through free play, is significant in another sense, too. It is a name that, because it is written, outlasts the speech situation. As a result, it can present a second and even a third homonym that also work in the story as written and that serve as further obstacles in the way of success. Vacassin may sound like *sein vacant*, but it also sounds like *seing vacant*, which is to say, empty signature, empty authorial seal. Furthermore, it sounds like an authorial confession of taking pleasure in the pastime of writing: *(je) vaque à seing*, I occupy myself with the signature.

What does it matter that there is more than one paronomasia here? We have been claiming that the empty signifier (*sein vacant*) has been exploited by Rousseau to pay homage to maternity by making saying a source of meaning even as he exposes the patriarchal notion of a proper language to ridicule. But with the second and third homonyms, we have a proliferating embarrassment of riches in the same spot. The single example by means of which Rousseau seeks once and for all to show the obstacle that language puts in the way of paying off one's debt to and for the other, turns out to hide further, unmastered instances of indeterminacy. Names are not just exploitable as empty signifiers that aesthetic play can make meaningful. They may also keep on functioning in that way beyond the possibility of the story to catch up with them, beyond the ability of the authorial instance to harness them.

The further set of homonyms that shift the attention away from saying the name to writing and the signature, suggest writing and the responsibility of the writer as the ultimate obstacle and the ultimate signified of the scene. Past all the testifying the scene does for the silent other, the name change of Mme Vaucassin blurts out a confession as to Rousseau's own preoccupations. They suggest that after all, the scene is not about restoration, about answering to and for Thérèse but about authorial response to a misfire in the gesture of homage supposed to wrap up the scene.

That misfire is inevitable, but not because in saying the word "saying" (*le Dire*) in a singular example, Rousseau has to set aside other examples where saying could also become meaningful. All examples of name play would operate according to the same logic and be subsumed by it. Rather, it is inevitable because the logic of the example, which privileges the singular and presents it as the model for the multiple, is presented in writing, which is not governed by that logic, but rather by a logic of simultaneity, insofar as it can deliver more than one saying, more than one example at once. Writing can deliver many examples in the same place; to speak about or explore them requires a narrative, the momentary forgetfulness or repression of some of the examples in order to explore them sequentially, one after the other. The logic of simultaneity ruins the logic of the example, which is ultimately a narrative logic. In the place of an adequate expression that still hopes to overcome all difficulties so converse can go on in a clarified atmosphere of understanding, and that implies a sequence, it sets a play of letters with a temporal logic that means that the text can at one and the same time restore and ruin the possibility of restoration.

There are several features to be noted as the text shifts away by virtue of these proliferating paranomasias, from a logic of the example to a logic of simultaneity that can help us toward some conclusions about Rousseau's embarrassed lie. The shift moves us away from what we have said so far: namely, that embarrassment is a matter of the I's failed attempts to account in speech for the other, toward writing and a recognition that, ultimately, one can only, ever, account for its reflexive structure which mirrors that of the self. That is what seems to be suggested, for example, by the paranomasic double *(je) vaque à seing*, which amounts to a kind of confession of masturbatory play with the signifier as breast. However, the fact is that the same name that confesses the pleasure of writing also evokes Rousseau's worst anxieties about writing, his worry that another's writings might circulate under his name, his fear of a falsified signature, his recognition that the self presented in his writings is always other than I: a vacant signature, *un seing vacant*. In other words, if the passage seems to be about the impossibility of writing about anything but writing and the writing self, it also seems to be just as certainly about the impossibility of writing about anything but the other, about writing as a place of a radical self-alienation. Embarrassment is no longer a matter of difficulties with the speech situation, but rather a problem of writing and reading a text, a problem of the Derridean double bind. In this scene, where Rousseau is trying, against his habit, to pay for both himself and his wife, the double bind states on the one side the impossibility of ever paying for the other in a language that self-refers; and on the other side, the impossibility of ever doing anything else in a language that consistently finds referents for the fictions it posits. This double bind linked to the signature is not a matter of the I's inhibitions, fears or desires, never mind his generosity, so much as it is a matter of how writing functions. And yet, because of it, because of Rousseau's play with it, we get a glimpse of a responsibility beyond the possibility of a subject responding, of a generosity beyond the notion of a generous subject, of an ethics that takes on the task of answering in advance for the double bind so that the alterity left out in speaking might make an appearance on the stage of language.

A final feature of the scene is worth noting. Our investigation of the embarrassed lie has suggested that the gap between saying and meaning explored by the scene does not lend itself to repair. As we follow the I caught by pitfall after pitfall, it has become apparent that the gap is rather a general condition, that at any moment the logic of simultaneity installed by writing can come to disrupt the sequential logic of exemplarity, and to allow the most literal, referential of language uses to appear as the most far-reaching of fictions. With embarrassment, the text is so knotted as to show both its inability to shake itself free of reference, and its inability to stave off the disruptive emergence of radically fictional dimensions. It is for that yawning gap that Rousseau seeks to make himself responsible in the *Fourth Promenade* in the scene of the embarrassed lie. Although it may be construed as defensive from the perspective of the discourse of the subject, insofar as it entails writing, the lie has to be thought as part of Rousseau's exorbitant response, a response beyond the very possibility of responsibly responding, for the double bind as it affects the I rendering its accounts with the other.

No less than the shame-driven performatives discussed by de Man, those of embarrassment explore textual indeterminacy. The difference is that they do so not in terms of the discourse of the subject so much as with respect to what that discourse leaves out of its reckoning; their accounts are made up out of regard for the other. "Other" includes here, besides the others to whom Rousseau owes a truthful answer, the silent other Thérèse of whom his discourse asks pardon, and finally the other in the I to which his words testify. For Rousseau, it is not so much through conversation with others, from their testimony as to their moods that we come to believe in other's minds, but rather through the possibility that our own words might exist simultaneously as expressive of us, and as foreign words, alerting us to the other within.

CHAPTER 3

The Shape before the Mirror: Autobiography and the Dandy in Baudelaire

The Dandy . . . must live and sleep before a mirror.

BAUDELAIRE, *The Painter of Modern Life*

Baudelaire's work is far from self-evidently autobiographical. *Les Fleurs du mal*, for instance, cannot be easily compared with a self-declared poetic autobiography like Victor Hugo's *Contemplations*, whose poems are of decidedly personal inspiration, bear dates that attach them to experience, and lay out a plausible narrative of poetic development. In contrast, Baudelaire's undated poems appear impersonal and, in their emblematic character, untethered to experience. Although the poet does give the collection the status of an expressive work in one letter to Ancelle: "Do I have to tell you, you who have guessed it no more than the others, that in this *terrible* book I have put my whole *heart*, my whole *tenderness*, my whole *religion* (travestied), my whole *hatred*?," it is only to take it back right away: "It is true that I will write the opposite, that I will swear by my great Gods that it is a book of *pure art, fakery, juggling*."[1] Whatever the principle of the "secret architecture" of the collection, it is not "the growth of the poet's mind."

Nor are the individual poems clearly self-expressive. It is true that the "Spleen" poems seem to indicate mood, but the mood in question is a dubious one where the poet's voice is cracked, incapable of striking anything but dissonant notes or sounding a death rattle. The enterprising reader who heads to a poem like "Confession" in search of a genuine

83

autobiographical moment will be disappointed to discover that the confession consists of a discourse overheard in the false note of someone else's voice. It is true that two of the poems—"*Je n'ai pas oublié, voisine de la ville . . .*" and "*La servante au grand coeur dont vous étiez jalouse . . .*"—are by Baudelaire's own avowal retrospective. And yet, even there, Baudelaire insists that he has done his best to generalize and to strip away the details that might make the intimate scenes identifiable.[2] The famous poem on memory, "Le cygne," starts out with a literary, not a personal, reminiscence ("Andromaque, I think of you!")[3] and moves on to recount an anecdote about an escaped swan wandering on a construction site that, although read by some critics as a literal event, has been thought by many too neat to ring true.

A similar situation obtains elsewhere in the work. Look to the *Artificial Paradises* for the soul-searching drug narrative of an experienced user, and you will be disappointed. Instead, you find stories the author, acting as a sort of social scientist who studies the effects of drugs on the human spirit, purports to have collected from others. In *Le Peintre de la vie moderne*, Baudelaire has eschewed the anecdotal style that his friendship with the painter Constantin Guys would have allowed, and has even effaced the name that would have anchored the portrait to a referent. Baudelaire's biographers Claude Pichois and Jean Ziegler will occasionally wonder whether the apparently most unproblematical of autobiographical texts, Baudelaire's letters to his mother, are not those of a mountebank who poses even in his most intimate moments.[4] In Baudelaire's texts, the personal style is all but dispensed with.[5]

The *Intimate Journals* is a more promising place to look for an autobiographical subject. Indeed, the main piece, *My Heart Laid Bare*, was projected as an autobiography perhaps unusual in tone, but not in structure—it was to tell the story of the education of an angry man.[6] But in the project as we have it, Baudelaire has avoided the narrative mode that Lejeune makes a crucial trait of the genre.[7] We don't find a story of the past events of a life, and the usual accouterments of the journal entry—names, dates, places that might somehow affix the fragmentary reflections to the happenings of a life—are mostly missing. Such names as do appear might as easily have been gleaned from a newspaper column as dug out of Baudelaire's own memory, so little do they tell that is personal. When, exceptionally, the poet dates a diatribe, he dates from the century.[8] Baudelaire systematically refrains from providing the sort of details—salty or sentimental—that spice Rousseau's *Confessions* and lend that text its aura of authenticity. Indeed, Pichois and Ziegler confess that at least one fragment of the *Fusées* strikes them rather as a fairy tale than a recital of the facts.[9] To most readers, these texts appear autobiographical only if one neglects the lapidary style, reminiscent of the philosophical fragment, which draws the attention away from the intimate detail toward the maxim, the sally or the sketch for a future work.

And yet, notwithstanding all that Baudelaire has done to minimize the reference to experience, there is a persistent, and surely not entirely wrong-headed, tendency in Baudelaire criticism to read his texts as autobiographical, and indeed to understand his persistent self-masking as prototypically Baudelairian. The tendency is not just represented by those readers of *Les Fleurs du mal* who have sought an anecdotal basis to the poems of the sonnet cycles, and have tried to explain them as so many confessions of the poet's relations to the various women in his life—from Sara to Jeanne Duval, Mme Sabatier, Agathe, or more crucially still, his mother. Alongside these crude attempts, there exists a more philosophically self- aware group who follow Genette's idea that language can always appear to be metonymically grounded rather than metaphorically motivated and, ranging themselves with Sartre, for whom Baudelaire's work is expressive of "the choice of himself that he made (to be this and not that) (*le choix de lui-même qu'il a fait* [*être ceci et non pas cela*])," read the text as documenting the I's fundamental gesture of self-constitution.[10] It is not anecdote but the family romance that attracts the attention; privilege is accorded the experience of loss, separation, and self-identification that lies behind the poet's most basic decisions. Recent works by critics of such widely divergent approaches as Bernard Howells, Didier Blonde, and André Hirt remain Sartrian in their concern with identifying a sort of cogito, a decisive coming into consciousness of which the poems are the expression.[11] This, despite Bataille's strong statement more than 50 years ago that it advances our reading of the poems not one whit to undertake such an analysis.[12]

The point here is not to reject the autobiographical reading as wrong-headed, but rather to ask about the problem that Baudelaire's marked preference for impersonal writing poses for an autobiographical reading, and more especially for a reading centered on identification. The discussion will center on the Dandy figure because it is with that figure that Baudelaire has usually been identified.[13] Running along with these questions will be the intertwined one of representation in poetic language, for it is certainly one of the prerequisites of narratives of identity that language be thought as representational. Even before a Mallarmé invokes the failure of representation and the undoing of voice, does Baudelaire move in that direction? Such a poetics might explain Baudelaire's failure to complete his autobiographical project and his general refusal of the personal style. If there is an autobiographical side to a nonrepresentational work, it would have to be located in the suicidal gestures where the poet disappears to foreground the mark, according to the logic of autothanatography we have been discovering.

By simply paying attention to the impersonal means of saying, we can find preliminary indications that this direction is justified in the very texts cited in proof of Baudelaire's self-expressiveness. Thus, the lapidary style of one much-cited fragment—"On the vaporization and centralization of the *Self*. Everything hinges on it." [*OC* I, 676] [*"De la vaporisation et de la centralisation du Moi. Tout est là."*]—gives it the air of an authorial admonishment regarding effective writing strategy, along the lines of those to be found in *Advice to Young Literary Figures*. The ironic distance opened by such a fragment between the author and the *moi* is worthy of attention. Similarly, in a passage like the following, where Bernard Howells finds incontrovertible proof that for Baudelaire literature is self-expressive, one can find, on the contrary, room for doubt. This is what Baudelaire says, in the *Salon de 1846*, as cited by Howells:

> . . . to be just, which is to say, to have its reason for being, criticism has to be partial, passionate, political, which is to say, made from an exclusive point of view, but from a point of view that opens the most horizons. . . . Thus one larger point of view would be individualism, properly understood [*l'individualisme bien entendu*]: the command to the artist of naiveté and the sincere expression of his temperament, aided by all the means with which his art can furnish him. (*OC* II, 418–9)[14]

Howells takes the passage to affirm as Baudelaire's view that the artist's task is "individualism, properly understood." But the passage, which is taken from a chapter called "What Good is Criticism?" (*A quoi bon la critique?*) and is far from a straightforward artistic *confiteor*, asserts something slightly different: Criticism can profitably adopt the perspective that art should be expressive. But that does not mean that Baudelaire himself professes "individualism, properly understood." He is simply noting individualism to be one potentially fertile aesthetic viewpoint from which to judge a work.[15] He retains the freedom to provide a different perspective, especially if the model of the work as self-representational fails to exhaust its meaning potential.

As a result of such passages, our approach to Baudelaire's perspective on art as self-expressive will necessarily seem a bit perverse because we will have to start by looking for evidence of a failure of the representational perspective before asking what other perspective Baudelaire might adopt and what can be gleaned from it about autobiographical writing. We can start no better place than with Sartre and Bataille, whose readings of Baudelaire's poetics in their relation to the Dandy, the type by whom Baudelaire is thought to be represented in his work, can allow us to set out the problems in a few broad strokes.

For to ask about representation in Baudelaire quickly leads to queries about the Dandy, figure at the heart of Sartre's critique and one that "must live and sleep before a mirror" (*OC* II, 678) [*doit vivre et dormir devant un miroir*]. Here, we must contend with Sartre's general suspicion of poetic language. Leiris, in an introduction on the whole very sympathetic to Sartre, nevertheless notes that the philosopher of liberty is "foreign to poetry . . . and sometimes of a singular rigidity . . . with respect to those who are its most passionate practitioners" (*Baudelaire* 15). And indeed, Sartre's few remarks about Baudelaire's poetics show us one who toes the Platonic line with respect to representation, at once accepting the premise that language represents what is and subjecting poetry to critique as secondary imitation. Thus Sartre, discussing Baudelaire's interest in evil, likens it to poetry in that both are "two kinds of creation with limited responsibility" (*Baudelaire* 69) [*à responsabilité limitée*].[16] Sartre spells out at some length why he judges *le mal* this way; in passages that Augustine might almost have signed, he says that it remains tributary to a preconceived notion of the Good. Just so, it may be inferred from his comparison, poetry is a language relative to the logos; its figures are luxuries derived from the intentional use of language as a language of proper names. This point is further borne out in Sartre's later discussion of the artist as parasite.

Whereas Sartre judges poetry with considerable distrust, a positive hostility breaks out around the image of the Dandy, as if that figure somehow posed a challenge to his project of determining the Baudelairian cogito. The sore point is the poet's self-representation in his function as poet. With the Dandy, Baudelaire advances masked, not as a living consciousness but as an ironic one, cognizant of repetition, aware of itself as factitious being—or, in Sartre's terms, as the object he is to others:

> We have seen that he assimilates the gaze that he directs toward the self to the gaze of Others. He sees himself, or tries to see himself, as if he were another. . . . Through a self-punishing lucidity, Baudelaire tries to constitute himself an object in his own eyes. [*Il se voit ou tente de se voir comme s'il était un autre. . . . Par la lucidité auto-punitive, Baudelaire tente de se constituer en objet devant ses propres yeux.*] (*Baudelaire* 105)

Now this mask is a privileged one, for its ironic lucidity masks the producer of masks, the poet. When Baudelaire projects an image of himself as Dandy, he does not simply tell us something derivative; he lies about his own nature, presenting himself not as the living, producing subject that he is, but as he appears to others, as object. He forebears to give us his cogito or to speak in his own voice, and instead provides a vision of an apathetic and insensible poet whose being lies entirely in appearance. The Dandy is "an ideal more elevated than poetry" an image of the self as

> Parasite of parasites: the Dandy parasites the poet, who himself is the parasite of a class of oppressors; beyond the artist, who still seeks to create, he has projected a social ideal of absolute sterility where the cult of the self is identified with the suppression of oneself. (*Baudelaire* 136)

In Sartre's idea, the poet creates something, even if it is only in figures, and as such can tell us a truth about the nature of the subject and its productions. But the Dandy is sterile and useless. Every bone in Sartre's body—let us not forget that of an artist-philosopher casting his lot in with the proletariat—protests against this image of the artist as nonproductive, or, more precisely, as projecting only new forms of ideas already in circulation rather than new ideas in adequate form.[17] The poet may deal with a subordinate mode of production, as Plato has it in Book X of *The Republic*, but at least he is producing something. With the Dandy, Baudelaire expresses himself in a figure for the death of self-expression, and more precisely of "individualism, properly understood:" He builds an altar to the "cult of the self" (*OC* II, 710) while evacuating the subject of its creative energies. Sartre finds this an impossible position inasmuch as the subject never can be anything but a subject for itself; its truth is always that of an active, creating being; and it is in vain that it tries to imagine itself as the mere appearance it is for the other:

> He sees himself or tries to see himself as if he were another. And it is certainly impossible to see oneself truly with the eyes of Others, for we adhere too much to ourselves. But if we slip into a judge's robes, if our reflexive consciousness mimes disgust and indignation with respect to reflective consciousness, if, so as to qualify the latter, it borrows from learned morality its notions and measures, we can for an instant fool ourselves into thinking we have introduced a distance between the reflected thing and reflection. By a self-punishing lucidity, Baudelaire tries to constitute himself an object in his own eyes." (*Baudelaire* 105)

Instead of re-presenting his constitutive gesture of self-consciousness, Baudelaire is guilty of writing from the position of the other: His horror of responsibility has him "choose to consider his life from the perspective of death, as if a premature end had suddenly fixed it. At each moment, while still living, he is already on the other side of the tomb" (*Baudelaire* 149). Again Sartre points to an impossibility: how to write with one foot in the grave, attached like Benedicta to the tomb, when one is still alive? It is impossible, so wrapped up are we in life, to compose our traits into a death mask.[18]

In a passage cited earlier, Sartre termed the idea of self-creation an "impossible" ideal for a being who has already to exist before it can serve as progenitor. Now he has told us that it is *impossible* to make oneself an object for others, *impossible* to make one's life into a destiny in advance. Impossibility boils down to a contradiction for Sartre: Baudelaire has set up an ideal image with which he can never fully identify. Instead of positing himself through a cogito, Baudelaire doubles himself, providing us both the productive poet he is to himself and the sterile mask he is to others. The Dandy is a self-representation by which the poet impossibly claims that the poet does not represent what is but what seems merely.

But is not impossibility, construed as the question of pure fiction and the nonrepresentational side to language, precisely the sort of thing that poetry is about? In his review of Sartre's essay included in *La Littérature et le mal*, Georges Bataille sees as the very crux of Baudelaire's poetry that he wanted "the impossible to the utmost" (*Baudelaire* 54), and makes that the centerpiece of his critique of Sartre. Writes Bataille:

> Sartre says about Baudelaire (it's the leitmotif of his essay) that the evil was in him of wanting to be the thing that he was for others: he abandoned thus the prerogative of existence, which is to remain suspended. But does man generally avoid that the consciousness that he is, becoming the reflection of things, become itself a thing like any other. [*Mais l'homme évite-t-il, en général, que la conscience qu'il est, devenant réflexion des choses, ne devienne elle-même une chose comme une autre.*] It seems to me not, and that poetry is the mode in which he is at liberty . . . to escape the destiny that reduces him to being the reflection of things. ("Baudelaire" 49)

Bataille poses the problem of impossibility otherwise than Sartre because he has doubts about our freedom to choose not to become objects. The problem is not the choice of inauthenticity, but rather, given consciousness's propensity to become thing-like, what can be the response. For Bataille, poetry offers a chance of thinking an escape from the usual lot. It, too, ultimately falls prey to reification, but it offers a task worth undertaking; and if it fails, it is nonetheless a proof of its value that it has correctly assessed its task as impossible to achieve and yet as impossible not to attempt. Baudelaire's answer is poetry because poetry is dissatisfaction, and, measuring itself against the immeasurable, takes on its task without flinching. Bataille writes:

> Inherent to poetry there exists an obligation to make a fixed thing out of a dissatisfaction. Poetry, in its first movement, destroys the objects that it grasps, it gives them back by destruction to the ungraspable fluidity of the poet's existence, and it is at that price that it hopes to discover the identity of the world and of man. But at the same time that it operates a dispossession, it tries to *seize* this *dispossession*. All that it can do is to substitute a *dispossession* for the *grasped* things of reduced life: it is not able to keep that dispossession from taking the place of things. [*Mais en même temps qu'elle opère un dessaisissement, elle tente de **saisir** ce **dessaisissement**. Tout ce qu'elle put fut de substituer le **dessaisissement** aux choses **saisies** de la vie réduite: elle ne put faire que le dessaisissement ne prît la place des choses.*] ("Baudelaire" 50)

Bataille traces poetry's double movement: On the one side, it dispossesses things of their prefabricated meaning and makes them fluid; on the other, it fails to remain an act of dispossession, instead substituting itself as formalized product, as reified value, for things. In this process, the accent is not on self-possession and self-recognition, but on dispossession and dis-identification. Baudelaire chooses poetry because of this restless dissatisfaction of poetry with itself. For Bataille, impossibility means something close to the aporias of Derrida, and it signals that poetry's task is the impossible one of giving a gift that cannot be given, saying a secret that is not a content, and so on. Poetry is a language external to the calculations and transactions of the logos: language that, in ceasing to represent things, returns them to their fluidity, and seeks to live up to our thirst for a life that is not bounded by what is.

Poetry's attention to manner put us in the neighborhood of the Dandy, and indeed, Bataille sees Baudelaire's Dandyism as related to his desire for the impossible. But for Bataille, Baudelaire's ambition to live as a Dandy was only a pale image of his desire for poetry:

> Baudelaire willed it . . . as it is fatal and fated [*comme il est fatal*] to will the impossible, that is to say, at once firmly, as such, and in a lying fashion, in the form of a chimera. Hence his moaning life as a dandy avid for work, bitterly bogged down in a useless idleness. [*D'où sa vie gémissante de dandy avide de travail, amèrement enlisé dans une oisiveté inutile.*] ("Baudelaire" 53)

"Willed the impossible as such . . ." that is, willed it in his poetry; "willed the impossible . . . in a lying fashion," that is, in a Dandy's existence. The ordinary assumption is that life is the given, the true, and art is its representation. But here that assumption is reversed: Life is the lie, the chimerical form or existential correlative, whereas poetry is the true, the authentic relation to the impossible. The Dandy's life as transgressor is a pale version of the greater transgressions of poetry. Baudelaire's constant reshaping of his image—his hair now cut short, now long, now dyed green, his demand for impeccable linen, his obsessive posing for photographer friends—are all substitutes of a desire for literature: that is, of a restless dissatisfaction with what is. Next to literature, the Dandy's life is a form compromised in advance because the dispossession it operates can never be complete: Although it is true that the Dandy's play with old forms allows a limited dispossession, appearances are never destroyed but are simply recombined and given different significance. He always remains on the near side of the impossible that the poet aims at and that requires a more thoroughgoing destruction, a sacrifice of reference itself.

One crucial difference dividing Bataille from Sartre over the Baudelairian Dandy thus concerns the status of the impossible with respect to poetry. For Sartre, poetry is representation, a rhetoric that substitutes for proper language, and the identification of the Dandy with the poet is an impossible: that is, a contradictory attempt to be both object and subject, judging consciousness and thing judged, image and consciousness, himself as he is for others and as he is for himself, mere representation and representing subject. But Bataille sees poetry as driven by a thirst for the impossible that necessitates the dissolving of representation, next to which it is *fatal* for the poet to identify with a given representation, in the sense that it kills the dream, but perhaps also, as we will be considering in a moment, in the sense that it is inevitable. Impossibility is not a matter of logical contradiction here but is rather a condition for poetry, which sets itself a double imperative: to dispossess oneself radically of what is through its dispossession of representation, which is an impossible task; and to seize that dispossession in a form, as it is impossible not to do, which means to resubmit it to phenomenality.

In an essay tending to adopt Bataille's position on poetic language, it may seem contradictory to privilege the Dandy figure in imitation of Sartre. Yet perhaps Bataille does not do full justice to the figure or indeed to his own insight. For Bataille's remark about Baudelaire's fatal identification with the Dandy is tantalizing: It seems to assert the ineluctability of such an identification without exploring the questions that would rise about it. What is to be learned—for autobiography, for identification, for poetic technique—from a representation of the impossible with which the poet *must not* be identified lest he lose his own best insight and yet with which he *must* be identified despite himself?

The Dandy as lying form of the poet's search for the impossible can conveniently be broached through a text Baudelaire knew very well, the 1845 *Du Dandysme* by Barbey d'Aurevilly, before we turn to Baudelaire's own fullest exposition of the figure in *Le Peintre de la vie moderne*. In his essay, Barbey differentiates between a mere clotheshorse and the Dandy. The Dandy distracts our attention away from the functional aspect of clothing to consider it as a problem of manner:

> It is not clothes that walk by themselves! On the contrary! It's a certain manner of wearing them that creates Dandyism. One can be a Dandy in crumpled dress . . . One day even—is it credible?—Dandies conceived the fantasy of *thread-bare suits of clothes [l'habit râpé]*. It was during Brummell's time. They had reached the end of impertinence, and they could do nothing more. They found the further impertinence, which was so *dandylike* (I can find no other word to express it), of having their clothes scraped [*de faire râper leurs habits*] before wearing them, along the whole length of the fabric until it was no longer anything but lace—a cloud. They wanted to walk in their cloud, those gods! The operation was very delicate and very long, and they used a bit of sharpened glass to carry it out. Well, there is a true deed of Dandyism. The clothes have nothing to do with it. They scarcely exist any longer. [*Eh bien! voilà un véritable fait de Dandysme. L'habit n'y est pour rien. Il n'est presque plus.*][19]

By placing the meaning on manner, the Dandy initiates a process of divestment and reinvestment. The arduous scraping away of the fabric until the suit is almost lace and can barely serve the minimal hiding and protecting functions of clothing is a sign of this double movement. The suit is all but liberated from functionalism and then worked on until it expresses the creative energy of its wearer. In refashioning the ready-made object, the Dandy disestablishes the god of function and sets himself up as a new creator, appearing as a god would, "trailing clouds of glory," "walk(ing) in (his) cloud" (*march[ant] dans [sa] nuée*).

It is clear from the anecdote that the scraped garment does not entirely lose its function. The garment "scarcely exists any longer," which is another way to say "is still a little bit" a garment. The Dandy has worked on it without making it disappear entirely. He rather re-presents the garment otherwise than dispossesses it of all meaning. He shakes the language of clothing loose from its referent of the body and makes it point to his own imaginative act.

In at least one section of *Le Peintre de la vie moderne*, "Pompes and Solennités," Baudelaire has resignification in mind.[20] There he discusses a picture entitled *"La fête commémorative de l'indépendance dans la cathédrale d'Athènes"* in terms of the painter's love of space, perspective and light, but it is chiefly the subject of the picture that interests us because what it is about is reevaluation, re-presentation. Here is the passage:

> M. G. excels in treating the pageantry of official functions, national pomps and circumstances, but never coldly and didactically, like those painters who see in work of this kind no more than a piece of lucrative drudgery. He works with all the ardor of a man in love with space, with perspective, with light lying in pools or exploding in bursts, drops or diamonds of it sticking to the rough surfaces of uniforms and of court toilettes. *Independence-day in the Cathedral at Athens* provides an interesting example of these gifts. That multitude of little figures, of which each one keeps its place so well, only goes to deepen the space which contains them. The Cathedral itself is immense and adorned with ceremonial hangings. King Otho and the Queen standing upright on a dais, are dressed in the national garb, which they wear with marvellous ease, as though to give evidence of the sincerity of their adoption and of the most refined Hellenic patriotism [*comme pour témoigner de la sincérité de leur adoption et du patriotisme hellénique le plus raffiné*]. The King's waist is belted like that of a the most coquettish of *palikars*, and his skirt spreads out with all the exaggeration prescribed by the national school of dandyism [*l'exagération du dandysme national*]. Towards them walks the patriarch, a bent old man with a great white beard, his little eyes protected behind green spectacles, betraying in his whole being the signs of a consummate Oriental impassivity. All the figures which people this composition are portraits, one of the most curious, by reason of the unexpectedness of her physiognomy (which is just about as un-Greek as could be) being that of a German lady who is standing beside the Queen and is part of her private suite. (*OC* II, 705)[21]

The costumes worn by the King and Queen, the central figures in the picture, are picked out by the "drops" and "diamonds" of light that bead them as sources of meaning. But it is not their individuality or sharpness of style that justifies Baudelaire's evocation of Dandyism, for the Royal Family wears traditional Greek costume. Rather, Dandyism is linked to the gesture of resignification, to the freeing of a signifier from its conventional meaning and its reinvestment through an imaginative effort. Indeed, the picture represents a kind of gala affair celebrating a national tendency to liberate and reevaluate signs. Consider the national dress, whose plethora of folds held by a belt is one indication of liberation and recapturing.

A king wearing the national costume on Independence Day would seem, at first blush, to affirm a resurgent national spirit, an investment by Greeks in the autochthonously Greek. But a little more delving—exacted by the enigmatic phrase of "national dandyism" and the reference to adoption— tells us that nothing is further from the case. To begin with, the war of independence from the Ottoman Empire celebrated here was not won by the Greeks, but ended only after the decisive intervention by Europe in the conflict. Victory was consolidated by the Conference of London, which established Greece as a kingdom independent of the Ottomans, and then immediately placed it under the protection of the European powers, setting on the throne Otto, the 17-year-old son of Louis I, King of Bavaria. The German face of the Queen's lady-in-waiting is a reminder of the present Greece, just as the oriental face of the patriarch gestures to the country's past as a Turkish dependency. By Otto's "adoption" of the Greek national costume, Baudelaire points to this European liberation and capture of "Greece" from the East as a "Greece for Europe." Resignification has taken place around the Dandy figure and a reevaluated Greece inhabits the traditional folds of the *palikar*'s kilt.

The constitution that established the new Greece with its enthroned monarch was of European manufacture. In the idea of at least one historian, the notions of nationalism and self-determination that Europe considers the modern legacy of Greek thought, in point of fact, were formulated in late Enlightenment Europe where they made emerge a new "ancient Greece." In this view, the Greeks had to go to school in Europe to learn what it was to be Greek.[22] Here, too, the King made a resignifying move that guaranteed his popularity. He took his name, Otto, out of the German context to which it was tied; and, respelling it as the Greek Otho, made it the name of the King of the new Greece, one that had rediscovered itself under European trappings.[23]

The Independence Day celebrated provides a further example of a sign liberated from a first context and assigned another meaning. In 1843, 11 years before Guys's picture was published in the *Illustrated London News*, there was a second Revolution, at the end of which Greek nationalists removed the hated Bavarian clique that surrounded the king and turned Otho into a constitutional monarch. The 1854 Independence Day thus celebrates a further re-presentation that makes Baudelaire's remark on Dandyism as national phenomenon particularly astute. Although Otho remains king at the time to which the picture refers, he is by then a figurehead in a country where the people have arrogated to themselves his kingly power in resignifying him.

In short, Baudelaire's vision coincides with Barbey's in that re-presentation is seen as a fundamental operation of the Dandy. It is the Dandy's signal ability to conceive of and capture the freedom of the signifier. The resignifying Dandy is a myth-maker who represents a failure of language to represent adequately to the spellbound audience. He dramatizes the availability of signs to mean otherwise.

Dandyism lies behind the rise of both individual and nation, for both depend on the liberation and recapturing of shopworn symbols. But innovation is not to be confused with creation or a limited economy with an open one. The resignifying attitude involves strategic power plays with the signifier's freedom; it liberates for the sake of recapturing, and turns that power to the benefit of the capturer. The constraints placed on freedom in the picture—as symbolized by the belt that cinches those exaggerated folds to the king's body—together with the calculating posture of the subject, suggest a limited economy in which self-interest dominates. Dandyism, Balzac has said, is "the art of expending one's revenues as a man of wit," and this notion of resignification goes along with the Dandy as spectacular consumer or recycler of signs who never destroys or invents anything.[24] The Dandy's gesture of resignifying interrupts the ordinary situation of sign exchange only long enough to establish him as exceptional being who lucidly masters the signs of a situation; all of his transformations are transformations in the meaning system. We can see the reason for Sartre's judgment that Baudelaire-as-dandy sacrifices his creative agency to the cult of selfhood, as well as why Bataille describes Dandyism as a reduced version of the desire for the impossible. The constraints placed on the signifier's freedom make it an occasion to be seized for personal glory. The subversive gesture of revealing an old fiction quickly redounds to the glory of the Dandy as having a privileged knowledge and power over signs. But according to Bataille, theoretician of sacrifice, the poet's desire is for the utmost in *dispossession*, for according an exorbitant freedom to language. The Dandy's gesture is indeed the gesture of making the impossible possible: It is a worldly, compromised activity that plays with representations rather than with things, while leaving the hierarchical relation according precedence to things over representations untouched.

Before leaving the scene, it is worth asking what can be learned from the resignifying moves of the Dandy in terms of Baudelairian autobiography. Ought we to hear an "auto" under Otto-Otho, as a sign that the Dandy king is a figure for the author Baudelaire? In this light, we note that Baudelaire's favorite figures of irony and allegory both entail exploiting an alteration in the status of a sign in the same way as does the Dandy's resignifying. With those figures, a sign bearing a conventional meaning is taken up into another context where it means in another way, through a disruption that moves away from the text as expression of a subject's view, to posit a superior, other worldly perspective. Be it through a rift opened up suddenly between what is said and the manner of saying it, or the ripping of a veil that invests an apparently anodyne natural figure with a supernatural charge, Baudelaire's favorite figures do not depend on likeness so much as on the difference within the sign. The Dandy's resignification is comparable with that accomplished by an ironist and allegorist like Baudelaire.

However, the limited action of the Dandy is very different from the way Baudelaire describes irony and allegory, whose action he sees as limitless. Absolute irony, *le comique absolu*, is endlessly self-lacerating; allegory's limitlessness also manifests itself in a melancholic self-dispossession, in signs exiled from their context that do not prepare the recuperation of the self through interiorization, but end in a metonymic scattering of the mind and a flood of exiles, as "Le cygne," for one instance, graphically illustrates: "I think of my great swan . . . / . . . and then of you / Andromache . . . // I think of the negress . . . // Of whoever has lost what can never, never / Be found again! of those who drink tears . . . / Of skinny orphans . . . // I think of sailors left forgotten on an island, / Of captives, the defeated! . . . of many others more!" (*OC* I, 86–7). The Dandy is the equivalent of the superior man who laughs at the other's fall in "On the Essence of Laughter," whereas in the work of art, a satanic, unlocalizable laughter that Baudelaire calls "absolute" is unleashed to shake the subject's masterful superiority.

It would thus be misleading to look for a self-portrait of the artist as triumphant Otto-man in the Independence Day picture. The Dandy figure with its calculations, its voluntarism, its lucid superiority, its narcissistic self-display, its self-conscious irony makes an incomplete figure for the artist because the artist's resignifying is always a preparation for an exorbitant sacrifice utterly carrying away the self and self-representation in its wake. In poetry, the poet meets with the incalculable in the form of accidents, and it is in that landscape where the very possibility of representation is dissolved that he must exercise his "fantastical fencing" "tripping over words as over paving stones / Bumping up against long dreamt poetic lines" (*OC* I, 83).

But there is another side to be considered. The Dandy also sleeps before a mirror for Baudelaire. Through figures for the sleep, fall or death of the Dandy another telling analogy between poet and figure can start to come into view. There is an absurdity to the thought that the Dandy bears a resemblance to the poet insofar as he *sleeps*. For that would be to say that the poet is most exceptional when, instead of depicting the world as it is or ought to be, instead of resignifying with the Dandy, like Homer, she nods off, goes mad, becomes insensible, and so on. If Bataille is right and poetry dispossesses, the Dandy letting his heroic vigilance relax in sleep might be a closer analogy for the poet.

Another passage from *The Painter of Modern Life*, this one culled from the section called "The Military Man" addresses the problem. In this section, Baudelaire is describing the particular beauty of the military man, which is in general, he says, distinct from that of women or of the Dandy. But the military man has at least one trait that allows a resemblance to the Dandy to shine through. He is with difficulty astonished, even by death, accustomed as he is to "the necessity of being ready to die at any moment" (*OC* II, 708) [*la nécessité d'être prêt à mourir à chaque moment*]. The Dandy, too, has "the proud satisfaction of never being astonished" (*OC* II, 710). There is thus this resemblance of attitude between the two that both are on notice that death is coming and indeed have already taken on some of its rigidity. Describing Monsieur G.'s watercolors and sketches, Baudelaire notes a good-looking staff officer, in whom we recognize a "sleeping" Dandy figure:

> Every type of soldier is there, the essence of each being *seized* upon [*saisi*] with a kind of enthusiastic joy: the old infantry officer, solemn and glum, overloading his horse with his bulk; *the exquisite staff officer with his pinched waist, wriggling his shoulders, bending unabashed over ladies' chairs, who, seen from the back, puts one in mind of the slimmest and most elegant of insects* [*le joli officier d'état major, pincé dans sa taille, se dandinant les épaules, se penchant sans timidité sur le fauteuil des dames, et qui, vu de dos fait penser aux insectes les plus sveltes et les plus élégants*]. (*OC* II, 708; my emphasis)

The vignette of the staff officer is striking because without actually naming him as such, Baudelaire presents us with an elegant military man who strikes one as an unaware Dandy, clinching the suggestion by way of a homonym (*se dandinant les épaules*) that says Dandy without exactly naming him one, using a style that in its allegorical allusiveness can itself be called dandified.[25] A translator with a good ear for the connotations of the scene, Jonathan Mayne, has set aside the readily available terms of "dandling" or "rocking back and forth," implying awkwardness, and has chosen the term "wriggling" more in keeping with the body language of an elegant Dandy figure.[26] This back and forth movement, together with

pinched waist and the turned back of the officer, justifies the comparison
to an insect pinned alive and wriggling to the painter's collection board.
We know it is pinned because Baudelaire tells us it has been "seized;"
rigor mortis has already started to claim the staff officer. Monsieur G.'s
painting lifts him out of the realm of the living and into that of art, where
he is eminently available to others, taken as he is from the back, and exhib-
ited not as the autonomous, self-conscious being he is to himself but as
elected all unknowing to mean for others. The officer does not present a
human figure, the face of a self-conscious subject; instead he is held, back
exposed, collected like an insect by a superior being, his destiny having
caught him unawares. In short, the exquisite officer is a specimen subject
captured and resignified by a superior allegorist just as King Otho had
captured and resignified the Greek kilt.[27]

The Dandy-like figure of the soldier as we see it here is already in the
process of succumbing to the machinery of death-dealing it sets into motion. Again, the particular beauty associated with the type is allegorical or
ironical. The scene plays on a noncoincidence between the world of the
salon inhabited by the officer, where wriggling is a sign in a courting
dance, and the world of the collector, where the same gesture points allegorically to death. It could be objected that the staff officer lacks the sovereignty associated with the Dandy figure. But the objection forgets that the
meteoric rise of the upstart is inevitably followed by a precipitous descent:
that the Dandy figure, too, is always a divided one. On the one side, he
appears a voluntaristic being who has imposed himself as sovereign subject, as I, in the minds of others. In his sovereignty, he rivals monarchs. It
is not just with Otho that the Dandy is a prince; Barbey notes a similar
rivalry between George IV and the famous Dandy George Brummell,[28]
and Baudelaire's princes are all Dandies. But on the other side, the Dandy
is characterized by a spectacular fall: Witness the exile and madness of
Brummell, the execution of Julien Sorel, the ultimate ousting of Otho in
1862. The staff officer, however alert and ready for death he may be, does
not escape it, any more than the Dandy who anticipates his fall by making
himself like a cadaver. The Dandy anticipates his allegorization or ironiza-
tion by electing those figures as his privileged means of resignifying.
Nonetheless, he inevitably finds himself caught in the mechanism he
thought to master. The Dandy asleep in the mirror represents the failure
of the notion that resignification, re-presentation is ultimately an expression of mastery. The paradox of the Dandy is that of an active, forceful
being who is disciplined and heroic, and is also a being seized from the
back, in the attitude of death.

His heroism can be distinguished from that of the military man, however, in that the latter dies the animal death of an insect on a pin, whereas the Dandy's death is that of consciousness. His superiority, Baudelaire tells us, is intellectual (*OC* I, 710). When he falls, it is in the mind: One thinks of Brummell gone mad in Calais, of Julien Sorel who literally "lost his head," or of the extraordinary attachment to form over substance that goes along with this decadent figure. Dandyism in general is an institution associated with the "setting sun" (*OC* II, 712) and thus with the disappearance of God and meaning from the universe (*OC* I, 149) by Baudelaire, in contrast to the resplendent sun of Enlightenment reason.

Earlier, the Dandy was identified as an incomplete figure for the active artist in that his relation to the sign is characterized by a limited dispossession and a self-interested recuperation. Now, with the appearance of the Dandy as a Sadian figure taken into the grip of the process that he has set into motion, the missing piece of disinterest and of a dispossession unlimited by the subject seems to have shown up, along with a closer resemblance to the artist. A dispossession that does not return to the subject characterizes the Dandy.[29] The Dandy asleep in the mirror is a limit representation indicating the potential for others to resignify the resignifying subject: It stands for the impossibility of consciousness fully harnessing the freedom of the signifier and opens toward the possibility of the I's own language being reappropriated by another. The Dandy awake and asleep before the mirror is the perfect expression of "individualism properly understood" in all its aspects, exhibiting the interest of consciousness in its representation and the potential for its dispossession in its images. Can we then conclude that Baudelaire does identify the artist with the figure, seeing the ultimate dispossession of the one as a clear point of analogy with the other?

Differentiating between Dandy and artist is the point of the prose poem "Une Mort héroïque." There an artist confronts a Dandy prince and, despite some strong resemblances between the two, ends by claiming his own death, as distinct from the Dandy's sleep. The poem shows us the mime Fancioulle, under sentence of death along with several other malcontents for having conspired to overthrow and replace the Prince. We know the Prince is a Dandy because out of *ennui*, he takes the sordid situation of political conspiracy with its predictable end in a round of executions, and recasts it as a dramatic spectacle of a buffoon miming for dear life. Fancioulle is commanded to give a last performance, attended by sovereign, co-conspirators, the public, and the *moi*, whom we ought not to forget, as we are dependent upon him for our account.

According to the observing I, the Prince's desire was probably to "judge the value of the scene-producing talent of a man condemned to death" (*OC* I, 320), his ability to keep on representing even as he enters his last agony. The audience, however, believes that Fancioulle is to be spared, perhaps because he is allowed to play before an audience, which suggests that his sedition has been forgiven, but also because the ease of his movement on stage expresses the idea it attributes to the Prince, "the idea of softness and pardon" (*OC* I, 321). The scene is thus perfectly set to demonstrate how an artist condemned to death will die, and how the ironical consciousness of the Prince, as opposed to the naïve consciousness of the audience, which simply doesn't believe that pretend people can "really" die, will understand that death in the terms of reflective consciousness. It is the perfect place to consider what distinguishes the artist (its own death) from the death of a Dandy Prince, or, for that matter, from the animal deaths of the fellow conspirators that will take place a few days later offstage.

Now the first thing to be noted is that while the Prince is doing his best to make Fancioulle mime the idea of death, Fancioulle is miming every idea but that one. Most of the prose poem is devoted to the description of Fancioulle's fabulous ability to defer the moment of death by acting as an incarnation of the idea of clemency and of life. Fancioulle starts by making death disappear: "Fancioulle was . . . a perfect idealization, which it was impossible not to suppose living, possible, real" (*OC* I, 321). He arrives on stage as an idea incarnate, and as such as a living work of art.

> Fancioulle proved to me . . . that genius can play comedy next to the tomb with a joy that keeps him from seeing the tomb, lost as he is in a paradise excluding any idea of tomb and destruction. . . . No one dreamt about death, mourning or torture any longer." (*OC* I, 321–2)

As for the prince, disappointed at the artist who keeps making him think of life when what he wants is to see what a condemned artist will do with death, his brilliant idea is to disrupt the illusion, to send a premature message of disapproval by way of a page, which will interrupt Fancioulle in his deferring idealization; and, by forcing him to face his approaching death while on stage, will require him to represent for observing consciousness its death, its becoming appearance or thing. A pounding on the door in "La chambre double," the chiming of the clock in "Rêve parisien," have the similar function of disrupting an illusion prematurely, of folding the end of the dream into the dream.

The Prince forces Fancioulle to anticipate death; like Lord Henry Wootton with Dorian Gray, he forces him to become "premature." What that anticipation means is one thing for the naïve members of the audience. For them, Fancioulle's death fits without a wrinkle as the return to the real. The whistle is the end of the play; Fancioulle's death takes place after the play is over, and is a signal of a difference between the world of illusion presented on the stage by the artist, and the bitter reality, which is presided over by the hard-headed and rather tyrannical Prince. In a sense, we can say that, for the naïve audience, as artist Fancioulle cannot die in the work. He can't die because death is reality, and that can't appear on the stage unless and until the play is over, the actor has stopped acting, and we've returned to reality.

But the Prince sees something more than the public because as ironic consciousness, he knows more about appearances and realities. He knows, for instance, that death does not necessarily mean the end of illusion. It is possible for characters to stage death, to represent it for consciousness without being actually flattened by it. When Fancioulle moves about on the stage, opening and shutting his eyes, opening his mouth "*as if* breathing convulsively" (*comme pour respirer convulsivement*), tottering about and falling down heavily, he may be pretending to die just as he has been mimicking life. The Prince wants to know how the artist will deal with death, and what he discovers is that the mime does not falter or fumble, as Shakespeare's "imperfect actor on the stage / Who with his fear is put beside his part." Instead, he incorporates the end or limit of representation into his representation. He shows the Prince the impossibility of anything that happens on the stage ever happening as anything but a heightened illusion. Fancioulle, we are told, is "awake *in* his dream" (*reveillé **dans** son rêve*), when he dies he "drops dead *on the stage*" (*tomba roide mort **sur les planches***), which is to say, dead within the representation. For the Prince, all the world is in theory a stage ("the great misfortune of this prince was that he never had a theatre vast enough for his genius"), and there never is anything outside of representation, unless it be perhaps the spectating consciousness watching the show, which is what the Prince wants to see about when he intervenes in the spectacle with his audible "comment" on it. We don't get a chance to see Fancioulle stand up to take his bow because the *moi* interrupts the scene right there. But the *moi* is fairly certain that the Prince expected him to do so, that he did not believe that by asking Fancioulle to represent death on the stage he would actually die. Few indeed are the sovereigns who ask pages to execute their disobedient subjects by whistling at them. What the Prince was doing was bringing the play to a premature end so as to see how the mime would fold that disruption, the idea of the end of idealization, into the play. What the

Prince cares about is the representation of the death of consciousness. He wants to see himself as he sleeps.

Here, too, Fancioulle is a consummate artist. One thing the death of consciousness means is not being able to "know" the difference—as in a hallucination—between a representation and a perception. That is exactly what happens in Fancioulle's death on stage. As the narrator has explained, Fancioulle has seemed a living statue, and the work of art is a paradise "excluding all idea of the tomb and destruction" (*excluant toute idée de tombe et de destruction*). Fancioulle's death does not happen as his singular death, with unrepeatable finality, nor as the appearance of worms and corruption. Instead, it has a physical appearance (the body falls), which appearance incarnates an idea of death as the departure of the spirit from the body, left suddenly bereft of purpose and animation. This is a hallucination: The body's fall is at once a perception of the real (of the body as such) and a representation, part of the illusion created by the artist to get across the idea of death. The figure of the body as "*roide mort*," the stiff, is significant here. The rigidity is a signal of the entrance of repetition onto the scene, as consciousness sees the limit of representation as just another representation. It is also suggestive of a certain apotropaic defensiveness that we have been associating with the Dandy with his likeness to a cadaver. The rigidity of the body stands very well for the last-ditch representation that parries the end of representation.[30]

Just as for the audience, the mime cannot die on stage because art is play and death is reality, so for the superior consciousness that is the Dandy, the mime cannot die because as artist he is always only representing death to consciousness. For the audience and for the Prince, the ideality of art contradicts death. Baudelaire comments in more than one place on the impossibility of dying, among other places in the final lines of "The Mask," where the statue's tears are cried at being condemned to live without possibility of dying. Are we to assume that Fancioulle somehow escapes death? The narrator does not say so but drops the curtain on the scene without letting the mime return to take a final bow. He does wonder, however, whether "the whistle, as rapid as a blade, had really frustrated the executioner?" (*OC* I, 322) [*le sifflet, rapide comme un glaive, avait-il réellement frustré le bourreau?*]. When a little later, the narrator calls the clown inimitable, however, it appears to be in part because he has managed to do the really incredible thing—unbelievable to the audience and unanticipated by the Prince—which is "to die" in his performance.[31] The *moi* seems to be saying that while Fancioulle represents the death of consciousness to the Dandy in a sheltering representation, he does not do his own dying by the light of that representation.

How does Fancioulle manage his death? At the end of his meditation on the story, the *moi* explains that Fancioulle had risen to the favor of the Prince (*"s'élever à la . . . faveur"*) (*OC* I, 323). The wording is odd here. One would have expected *"être en faveur"* or even *"s'élever en faveur,"* to be or to rise in favor if Baudelaire were simply talking about the Prince's favorable attitude toward him. As expressed, the Prince seems to have tendered him a mark of his favor, maybe even accorded him the looked for clemency, and Fancioulle has risen to the occasion and has wrested his own death regardless of the impossibility of representing it from his art. He has gotten a favor, and he has given one in return. How does he get his death?

The misfiring of the sovereign's sign of disapproval can help make the point. We have shown that to the Prince, Fancioulle grasps the sign as a Dandy would, as the occasion for a heightening of his prestige as artist as figure for the Prince. Fancioulle makes the sign of disapproval into a means to represent the end of representation, and thus into a sign of the Prince's favor. We must remember, however, that we are not looking at things from the Prince's perspective, but share that of the I writing the story, whose problematic identification with Prince or buffoon is thus the hidden center of the prose poem. That perspective is significantly different from that of the Prince at various points, and increasingly so toward the end of the story, where we are reminded that his pen trembles and his eyes are blurred by tears "while I seek to describe this unforgettable evening to you" (*OC* I, 321).

Now, to the I, the whistle is significant because it disrupts, over and above the illusion of the mime's mastery over the spectacle, the narrative illusion that the I is telling a story to a listening community of hearts: "a sharp whistle blow . . . *rent* [*déchira*] both ears and hearts" (*OC* I, 322; emphasis mine). The noise of the whistle, like the subsequent laughter of the child in the corridor off stage, breaks the silence the better to remind of it. Baudelaire's term *déchirer* is of particulate note in accomplishing this reminder. Its primitive meaning is to rip, or tear, as a fabric or other flimsy material, and it bears connotations of revealing truth, as in the expression *déchirer le voile*, "to tear the veil," as an idiom meaning "to reveal the truth." But here, through a catachrestic usage, also perfectly normal in French, the term is transferred as if there were an analogy between revealing to eyes that can now see what was hidden before and revealing to ears that can now hear what before was kept silent. In fact, the term involves a wild naming because there is no corresponding term to exchange, and we find ourselves moving not toward greater understanding but toward deafness. The effect of the whistle is not to bring the ear into its own but rather to split or rend it. The whistle doesn't teach the ear to remember language as about sound; it breaks the eardrums, and reminds narrator and listener that the mime has been miming silently all along, as in a text. In short, so far as the I's perspective is concerned, the mime is suddenly miming his deafness to speech, the sign as given him by a *page*, and not by consciousness.

He's remembering about reading and writing. Signs are not perceptions only, appearances to eye or ear; they have a material aspect and as such are another matter for representing. It is as though Fancioulle had reached a point where he no longer had any ideas to represent but had kept on going past the point of providing a signifier for a previous signified. He's literalizing a figure, *mourir de honte*, perhaps. Or perhaps he's inspiring himself from a term of English theater slang that made its way into the language around the time Baudelaire was writing, "corpsing," with the sudden shuddering fall of the actor out of his part into the disseminating laughter of absolute irony. Or with his body, he's simply giving shape to the fall of a figure into literality, making his body into the inkjet fixed onto the page as a letter; he's materializing the letter, remembering literality, so far excluded from the spectacle, drawing our attention to what we can only read, like the difference between what sounds the same, the homonym of "page" and "page." Fancioulle has been parading idealist art as the highest art; now, with him, with the rip in the illusion that we are hearing a story about a spectacle and the reminder that we are reading one, dies idealist art, replaced by an art that operates otherwise, not as the representation of a deed, nor as the incarnation of an idea, but as the miming of the difference that writing makes between the spectacle and the written page.[32]

In the figure of the artist undone, we have a figure that resembles the Dandy in resignifying and in dying as expressive subject, but who chooses another death in turning to literature for inspiration. Thinking back for a moment to Baudelaire's statement that the Dandy "has to live and sleep before the mirror," we can say the Dandy is indeed the representing subject both in its apotheosis and in its subsequent fall.[33] The artist, however, represents without a prior represented; his death and his afterlife both spring straight from his anticipation within his work that his work will have survived him.

To the extent that the writing I identifies with one of his characters, it is surely with the mime Fancioulle who reaches the apogee of his art only in his falling. The artist cannot identify with the Dandy as mastering consciousness because that is to identify with an idealist, whereas the artist's inspiration comes from the material. Nor can he identify with him as sleeping figure because the sleeping Dandy stands for a limit to consciousness, whereas the artist, even in dying, "knows" his double nature. That is what Baudelaire says of the artist in his text on laughter: "(Artists) know that a given being is comic, and that he is so only on condition of not knowing his true nature, just as, by an inverse law, the artist is an artist only on condition of being double and of ignoring no phenomenon of his double nature" (*OC* II, 543).[34] The doubleness of the artist, his simultaneous activity of rising and falling, allows the mime to make the difference between the spectacle on the stage, and as it will be read in the text of "Une Mort héroïque." The Dandy figure thus appears as one of the numerous doubles parading through Baudelaire's text that invite us to look for resemblances to the artist, while refusing identification.

And yet, is the Dandy just one among the array of doubles? Note that the Prince has, unwittingly, through the page, tendered the sign from which Fancioulle wins his death. The Dandy is more than a figure for self-consciousness. It is his double decision to command the spectacle and to put an end to it that provides the necessary stage. That is what Baudelaire says when he tells us that the Dandy is situated before the mirror, *devant le miroir*, in the liminal position of one who allows and forbids access to literature as representation. Through the Dandy as subject, we get access to the spectacle given that it is consciousness, self-consciousness, that the spectacle represents. But as shape before the mirror, as suit of clothes, he blocks the play of appearances. He can stand in as the shadow cast by a not yet-arrived, nonrepresentational poetry; his decisive command has let Fancioulle seize his death as the death of a writer in "Une Mort héroïque." We can think of this Dandy shape as a placeholder. He is a stop-gap for a new manner that steps out as motive when representation fails. Like the eponymous hero in *The Picture of Dorian Gray*, he represents a new motive for art. He lets the mime foreknow the future death awaiting him, foreknow his double nature. In short, the modern artist identifies with the Dandy's decisive act that puts clothing ahead of the mirror, and thus ends by obliterating the play of representation.[35]

It is literally true that the story "Une Mort héroïque" spins out from the mime's having identified with the Prince. This identification is mistaken in almost every respect, and the mime is punished heavily for it: first, by the sentence of death pronounced against him for daring to conspire to substitute another leader for the Prince; and then, by the derisive whistle that greets his perfect representation of the princely thought of pardon. But in one particular, in the Dandy's having made manner a motive, in his having grasped a radical freedom to the signifier that spells the end of the representation of what is and the beginning of a representing without a represented, the artist indeed identifies meaningfully with the Dandy Prince. It is not the superiority and lucidity of the Dandy, nor is it his being for the other, that attracts this Mallarmean Baudelaire; he identifies with him insofar as the latter all unknowingly signals the end of representational art and the arising of a representing inspired by the sign.

Now we can see why Bataille finds the artist's foreknowledge of his death as idealist artist, his identification with the Dandy blocking the mirror, ruinous, fatal with respect to the dispossession aimed at by poetry. For such foreknowledge reanimates what had to be without speech or consciousness for the identification to occur. It reactivates the representational poetry that is over and done with. In the identification with the Dandy, the art of representation that is finished survives itself.[36] In what speech could the subject claim its resemblance to an evacuated, dehumanized subject? The Dandy is a figure for the discursive I.[37] To identify with the evacuated Dandy is to make it rise again, to possess it one more time with the attributes of the discursive subject whose dispossession has allowed Baudelaire to foreknow his fate as artist with respect to the work, to forget about the critical distinction between an art of appearances that reveal consciousness and an art inspired by the written sign.

But Bataille is also right to say that identification is ineluctable and is to be welcomed as such. The poet welcomes what he cannot help because his identification will set into motion the dissolution of the analogy and will get him the freedom to anticipate his death by writing. The poet is inevitably, fatally, attracted to the Dandy as provider of a material of the sort needed to feed his poetry, a material that will let him stage the death of idealist art. The Dandy as the idea of a manner in the way of the mirror opens a horizon outside of those covered by "individualism properly understood," and as such, it opens another horizon for poetry.

Baudelaire's texts appear to eschew the autobiographical, written as they are around the I's death, around the failure of representation and particularly self-representation, and foregrounding as they do the claims of the text to be written from language. But in the repeated emergence of a shape blocking the mirror, of an autothanatographical writing, where a language of representation repeatedly gives way to a language that represents "only" more language, we find a Baudelairian signature.

II

Writing Death, with Regard to the Other

CHAPTER 4

Hospitality in Autobiography:
Levinas *chez* De Quincey

What would a Levinasian autobiography look like? Is such a thing imaginable? The question is directed in the first instance at autobiography, as a question concerning its ability to go beyond the representation of the subject to write the encounter with the absolutely other for which Levinas's ethical philosophy calls. But it is also, in the second instance, a question for Levinas, concerning the potential of autobiography to represent an alterity perhaps not fully accounted for by his philosophy. This double question presides over the reflection that follows.

Certainly, the notion of Levinasian self-writing is, at first blush, unpromising. In the accepted notion of autobiography, the aim of the genre is the disclosure of the I's self-sameness through the representation of its experience. Experience can be thought only as my experience; as De Quincey says in the *Confessions of an English Opium-Eater*, "No man surely, on a question of my own private experience, could have pretended to be better informed than myself." We assume that autobiographical knowledge comes through the consciousness of an individual subject standing apart: "each man's consciousness [is shut up] into a silent world of its own, separate and inaccessible to all other consciousness."[1]

But Levinas's ethics, as he explains in *Humanisme de l'autre homme*, contains a critique of experience, representation, and the isolated individual:

> *It is rather a matter of the questioning of* EXPERIENCE *as the source of meaning,*
> of the limit to transcendental apperception, of the end of synchrony and its
> reversible terms; it is a matter of the non-priority of the Same and,
> throughout all these limitations, of the end of *actuality,* as if the *untimely*
> [*l'intempestif*] were come to upset the agreements of representation.[2]

To quest after meaning in representation misses the point for Levinas.
Thought is not equivalent to a knowledge derived from experience, and
the subject's aspiration to knowledge of objects always neglects something
more fundamental—the question of the other as source of a meaning that
is not reducible to my representation. As for the self, self-identity (*le
Même*) and self-presence (*l'actualité*) stand indicted. In short, if we accept
that autobiography is indeed limited to the representation of the egocen-
tric subject's experience with a view to securing self-sameness, it would
seem quite impossible to conceive of it along Levinasian lines.

Perhaps, however, Levinas's concern with the other might link his
thought to another aspect of autobiography: namely, its performative dimension. Without an address to the other—be it Augustine's prayers to
God, Lazarillo's ironically obsequious "Vuestra Merced," Rousseau's
over-the-shoulder references to *le lecteur,* or Jane Eyre's abrupt addresses
to "Reader"—there could be no autobiography or autobiographical fiction. As Gusdorf already understood, the autobiographer does not write a
treatise on experience, but rather testifies to it or gives its apology.[3] In
saying experience, the I attests, excuses, premises, promises, confesses, testifies, or otherwise translates the discourse of knowledge into that of
power and justice. And Levinas's insistence on the "pure sign made to the
other; sign made from the giving of the sign" (*HAH* 13), his concern with
a language that is not one of message ("an incessant unsaying of the said")[4]
but of address "from the revelation of the Other," places him squarely in
the domain of the performative.[5] A consideration of the performative
might allow Levinas and autobiography to be linked.

Besides, as Levinas knows very well, there is no escaping the subject,
even if that subject has to be conceived as in crisis, a subject whose unstable horizon is given and threatened by the other. In its address to the
other, the subject constitutes itself as an ethical being, while violently
usurping the former's place in the world by the same speech act. At least
one reading of the performative in Levinas makes it a privileged form of
the face-to-face with the other. There, the I comes to be responsible for
the other that both constitutes and menaces it. Levinas explains the double
relation: "the subject is hostage," and also, the "subject is host" (*AE* 142,

276) [or guest, *hôte*]. Levinas's subject in crisis, his subject constituting itself as ethical in the face-to-face, provides a promising avenue for approaching the relations of the subject to the other in autobiography. For Levinas, the I determined as self-knowledge is deprived of its origination in the encounter with the other. That is as much as to say that a Levinasian autobiography would bring the subject into remembrance of its vexed relation of violence and gratitude to the other.

After all, then, we may be able to imagine an exemplary Levinasian autobiography. It would tend to feature the subject in crisis, prey to the untimely occurrence (*l'intempestif*) in a narrative troubled by discontinuity, where experience is a moot point and the account of the I's relations to the other is central. I'd like to put forward as an anachronistic candidate for this role of Levinasian autobiography De Quincey's *Confessions of an English Opium-Eater*. Already on the score of style—De Quincey's digressiveness is generally agreed second to none—the *Confessions* rate our consideration. As De Quincey explains it, the rambling, disjointed narrative is the effect of his having privileged not his experience, but its detritus and the extraneous ornaments that are its trappings: "parasitical thoughts, feelings, digressions . . . spread a glory over incidents that for themselves would be—less than nothing."⁶ This digressiveness, moreover, can be associated with De Quincey's concern with what he baptizes, in contradistinction to a "literature of knowledge," a "literature of power." As spelled out in "The Poetry of Pope," the literature of knowledge is a teaching literature addressed to the discursive understanding. It has truth as its aim, and it interests through novelty. The literature of power, on the other hand, is addressed to "the higher understanding or reason, but always through the affections of pleasure and sympathy."⁷

There are other reasons besides style for seeing the *Confessions of an English Opium-Eater* as quintessentially Levinasian. Chief among them is that fact that De Quincey's I does not come into existence alone, nor claim the relative autonomy we are accustomed to granting it in autobiographical literature of the Rousseauian variety.⁸ De Quincey's confessions proceed from other motives and develop other motifs than those that characterize the self-sufficient I. Nowhere in the text will the portrait of "a man in all the truth of nature . . . Myself alone" even be attempted.⁹ Instead, his I is dependent upon the other for its emergence. This is true at the anecdotal, experiential level, as represented in the story, as well as in discursive, performative terms. The preface provides a good example of the way that the address to the other motivates the story. The I does not emerge as a Romantic subject reflecting upon sensation or emotion.

Rather, it emerges in a Modernist pose, in nervous reaction to an imagined accusation. This is what De Quincey says to justify his writing an account of "a remarkable period" in his life:

> I trust that it will prove, not merely an interesting record, but, in a considerable degree, useful and instructive. In that hope it is, that I have drawn it up: and that must be my apology for breaking through that delicate and honourable reserve, which, for the most part, restrains us from the public exploration of our own errors and infirmities. Nothing, indeed, is more revolting to English feelings, than the spectacle of a human being obtruding on our notice his moral ulcers or scars, and tearing away that "decent drapery," which time, or indulgence to human frailty, may have drawn over them . . . *All this I feel so forcibly, and so nervously am I alive to reproach of this tendency, that I have for many months hesitated about the propriety of allowing this, or any part of my narrative, to come before the public eye* . . . and it is not without an anxious review of the reasons, for and against this step, that I have, at last, concluded on taking it. (*OE* 1, my emphasis)

This is not the calm, rational power of a self-conscious subject reviewing a lived past in a narrative. Rather, the fragmentary narrative will feed off the anxieties of a being whose main claim to our notice is that he worries about whether and when to obtrude himself on us. It is first and foremost De Quincey's present act of confessing rather than his addiction that is to be judged. We even see De Quincey tying his very existence to the other's call in the passage, literally springing to life to write a response to the reproach that he should be contemplating writing an autobiography: "All this I feel so forcibly, and so nervously *am I alive* to reproach of this tendency"(my emphasis).[10]

A dependency on others for survival is characteristic and, reaching sublime and ridiculous proportions, makes the De Quinceyan I into the counter-example of the self-reliant man. Instead of looking for a job to tide him over during a period of want, for instance, De Quincey works hard to collect the largest possible chain of people on whom to rely, always deferring the actual pocketing of money: He wants to borrow on his paternal expectations from moneylenders; to do so, he obtains money from a family friend so as to be able to travel to solicit a letter of attestation to his identity from a noble friend, finding sustenance for his journey in Ann's tenderness and on the shoulder of a stranger. The friend turns out to be absent, but another provides him the needed letter instead. All of this effort comes to naught in literal terms—the money is not forthcoming from this quarter, and comes instead unexpectedly from another. However, the gathering of support works to fuel the narrative with a good deal of lively incident.

It is moreover evident that the others on whom the I relies will not be those to whom he is related by nature or friendship. From the first lines of the narrative proper, our hero is deprived of home, family, and friends; and gone among strangers: "My father died, when I was about seven years old, and left me to the care of four guardians. I was sent to various schools, great and small; and was very early distinguished for my classical attainments, especially for my knowledge of Greek" (*OE* 6). One can hardly emphasize enough the lengths to which De Quincey goes to depict the I as deprived by circumstance of any sense of rootedness in the family group. In the 1821 *Confessions*, we never once see him at home with his mother and siblings.[11]

His youth is spent at school or as a runaway living precariously in the houses of others. Even where his actual circumstances were of a rich family life, the narrative deliberately seizes him apart from them (in London while they are in Grasmere); or, where he is himself at home, his family is most often absent—evoked at most by a tea-table laid for two, or by an interior scene peopled by servants and strangers. When his children do briefly haunt his bedside, it is to sharpen the contrast between his nightmares and the peaceful life from which he has been exiled. His wife is mentioned as an amanuensis whose absence helps explain the sorry state of the finished manuscript. It would be very hard to imagine a hero more deprived of the ordinary sources of autobiographical pathos, or a narrator working harder to make do without the literary resources a rich personal experience provides.

De Quincey's hero lives instead on intimate terms with strangers. As a runaway, he occupies a makeshift bed for weeks with a forsaken child about whom he knows little, but whom "I loved . . . because she was a partner in my wretchedness" (*OE* 20). Ann is the very type of the stranger, the human being "that chance might fling my way" with whom "it has been my pride to converse familiarly" (*OE* 20), and she is "loved . . . as affectionately as if she had been my sister" (*OE* 27). Ann's very name suggests her status as first comer; not only does De Quincey not know her family name, but her given name hints by paronomasia at the indefinite article, as if she were an example of the undetermined other, An(n) Other.[12] One of the most affecting moments in the early part of the *Confessions* shows the I, on the verge of running away from school, mournfully taking leave of "a place which I did not love, and where I had not been happy" (*OE* 8). The elegy reaches its apogee as the hero plants a filial kiss on the portrait of a woman who is a total stranger to him. In brief, the others the hero encounters bring out the bonds that tie him to a community rather than to a family, and are correspondingly ethical rather than erotic in nature.

Even his preferred language is not the familiar, maternal language of English. De Quincey picks out as the distinguishing characteristic of his boyhood his development of a remarkable ability to speak the dead language of ancient Greek. Generally speaking, we think of the newspaper as a matter of knowledge, where content is all. But for the young De Quincey, the content was merely a pretext. If he read the news, it was so as to translate it into Greek, a written language of no earthly value for communicating knowledge but having great symbolic power.[13] In short, the *Confessions* show De Quincey deprived or depriving himself of the familiar, actively seeking out the other, estranging himself habitually even from his own tongue. It is in the company of strangers that De Quincey is at home, on others that he depends for his existence and sustenance. Like Baudelaire's poet, whose soul wanders in the gutters outside its apartment, De Quincey is always wandering outside home.

The connection between the I's state of deprivation and his reliance on the other can be variously understood, resulting in two distinct narrative structures. It can be thought as causal. The I may live with strangers because it cannot rely on itself. Its recourse to others, meanwhile, further impedes it from developing its own resources. Thus, in trying to borrow against his paternal inheritance, the young De Quincey dissipates his money on a vain journey to find a friend to stand him surety for the loan. What is true of the hero is also true of the narrator, whose dearth of material leads him to lay hold of topics and texts extraneous to his subject that, while meant as stop-gaps, end by replacing and thus further depleting his life narrative.

The connection of the I to the other can also be viewed within a teleological framework. There, the structure would not be one of debilitating dependency but of a reenergized relation where the subject is infinitely grateful to and responsible for the other that helps it to transcend its natural state. De Quincey's I is hungry for the relation to the other that lets it come into being, with self-destitution a step that will bring it again into that more primordial relation. Had the hero not deferred the moment of touching his inheritance—had he never run away, met Ann, and nearly died of hunger—he would never have owed his life to her, and thus could never have discovered gratitude and the longing for a transcendence of the here and now that accompanies that feeling. Each instance of suffering recounted is an opportunity from the narrative point of view to repay an obligation to the other on whom the I depends for its existence as ethical subject. That can be seen in the gratitude expressed for Ann's having spent her few pennies on a glass of wine to revive the hero:

> O youthful benefactress! how often in succeeding years, standing in solitary places, and thinking of thee with grief of heart and perfect love, how often have I wished that, as in ancient times the curse of a father was believed to have a supernatural power, and to pursue its object with a fatal necessity of self-fulfillment,—even so the benediction of a heart oppressed with grati-tude, might have a like prerogative; might have power given to it from above to chase—to haunt—to way-lay—to overtake—to pursue thee into the central darkness of a London brothel, or (if it were possible) into the darkness of the grave—there to awaken thee with an authentic message of peace and forgiveness, and of final reconciliation! (*OE* 22)

The speaker wants to render to the other the favor the other has done it. Ann has resuscitated the hero with a glass of wine, a "powerful and reviv-ing stimulus . . . [without which I was convinced I] should have died upon the spot" (*OE* 22). Nor is the narrator content to remember her merely. He wants to pursue his benefactress into the grave, to revive her as Christ did Lazarus, and that desire emerges in the shift to a transcendental regis-ter, expressive of a sudden recognition on the part of the I of a relation to the absolutely other.

In short, both causal and teleological ways of structuring the I's connec-tion to the other fall in with Levinas's discussion of the proximity of the other. The encounter with the other sets the I in crisis, shaking it out of its narcissistic complacency and endowing it with a sense of responsibility and of dependency not limited by experience.[14]

The resemblance between Levinas and De Quincey is clinched by the fact that both think the I's relation to the other in terms of hospitality. That relation is not fully exhausted by interest, appropriation, exchange, or any of the terms that characterize a limited economy. Instead, Levinas, as Derrida has shown, has recourse to terms like "hospitality" and "the gift" to describe an encounter that has an unlimited, an an-economic side.[15] For De Quincey too, perhaps under the influence of Kant's essay on *Perpetual Peace*, scenes of hospitality frame the hero's entrance into the world as well as the scholar's retreat from it. The theme of drug addiction also involves an intact space—the home, the family, the self—exposed to an alterity that at once threatens its healthy functioning and provides that intact space with a potential to expand beyond itself, to gain a window onto the infinite, as Baudelaire puts it.[16] De Quincey even conceives his text in terms of hospitality. The most cursory of readers cannot help but notice the preponderance of foreign terms and citations in a work that purports to contain *English* confessions.

Identifying De Quincey's autobiography as Levinasian in cast lets us consider the problem of the other in De Quincey in a new light. In his illuminating study, John Barrell diagnoses De Quincey's fascinated repugnance for the orientalized other as the illness of British imperialism, and in the process, analyzes the lurid details of the text in terms of a xenophobia and hysteria he attributes to De Quincey.[17] Imperialism, too, is diagnosed as a pathological condition, against the normal condition of a self-contained, autonomous state. But in his hurry to assimilate De Quincey to the worst ideologues of his time, Barrell does not consider De Quincey's rhetoric within an ethical framework, which seems necessary given De Quincey's interest in Kant and which a Levinasian reading would encourage. Following out the problematic of hospitality will allow a fresh approach, and one that attends more closely to considerations De Quincey himself deemed central. There is a further possible benefit. De Quincey's views on hospitality might reveal some crucial differences with Levinas that could lead us to a critique of the latter's philosophy. For instance, Levinas allows the I only a certain internal difference, which—subsumed as it is by the subject as it transforms itself—is ultimately left behind. But De Quincey, for instance in the drug motif where the I takes in a killing negativity, suggests a self-alteration more shattering.[18]

In order to examine what hospitality means for De Quincey, we will take two contrasting scenes where it is central. In the first of these scenes, "casual" hospitality is at issue, and the incident shows a reciprocal relation, a give and take between host and guest who are similar and potentially substitutable for one another. In the second scene, which I think ultimately exceeds the Levinasian framework, violence and misunderstanding threaten. There, the gulf between guest and host is too great for exchange—indeed guest and host appear almost to be subject to different physical laws—but what De Quincey calls the "laws of hospitality" (*OE* 57) are nonetheless invoked.

The Kindness of Strangers: Casual Hospitality

The first scene recounts an episode in which the runaway hero, his money having given out, becomes dependent on the hospitality of Welsh villagers. A family of brothers and sisters take him into a cottage where he meets with an "affectionate and fraternal kindness that left an impression upon my heart not yet impaired" (*OE* 14). But after three nights, his hosts' parents return, and rudely rebuffing his addresses, force him to take his leave. Reciprocal exchanges are evident throughout the passage. The hero subsists on "the casual hospitalities which I now and then *received*, in *return* for such little services as I had an opportunity of *rendering*" (my emphasis). Through the literal services of bed and board for conversation and letters in English, hosts and guest exchange the mutual recognition of a common kindness and gentility. The narrator has singled out, among the "humble friends" who received him in Wales, a genteel group: "four sisters, and three brothers . . . all remarkable for elegance and delicacy of manners. So much beauty, and so much native good-breeding and refinement, I do not remember to have seen before or since in any cottage" (*OE* 14). On its part, the Welsh family treats the impecunious scholar as a gentleman, "as if my scholarship were sufficient evidence, that I was of gentle blood." Hosts and guest appear elevated by the mutual recognition that both belong to the *genre humain*. The stranger one treats as a fellow human confers in return the sense of acting as a gentleperson (*gens*). The theme of kindness, mentioned no fewer than four times in the passage, with its etymological link to species or lineage, provides further evidence in the same vein. To be human is to be humane: that is, hospitable to others who, although strangers, one knows to be like oneself. The seven brothers and sisters of the Welsh family can not only substitute for De Quincey's own of seven siblings, but is preferable to it because he is divided from his own natural family by differences in a war of interests, as we discover in the *Autobiographical Sketches*.[19] With the Welsh family by contrast, De Quincey finds the uplifting recognition of a common humanity, and discovers the social affections.

Émile Benveniste can help delineate a few traits of conditional or casual hospitality, described in *Vocabulaire des institutions indo-européennes* as the situation of the *hostis*, with whom a pact allows exchange, in contradistinction to the *peregrinus*, who is outside any pact:

> A *hostis* is not a foreigner [*l'étranger*] in general. Unlike the *peregrinus*, who lives outside the limits of the territory, *hostis* is "the foreigner, [*l'étranger*] insofar as he is recognized to have rights equal to those of Roman citizens." This recognition of rights implies a certain relationship of reciprocity, supposes a convention: whoever is not Roman is not called *hostis*. A link of equality and reciprocity is established between *this* foreigner and the Roman citizen, which can lead to a precise notion of hospitality. From this

representation, *hostis* would mean "he who is in relations of compensation;" this is indeed the foundation of the institution of hospitality.[20]

Benveniste emphasizes that it is Roman law—or more generally, Roman discourse—that decides which foreigners are equal and capable of entering into exchange with the citizen. Not just any foreigner will be treated as guest but only those named foreigners who have been previously determined by pact to be capable of entering into exchange. In the Benveniste text, the true host, the master of the house of hospitality itself, is Roman law given that it determines the exchange partners. De Quincey's hero often operates within just such a previous political pact. A prior treaty is evident first of all in the fact that the common tongue is English, which the Welsh hosts have learned because it is the language of the nation that annexed Wales in the thirteenth century. The "guest" is thus no homeless wanderer, but rather the scion of an earlier wave of English empire-makers who had subjected Wales to English law and made of it a political and economic dependency.

In this passage, hospitality is defined as English hospitality. The ideal of reciprocity and equality has preceded the hero across the border, as part of the baggage of the history of English expansion. But it does not mask that history for the narrator, who is not to be confused with the hero in this. The former accumulates details that remind us that the heart of the scene for him, as avid reader of Ricardo's *Political Economy*, lies not in the manifest content—the hero's dream of a lovefest among gentlefolk—but rather in the hidden message of economic repression and violent annexation. The family members speak English because they have been in service in England. Indeed, the letters De Quincey writes aim to get native English-speakers to pay extra obligations incurred to the Welsh in their service: Apparently, the young women have "lived as servants in Shrewsbury, or other towns on the English border," where they have fallen in love with Englishmen; one of the brothers "had served on board an English man of war" and is owed prize money for his exploits. We have thus to consider the use of a predictable set of oppositions and cultural stereotypes dividing Welsh and English as a sign that we do indeed have to do with a social fantasy, but not that that fantasy is the mature De Quincey's. For De Quincey's narrator, the hero's fantasy of reciprocity is a delusion that masks the political reality of economic and political dependence. The hostility missing from the young people's meeting is immediately in evidence upon their parents' return.

All of this suggests that De Quincey's casual hospitality converges with Levinas's critique of the I who, in positing the other as a subject like him, reduces difference and turns the other into an object of knowledge. In autobiography, the subject is master of the house; and wherever he goes with his language, whether he calls himself guest or host, his sovereign gesture of speaking first determines the other as the other for him. De Quincey's first move is to bring the I into crisis by pointing to his hero's delusive belief in his own autonomy. Instead, he is a puppet of his language, which speaks through him, imposing its categories on him.

Because this hospitality so visibly takes place on the subject's terms, it is something other than hospitality. It is a visit paid by the colonizer to an already-colonized other, a visit in which he comes across oppositions that are entirely familiar because he has brought them with him. It is as though the I had said to the Welsh family, make yourselves at home in my house, even to the point where you act as the hosts and I as the guest, so that we may—each in his own way—enjoy my beneficence. In short, the scene tends to suggest the ready availability of hospitality only in impure forms. It is present as a welcome extended to an other already readied to enter into exchange with the subject, but it is not a pure welcome, beyond exchange, extended to the other as such. De Quincey's "casual hospitality" confirms Levinas's insight into the subject's reduction of the other.

However, the passage suggests that the I does catch sight of a beyond to self-interest, for the episode left "an impression upon my heart not yet impaired" (*OE* 14). Moreover, despite the preponderance of economic metaphors, De Quincey calls the young people's action an act of *hospitality*. We must look elsewhere, away from the logic of exchange, to understand why that should be so. De Quincey says, "the reception one meets with from the women of the family generally determines the tenour of one's whole entertainment" (*OE* 14). To understand why De Quincey finds the experience one of hospitality, *il faut chercher la femme*.

For the Levinas of *Totalité et infini*, "the welcoming [*l'accueillant*] *par excellence*, the welcoming in itself" is feminine (*TeI* 131).[21] The feminine stands for what Derrida, reading Levinas, calls "inviolable violability."[22] By this is meant a simultaneous interdiction of and vulnerability to violence: specifically, the violence of the subject. It is related to woman who, in Levinas, is the figure for the other's alterity, as tantalizingly out of reach and also as vulnerable, as simultaneously open to reduction and irreducible by the subject. The Welsh young women are exactly in that position. On the one side, they are open to the Englishman's approach. They have English-speaking "sweethearts," and the I himself has easily "penetrated" their love secrets. On the other side, they are utterly aloof. They maintain their "maidenly pride" in writing to their sweethearts and shut the I out of the unoccupied bed that stands in their apartment. This empty bed has particular significance. It figures a reserve of Welsh autonomy that resists all encroachment, a place set apart where the visitor's contaminating presence is forbidden.[23]

Within a house that has, as it seems, been entirely taken over by the visitor even before his arrival, the bed that is set off-limits stands for the inviolable alterity of the other. It therefore allows the representative colonizer to understand his experience as one of hospitality: that is, of encountering the other as withdrawn from and resistant to his appropriation. Through the empty signifier of the set apart bed, the I learns of the impossibility of hospitality. It is compromised because the other is the other for the subject, and hospitality has become a matter of exchange. It is truly impossible because as the hero learns, it only comes into view as desirable through the withdrawal of the other behind a closed door into a forbidden place whose limits must be respected. In short, an experience of the limits of hospitality, of respect for the other's intactness, seems to constitute for De Quincey the core of casual hospitality. In one's meeting with the other, one enters into a perverted and contaminated hospitality as exchange, while yet recognizing the other and pure hospitality as such through their withdrawal.[24] Ann, the streetwalker with a "plundered . . . property" who is treated as a sacrosanct sister by the impecunious hero, is another good example of woman-as-other at once off limits and vulnerable (*OE* 21).

The logic has been laid out by Derrida as what he calls the "paradoxical and perverting law" of hospitality. In *De l'hospitalité*, he says that "inviolable immunity is the condition of hospitality"[25] and then goes on to explain its necessity:

> I want to be the master in my home (*ipse, potis, potens,* master of the house . . .) so as to receive whomever I want. I begin by holding as an undesirable foreigner, virtually an enemy, whoever encroaches upon my home [*chez moi*], my ipseity, my power of hospitality, my sovereignty as host. The other becomes a hostile subject whose hostage I risk becoming. (*Hospitalité* 53)

In the passage from the *Confessions*, refusing to welcome the I into the bed in the women's apartment is the equivalent of holding him an undesirable encroacher, and setting up the private apartment as the *sanctum sanctorum* by means of which the other's sovereignty is confirmed. The English subject encounters a limit at their door, a limit of interest to him as ethical subject because it introduces him to a division within himself, between

imperializing reason and the heart, the logos and rhetoric, his consciousness as a reservoir of knowledge and his heart as reserve of love and feeling. De Quincey's casual hospitality gives us the wherewithal for a
Levinasian critique of the narcissistic subject moving about in a stale world
it has determined for itself; it also shows the I recognizing the other as
outside and untouched by its determination, and so coming to long for
self-transcendence.

De Quincey's picture of casual hospitality has implications for the relations between constative and performative, and more especially for the
exchange and translatability associated with the former, as for the particularity and untranslatability associated with the latter. In the passage, English has the status of *lingua franca*, a universal language of meaning and
commerce, of common nouns, of knowledge, into which all messages—be
they of business, friendship, love, or maidenly pride—can be translated. In
contrast to that language of universal message-bearing, Welsh appears as
a language of proper nouns ("the village of Llan-y-styndw [or some such
name]" [*OE* 14]). To De Quincey, it is a language that bristles with conso-
nants and names that point but do not mean. It has another characteristic
that filters through in the young people's English and is found in even
greater purity in the parents' Welsh. It is a performative language that
invites or welcomes ("on my first introduction"), urges ("I was pressed to
stay"), pleads ("he begged. . . . I would not take it amiss"), entreats ("they
spoke warmly to their parents"), apologizes ("and excused the manner of
the old people"), and denies ("*Dym Sassenach* [no English]") (*OE* 14–5).
The dividing line between the constatives of English and the performatives of the Welsh is not absolute, for English performatives are spoken by
the Welsh brothers and sisters; and the I, under the influence of the
Welsh, makes performative overtures to the parents ("my addresses").
There is a difference between the Welsh-accented performatives spoken
in English by the young people and the Welsh performative of the parents.
When the young people use words, they are indeed using them. Their
speech is conventional and aims at exchange. The fact that they speak
English, the language set up as that of knowledge and common currency,
helps hedge those performatives in as accepted procedures, consistent with
and useful for the circumstances in which they are uttered. Their performatives work within already established rules, and as such are appropriate to
the relations of contaminated hospitality. An image of what is entailed in
such a performative can be found in the homosocial bond formed between
the brothers and the I, which becomes evident when one of the brothers
invites the hero to sleep in his bed. It is not just a matter of like lying

down with like, for if the I does so, it is ultimately a sign of his having agreed to respect the incest taboo, forbidden as he is, like the brothers, from intercourse with the sisters. He is signing onto a pact rather than initiating one.

But the old people's Welsh works differently. Their gesture of refusal does not consist in saying words that have a conventional power to invite, promise, welcome, and so on. It consists, from the I's perspective, in opposing incomprehensible foreign words to comprehensible, English ones. They refuse to enter into exchange with the I, refuse the "paradoxical and perverting laws of hospitality," refuse to have truck with the colonizing subject or his chief instrument of domination, his language. There are and can be no accepted procedures for action where no common law and language are admitted. We can say that this refusal that shuts Welsh off from English is a performative in a sense, but not that it is conventional. The Welsh parents speak for an otherness that, withdrawing into itself, forbids determination and with it translation or exchange. *Dym Sassenach* closes the door as effectively against English as the sisters closed theirs against the Englishman. Their verbal gesture lays down the law in laying down a limit beyond which Welsh rules reign.

The impossibility of translation finds a literal form in the narrator's attempt to translate the old people's Welsh into English. What does his translation—No English—mean exactly? Are the parents, according to him, saying that they do not know English ("[we speak] no English")? Are they forbidding the speaking of English ("No English [is to be spoken here]")? Are they denying Englishmen entrance ("No English [people welcome here]")? Are they telling the truth about their own language ("[*Dym Sassenach* is] no English")? Is the translator perhaps expressing his own befuddlement, a gap in his translating skills or even a more general untranslatability ("No English [can render this]")? Has the narrator perhaps translated things for us in another sense, giving access to what might have been the hero's hallucinatory perception, responsible for his remembering the tag, that the parents were, after all, speaking a broken English—Dim Sassenach, Stupid Englishman? The Welsh performative passes into English in an overdetermined utterance. When De Quincey returns to England, his English will be host to a sudden and violent foregrounding of the performative dimension, here picked up from the Welsh.[26]

The exchanges of citizen and *hostis* imply a common understanding of what language is: translation, exchange of contents, of thoughts, acts of welcome that do not transgress the limits provided by the founding pact. Much can be learned from conditional hospitality then. We have uncovered a possible impossibility to hospitality, a violable inviolability to the other, both of which lend themselves to the critique of the subject in its appropriative tendencies. We have also seen that language participates in and perhaps helps determine the same logic. The subject's relation to the other is carried in a familiar language that tries to make everything exchangeable but that has within it, parallel to the withdrawal of the other, a resistance to exchange. All of this is very Levinasian, and anyone finishing reading De Quincey here might well conclude that in his own way, the author is concerned with the ethical subject *à la* Levinas; and with a discourse that, in the latter's vocabulary, unsays the said—that is, critiques the idea of language as content-based—foregrounds the performative aspect, displaces meaning through the movement of transcendence—all in the name of the human other as such.

The Foreign Visitor: The Law of Absolute Hospitality

The episode of hospitality in the *Confessions* I now want to turn to leaves a different impression, and one that will allow us to distinguish, amidst more structures that can be read as Levinasian in De Quincey, room for critique of the Levinasian vein. The scene, which is situated squarely in the midst of De Quincey's discussion of opium, features a subject at the turning point between its joys and pains and is told with a wry humor at odds with its somber theme. It takes place in Dove Cottage, which De Quincey rents after the Wordsworths, a cottage "populous with books," and concerns a Malay who knocks on his door on his way to an unknown destination (*OE* 60).[27] The hero holds a "conversation" with the visitor whose language he does not speak, by reciting "some lines from the Iliad." After a short rest, the Malay departs but not before De Quincey has given him three pieces of opium, enough to fell "three dragoons and their horses," which he swallows in a single gulp (*OE* 57). The host, afraid the man will die from so large a dose, even more afraid to force an emetic down his guest's uncomprehending throat, allows him to depart but remains anxious about his fate.

In lieu of conditional hospitality, the scene is concerned with the absolute "*laws* of hospitality" (*OE* 57, my emphasis). Instead of likeness and kindness, the scene is marked by difference, as is attested to by its violence, visible in the Malay's look of ferocity, the hero's murderous gift, and the Malay's "vengeful" haunting of the hero by dreams of other Malays, "worse than himself, that ran amuck at me, and led me into a world of troubles" (*OE* 58). Instead of a celebration of universal humanity according to the English traveler, the passage flirts with racism. Moreover, whereas we saw a prior pact and a shared language connecting guest and hosts in conditional hospitality, here "there seemed to be an impassable gulph fixed between all communication of ideas" (*OE* 56). The Malay is not a guest but Benveniste's *peregrinus*; his existence outside all exchange will raise the question of the limits imposed by exchange and a need for its transcendence. With the *peregrinus*, we will see the need for an absolute welcoming beyond all the welcomes already programmed as sayable. There will arise a wish for a saying without a said, a performative that does not act within an already determined context but creates a new one.

A less-obvious contrast concerns the problem of the limits of hospitality. Conditional hospitality sets spatial and temporal limits. In the earlier passage, it relied on limits, be they the spatial limits set up by the women's apartment and the borders between England and Wales, or temporal limits—the proverbial three days of the hero's visit—or the limits imposed by the parents' *Dym Sassenach*. But here, limits are rendered indefinite or inoperative. Whereas the Malay spends only "about an hour" in the house, he proves at once remarkably elusive and hard to extricate. Viewed by the servant as a demon to be exorcised, he seems to obey physical laws different from those of the host country, swallowing an overdose of opium without apparent ill effect, appearing magically in and passing through the Lake Country without leaving a trace. While one might assume the guest's body would entail spatial limits, in fact, the body does not serve as a figure for a limit between inside and outside so much as a signal of the other's absolute inviolability. Even at the price of killing him, the hero must not force him to vomit the deadly dose of opium. Discursive limits are also being pushed, not only in the scene where the "dialogue" between host and guest is implicitly compared to a "lunar language," but also in the way the narrator tells the episode—as an ironic aside, an anxious moment intercalated in an otherwise happy period, that all but swallows up the space that was to have been devoted to the description of happiness.

Kant, whom De Quincey claims to have been reading at this time, links hospitality indissociably with finitude. Kant says:

> *Hospitality* (hospitableness) means the right of an alien not to be treated as an enemy upon his arrival in another's country. If it can be done without

destroying him, he can be turned away; but as long as he behaves peaceably, he cannot be treated as an enemy. He may request the *right* to be a *permanent visitor* (which would require a special, charitable agreement to make him a fellow inhabitant for a certain period), but the *right to visit*, to associate, belongs to all men by virtue of their common ownership of the earth's surface; for since the earth is a globe, they cannot scatter themselves infinitely, but must, finally, tolerate living in close proximity, because originally no one had a greater right to any region of the earth than any one else. Uninhabitable parts of this surface—the sea and deserts—separate these communities, and yet ships and camels (the *ship* of the desert) make it possible to approach one another across these unowned regions, and the right to the *earth's surface* that belongs in common to the totality of men makes commerce possible.[28]

For Kant, it is the finiteness of man's dwelling place that obliges us to be hospitable, and the right to hospitality has temporal limits. The episode of the Malay visitor who returns endlessly multiplied in dreams, tests these limits.[29] As De Quincey conceives them, the relations between England and the Orient are those between a place where there are limits and boundaries and a place where broods "a sense of eternity and infinity" (*OE* 74).

Also missing from De Quincey's passage is any dominant sense of likeness or "kindness" between host and guest. The Malay is not a guest with whom, as per Benveniste, one can enter into exchange. On the contrary. He is unknown, unnamed; his social class and business are question marks; even his origin, as we will show in a minute, is suspect. The passage can be seen to provide an example of what Derrida terms "absolute hospitality," that is:

> *The law* of hospitality, the unconditional law of unlimited hospitality (give the arriving one one's whole home and one's self, give him one's proper being, our proper being, without asking his name, or for a countergift or to fulfill a single condition). (*Hospitalité* 71)

The law of absolute hospitality is a law that gives over everything, one's house and oneself, to the other, to alterity without contract and without return. It is distinct from—indeed, the antinomy of—"the *laws* of hospitality," which are conditioned and conditional and as such take place within the contractual space defined by Derrida, as we saw, in keeping with Benveniste:[30]

> [T]he *laws* of hospitality, its rights and its obligations that are always conditioned and conditional, such as they are defined by the Greco-Latin tradition, that is, the Judeo-Christian tradition, all of law [*le droit*] and all of

philosophy of law [*la philosophie du droit*] up to Kant and Hegel in particular, through the family, civil society and the state. (*Hospitalité* 71)

There is a further point—this time, a matter of aesthetics—that can help in understanding the difference between conditional hospitality and unconditional or absolute hospitality. In the Welsh scene exemplary of casual hospitality, the narrator insisted on beauty ("So much beauty. . . . I do not remember to have seen before or since in any cottage" [*OE* 14]). But the Malay is part of a "*picturesque* exhibition" (*OE* 57, my emphasis). Any number of authors from the period have commented on the differ-ence between the picturesque and the beautiful; Thomas Doubleday does so in a brief essay on the topic first published in *Blackwood's Edinburgh Magazine* soon after the *Confessions*:

> [T]he pleasure we derive from the contemplation of objects which are styled Beauti-ful, as opposed to Picturesque, arises from the unexpected ease and readiness with which we comprehend the distribution of their parts. Take regular architecture as a specimen. . . . Let the minor parts be ornamented as they will—let the details be ever so elaborate, ever so diversified, still the general design is at the first view fully present to the mind. Let any one look at the Parthenon, at St. Peter's, at St. Paul's, at Blenheim or Versailles, and he comprehends their plan at once. . . . He is struck with the triumph of order. (my emphasis)[31]

The beautiful appeals to our sense of ease of enjoyment, and bespeaks regularity, method, order. The beautiful object is viewed as a totality, the fruit of a single plan. On the other hand, the picturesque, a more difficult and puzzling source of enjoyment, has an irreducible variety:

> The most picturesque object, perhaps, in nature, is a tree. Why is it so? Because the distribution of its parts is so infinitely complicated, and so wonderfully diversified, that *the mind cannot, even by the longest-continued efforts, attain to a full and complete idea and remembrance of them.* No painter could ever delineate a tree, branch by branch, leaf by leaf. If he did, no spectator could decide whether he had done so or not. Our most distinct idea of a tree is only general. We have little more than an outline. The greater and more superficial indentations of its foliage, its larger interstices of branch, its masses of shadow, and its most pervading hues, are enough for us. We are compelled to *lump* and sloven over a million of beautiful particularities, exquisite minutenesses, which our apprehension is not mi-croscopic enough to seize in the detail. In spite of ourselves we *make a daub of it* even in imagination. Hence, in the contemplation of masses of foliage,

there is a perpetual excitement and struggle of the mind to obtain a complete idea—a constant approach with an impossibility of reaching the de-
sired goal. DIFFICULTY, then, is the source of the Picturesque. Irregular
variety is its life. (first emphasis mine, other emphases in the original)[32]

The picturesque involves a struggle to attain a complete idea, with the
idea to be attained less that of an object than of what impedes totalization.
It implies a complex, diverse material, having "the infinite divisibility of
matter,"[33] and too many parts to fit into some general plan. Or, the idea
we have of it is too general, too abstract—an outline or a silhouette—to
account for any but the largest divisions. The tree is represented crudely,
"made a daub of;" its diversity has been, as in the literal meaning, plastered
over. The mind struggles with the heterogeneous without overcoming it
in a synthesis.

The vision of the Malay visitor in the kitchen involves a conflict, resolved in favor of the picturesque, between these two sources of aesthetic
pleasure. Eyes center on the mysterious guest come from the Orient to
visit the typical English house; and on the servant girl, who is lifted out of
her ordinary function to stand for the Lake Country home, and indeed—
through her "beautiful English face," her intrepidity and independence—
for England itself (*OE* 56). This couple is the focus of a conflict between
principles and is framed by two watchers. One is the master of the rented
cottage, to whom it falls to greet the guest with whom he is most closely
coupled. The second is the crouched child whose gesture of catching at
the girl's skirts situates him as under her protection. The scene gets its
tension from the difference between two couples: the first couple of the
girl and the child under the aegis of beauty; and the second, that associated
with the Malay and the I, under the aegis of the picturesque. The ultimate
disappearance from the account of the first couple signals the victory of
the second principle.

Key to the passage is the extraordinary guest around whom the others
gather. He speaks not a single word of English and wanders from the
straits of Malacca into the opium-eater's cottage in the isolated Lake
Country in the year 1816. De Quincey cannot imagine what could have
brought him there: "What business a Malay could have to transact among
English mountains I cannot conjecture" (*OE* 55).[34] How did the Malay get
to his kitchen? Why, if he has any business in the area, is he so manifestly
unable to transact it given that he speaks no English? All these questions
raise another: Whence comes the narrator's certainty that his visitor is a
Malay at all? Given that he does not share a language with the visitor, how

does he know what to call him? The hero is guessing: "He . . . replied in what I *suppose* was Malay" (*OE* 57, my emphasis). What is a Malay, that De Quincey should conjecture his unknown visitor to be one?

Owing to its location on the major sea lane of the Straits of Malacca, the area of Southeast Asia known as Malaysia has long been a country at the crossroads, a meeting place of peoples, languages, and religions, as well as a busy marketplace for barter and exchange that was early coveted by Europeans. As a result, in West Malaysia alone are found groups of aboriginal Orang Asli, Malays, Chinese, Indians, and Pakistanis. Religions include, besides the dominant Islam, native religions, Confucianism, Buddhism, Taoism, Hinduism, and Sikhism; and, following the sixteenth-century Dutch occupation of the area, Christianity. The languages spoken are correspondingly diverse. Perhaps De Quincey has called his visitor a Malay because like a painter on a mission to delineate a profuse diversity, he has gone for a general outline. The term "Malay," designating a citizen of a country inhabited by groups from all over Asia, is apt, for in him live variety and indistinctness.[35]

Certainly, the way De Quincey deliberately piles up hodgepodge bits and pieces of Asian culture would suggest the name "Malay" had been chosen for that reason. The guest's turban and loose trousers suggest a Muslim or a Sikh. Tigers (the Malay is compared to a tiger-cat) can be found throughout China, India, and Southeast Asia. The mahogany said to veneer his skin is native to America, Africa, and the Philippines; the enamel work to which it is also compared is found in Asia Minor and Egypt, and is a well-known product of Japan and China. In short, what better way to signify the picturesque, that mixture of variety and indistinctness, than by the name of a country that assembles the utmost exotic or Asian peoples, languages, and religions?

In the later dream sequence devoted to oriental motifs, De Quincey notes this tendency to assemble the most heterogeneous of things when it comes to the Orient:

> Under the connecting feeling of tropical heat and vertical sun-light, I
> brought together all creatures, birds, beasts, reptiles, all trees and plants,
> usages and appearances that are found in all tropical regions, and assembled
> them together in China or Indostan. From kindred feelings, I soon brought
> Egypt and all her gods under the same law. (*OE* 109)

In the passage that concerns us, the connection is not made by heat or sunlight but the principle of association still holds. Whether we say that the picturesque appears in De Quincey whenever the Orient is in the offing or that the Orient appears wherever the picturesque rears its head doesn't much matter for the analysis. What matters is first that the principle of assembly is metonymic, leaving heterogeneous pieces to their heterogeneity, in contrast to the scene of casual hospitality where difference was taken in as likeness through metaphor. The proliferating heterogeneity that belies appropriation or exchange and that threatens totalization and intactness begins to delineate an understanding of hospitality very different from that of casual hospitality.

The idea that appears to assemble the heterogeneous figures in this passage about the reception of the Malay is that of looking, in both the transitive and intransitive uses of the verb. Servant girl, child, and—even more ostentatiously—master, are all spectators. As for the Malay, around that central figure clusters a vocabulary of appearance, simulation, of looking and looking-like. If the servant, tutelary spirit, wants her master to exorcise him, it is because he brings out the simulated side of that prototypical English home that is Dove Cottage. The cottage, we are told, is "unpretending" (*OE* 55). Modest it may be, but without pretense or show it is not; next to the "ferocious-looking" Malay, a number of salient details that denote pretense and seeming appear: The kitchen's paneling is of "dark wood that from age and rubbing *resembled* oak," and the kitchen itself "*look*(s) more like a rustic hall of entrance than a kitchen" (*OE* 56, my emphasis). Good old English oak, the very timbers of the house, can be simulated, and the kitchen can look like an entrance hall. There is no need to invite the guest into Dove Cottage: He is already inside in the sham of the house's very walls and structure. The violation of the house does not take place in the same way as it does in casual hospitality where it is never a problem to draw a clear boundary between inside and outside the house, between the women's and the men's apartments. Here, the integrity of the house is so affected as to make the very possibility of drawing a line or closing a door against the visitor problematical. The Malay's visit brings out a fakery that the inhabitants of Dove Cottage, by dint of habitual intercourse with the Romantic clichés associated with the cottage, have come to forget. That fakery cannot be driven out without taking down the walls, setting into question the limits and conditions of the prototypical English house.

An awkward sentence reinforces the point. The sentence reads: "In a cottage kitchen, *but panelled on the wall with dark wood that from age and rubbing resembled oak and looking more like a rustic hall of entrance than a kitchen*, stood the Malay" (*OE* 56, my emphasis). In terms of a meaning based on representation, the italicized clauses clearly modify "kitchen."

The sentence defers the arrival of subject and verb through clauses that describe the kitchen where the act of hospitality is to take place. But the unusual structure of the sentence allows, even invites, other readings. A kitchen "panelled on the wall" already sounds rather more a depiction of a kitchen than an actual room. Furthermore, considered from a grammatical standpoint, the clauses read plausibly as a series of adjectival phrases building a description of a deferred subject—here, the Malay: "In a cottage kitchen, but panelled on a wall . . . looking like an entrance hall . . . stood the Malay." It is as if "Malay" were the figure for some part of the house, say, a frieze or screen. The construction works grammatically but is askew from the point of view of representation. How can we think of the Malay as paneled on a wall or looking like an entrance hall? And yet, given that the Malay's skin is likened to veneer, which, like paneling, is a form of wood overlay, and given the identification of the walls that *look like* oak and the kitchen that *looks like* a hall with the central figure of simulation that is the Malay, given the Malay's tendency to show up where he apparently has no earthly business, the reading is sustained by the passage. The Malay is confused with the house, as much a figure for simulation in its structural components as a literal visitor. The guest makes himself so at home that the house ceases to be home to the host, who discovers it to have been always already haunted by an alterity of which the present visitor serves as a reminder.[36]

There is a literal, referential way to understand the point, in keeping with our conjecture that the house itself is at stake. By the 1820s, long trade with the Orient meant its goods had been embedded into English life: the turban, a stylish hat for women by Jane Austen's time; or the exotic woods imported for paneling; or the tiger-cat, the familiar animal of the hearth with its Egyptian past and its name redolent of the jungle; or the Turkish carpet covering many an English floor ("[the Malay] lay down upon the floor" (*OE* 57); or opium with its myriad preparations and outlets, or the accoutrements of De Quincey's later vision of happiness—"a tea-table . . . the tea-tray . . . an eternal teapot . . . for I usually drink tea from eight o'clock at night to four o'clock in the morning" (*OE* 60).[37] It is as though De Quincey, descending to his kitchen, had noticed the Asiatic provenance of English home furnishings—tea tray, Turkish carpet, exotic wood, cat—and had conjured up the appropriate *genius loci* for these exotic products.

It is not only the house that is affected by the Malay. The other figures, too, become stagy and sham near him. This is generally true: The house's inhabitants are caught playing roles in a tableau around a glowing hearth that serves as a stereotypical element in a dramatic picture of the English-man surveying his castle. As for the I, his omniscience is a matter of show; he does not truly master "all the languages of the earth, besides, perhaps, a few of the lunar ones" (*OE* 57) but merely makes believe to do so. There is a similar effect on De Quincey's English, that language of commerce and translatability. Already endangered in the syntax of the sentence de-scribing the kitchen, its ability to represent becomes thoroughly unhinged after we take into account insistent poetic patterns to be found in the passage and its frame. What are we to make of the rhyming effect of "the Ma*lay* had no means of bet*ray*ing the secret . . . he *lay* down upon the floor" or of the opening sequence when, speaking of his happiest *day* and of giving *away* laudanum, De Quincey begins the digression: "By the *way*, now that I speak of giving laudanum a*way*. . . . One *day* a Ma*lay*" (*OE* 57, 55, my emphasis)? What is the significance, if any, of the fact that it is after declining to describe his stomach *malady* that De Quincey begins to talk of the Malay? What to make of the haunting of the passage by the French language in the idea of assemblage, of mixture (*mêlée*) associated with the picturesque and the mixture of tones, or in the feeling of queasy anxiety (*malaise*) that reigns here? These patterns are evidence of language that does not speak in intelligible sentences but is not unmeaningful. In that respect, it is a language not unlike the "Malay" the I supposes his guest to speak: that is, deduced to be meaningful language on the basis of sound patterns. The passage points to a poeticity to language at the root of the hallucinatory perception of visitation by the other that explains the mind's unease with the picturesque. The Malay stands for the potential of a representation, however apparently anodyne, to be taken over by a defamiliarizing spirit. Certainly nothing is more extrinsic than the intru-sion within a seamless narrative of events and descriptions tied to and perhaps derived from the written frame. The Malay's "visit" brings home to the narrator how little his language and memory are his own.

The Malay, then, is the figure revealing a repressed or forgotten heter-ogeneity within the house boundaries themselves. This is as much as to say that the scene is about bringing out an awareness that what has been taken as nature is in fact something else: art, ideology. The Medusal flavor of the text supports this reading, according to which the *Confessions* stages the rigidified ideological fictions of the early nineteenth-century English-man. The other has always already made himself at home in the house; through the unrepression of the forgotten alterity, the subject's fantasies of naturalness and familiarity can be revealed to be just that—wishful fantasies.

The passage reveals that, as Derrida has stated, the law of hospitality commands the giving over of the I, his home, his being, his language, to the other without limit or condition. This includes even the temporal conditions that Kant has placed on hospitality that allow him to distinguish, for instance, the "right to visit" from that of inhabiting. This openness is a source of danger but also of potential. Notice that the violability of the house is not to be understood in terms of an inside penetrated by an outside so much as by an inside shown to contain a simulation that situates it outside the outside-inside distinction—in other words, a familiar space is defamiliarized by both its frame and conditions being brought into view.

A word should be said about the Malay's host, because it is that host who—faced with the realization that he has taken a construct as nature, charged by the servant girl with exorcising simulation from the house— acts in a peculiar way: He deals with sham by himself dealing in it to supplement his failing knowledge. There is a veritable cascade of suppositions in the passage:

> What business a Malay could possibly have to transact amongst English mountains, I cannot *conjecture*; but *possibly* he was on his way to a seaport about forty miles distant. (*OE* 55, my emphasis)

> In this dilemma the girl, recollecting the reputed learning of her master (and, *doubtless*, giving me credit for all the languages of the earth, besides, perhaps a few of the lunar ones . . . .). (*OE* 56, my emphasis)

> He . . . replied in what I *suppose* was Malay. (*OE* 57, my emphasis)

> To him, as an Orientalist, I *concluded* that opium must be familiar: and the expression of his face *convinced* me that it was. (*OE* 57, my emphasis)

> As I never heard of any Malay being found dead, I became *convinced* that he was used to opium, and that I must have done him the service I designed, by giving him one night of respite from the pains of wandering. (*OE* 57, my emphasis)

To this group can be added the "dialogue" the I makes up with the Malay's help. We could even point forward to the next section, a long hypotyposis that describes the ideal happy day on opium: "Let there be a cottage . . . let it be a white cottage. . . . Let it be in winter. . . . Paint me the room. . . . Therefore, painter, put as many (books) as you can into this room . . . paint me a tea-table . . . place only two cups and saucers on the tea-tray . . . paint me an eternal teapot . . . paint me a lovely young woman . . . you

may paint 'the little golden receptacle of the pernicious drug' if you choose
. . . paint me, if at all, according to your fancy" (*OE* 58–61). The I's status
as master of discourse goes along with an awakened capacity for spinning
fictions.

Making fictions has two separate but related functions with respect to
the mind's attempt to bring harmony to heterogeneity. In the first place,
it is an index of the unknown that confronts the I. That unknown is not
a simple matter of ignorance of the facts. It might better be called an
indeterminacy, for in it facts taken for granted are revealed potentially to
be fictional—as the kitchen fleetingly appeared a mural of a kitchen, or
the Malay momentarily seemed a figure for the simulation inhabiting its
very timbers. A question subject to historical verification—where did the
visitor who dropped in at Dove Cottage in 1816 hail from?—takes on a
more mysterious ring, as if one were asking like Baudelaire about a visitor's supernatural origins, "Do you come from the deepening sky, or
emerge out of the abyss?"[38] A prosaic answer—the Malay was in fact a
Turk, a Sri Lankan, an Indian, whom De Quincey called a Malay because
he shared the cultural blindness of his time—can't allay a deeper suspicion
that the scene in its entirety may well be a phantom of its author's brain.
It could have been born of "mighty opium" perhaps, or even of its analog,
textual malaise, in an anthropomorphizing move that has given human
shape to the productive operation of the poetic function of language. The
memory of this incident, which is, we recall, told "as furnishing a key to
some part of that tremendous scenery which afterwards people the dreams
of the opium-eater," is suspect (*OE* 5). It is so neat and so unlikely an
experience as to suggest doubts about whether it is not a fantasy. This is
the last memory recounted of an incident with the apparent status of a
lived experience, and it is followed by a broken and fragmentary series of
dreams. Why not then consider this last episode the first of the dream
sequences? In sum, the I's conjecturing is an indication that the story recounted as if it were lived experience might instead have a conjectural
basis.

The fictions do not only stand as testimony to indeterminacy. however.
They also attempt to ward off the fear of that unknown by reducing it to
a manageable—that is, determinate—size. To say that the encounter with
the Malay is a fiction is to claim to know the difference between fact and
fiction, which is precisely what is in question. Thus, the I's determinate
conjecture that the visitor is on his way to a seaport masks and reduces the
more disquieting question of what business the other continues to have
with the house; the conjecture that the girl believes her master able to

communicate in all of the earthly and some of the lunar languages masks and reduces the question of whether his language is communicative; the fiction of a visit from a Malay hides the larger question of whether the I can ever know the status of its autobiographical representations; the assumption that the Malay is familiar with the properties of opium hides the problem of what sort of unknown opium stands for; and so forth. The subject's conjectures reduce indeterminacy to a knowable unknown, even as they gesture toward it. The stake of that reduction is the subject's mastery over the house in which the guest has made himself so thoroughly at home. In the mind's struggle with heterogeneity, it indeed "makes a daub of it:" that is, "represents crudely," "plasters over." What it tries to plaster over is doubt as to its sovereignty. It is indeed in crisis.

For equally affected by fiction is the host, in whom a double relation to hospitality can be discerned. In one perspective, the host gives up everything to the guest as representative of indeterminacy in an open-armed gesture of greeting—everything, including property, identity, memory, sanity. But, looked at from the perspective of the servant girl as representative of neighborhood, his same gesture can be said to redraw lines, accentuate difference, and deepen the hostility between the Malay and the Englishman. Both of these tendencies appear in the lunatic "dialogue." Whatever can the host be doing, quoting lines from the *Iliad* to the Malay? Whatever can the Malay mean by his response? After all, neither understands the language of the other. In this dialogue, the host gives up what was the essence of English in the earlier scene of conditional hospitality— commerce, exchange, meaning—to quote a text in a dead language that can convey no determinate content to anyone but himself. As an excellent scholar of Greek who could harangue an Athenian crowd (*OE* 7), he might have said something from the heart. Instead, he's just "saying words." And those words not from the *Odyssey* with its abundant scenes of hospitality but from the bellicose *Iliad*. Simulated as it is, the speech act ought to be an utter failure.

But from the Malay's response, ironically reported by the narrator— "he worshipped me in a most devout manner, and replied in what I suppose was Malay" (*OE* 14)—we can divine that the visitor has understood the speech as on one level it seems to have been offered, a speech of welcome from a host so eager to make the *peregrinus* feel at home that he speaks the closest he can come to the latter's language, which is to say, not just a language geographically close to an Eastern language but a quotation in which iterability is the central feature. The host gives his house over to the guest in a mad performative that takes on the signified of welcome insofar as it is taken up as human speech. On his side, the Malay knows well enough that the master of the house is welcoming him to respond with gestures of thanksgiving, thereby effectively taking over the role abandoned by the host of speaking an expressive language. The performative has the effect of producing a complicity, a shared secret or bond, where none had previously existed. The host and the Malay alone know that their exchange has taken place in two languages: indeed, that their exchange has in a sense consisted of the exchange of two languages (a language of communicative response, however codified, is spoken by the guest; a language of simulated saying, however meaningful of welcome, by the host). As if for the benefit of the watching child, the host's speech act is thus liminal in extending hospitality to cover a *peregrinus* with whom no prior covenant has been signed. The passage treats the act of welcoming the other as the purer because there is no content passed, and the subject's declared intention of saving his reputation is independent of the way it is taken up by his interlocutor. In short, De Quincey's speech act is an extreme case of a Levinasian "Saying without a Said" (*AE* 133), a gestural speech act where "to present oneself in signifying is to speak" (*TeI* 61). A pure fiction of hospitality, of welcome and thanksgiving, links the two figures, one of which has given over its mastery to greet the other and the other of which, in signaling its indebtedness, has given—in the paradoxical salaams—a token of human understanding. With absolute hospitality, the speech act is inaugural by virtue of its repetitive, imitative quality.[39]

But we must notice as well the determinate side of the feigned dialogue, visible through the meaning it will immediately gain in the neighborhood by the servant's report, and compatible with Levinas's recognition of usurpation of the other's place as the subject's consistent mode of action. The servant girl's ignorance of what she is seeing is almost total. She would not understand Greek and would probably not know that it is Greek that her master is speaking; unlikely to grasp that the Malay's language was not the same as her master's, she would certainly not know what his salaams mean, but most probably will interpret them as worship; she would ignore the secret that De Quincey's speaking was a feigned speaking, even a feigning of feigning (if we take it that all speaking is to lie, as we can if we take seriously Levinas's idea that the subject usurps a place in the world). For the servant girl, the dialogue can thus be reassuring: Her master does indeed speak all languages and in his omniscience stand as the most recent incarnation of Western civilization and the logos; as for the East with its productive fictions, in the person of the Malay, it slavishly adores Western rationality and universalism. Insofar as the determinate context into which it is taken up is concerned, the fiction of absolute hospitality that undoes mastery, that welcomes the exotic stranger and makes the house over to him, will be taken to reenact and make believable the fiction of the English master and colonial. In doing so, it redraws the boundaries and increases the distance between the Malay and the English neighborhood. The fiction of absolute hospitality, in which the subject gives over his house to the *peregrinus*, will be received by that context as a reassertion of English mastery.

Given the pervasive indeterminacy of the scene, which is such that we cannot even be certain that it constitutes a genuine confession, suspense and vacillation might be expected. Our analysis has shown that nothing is further from the case. The scene is very productive in the context, and what it produces—even while signaling the recognition of dissimulation and a failing ideology—is new ideology. The host no sooner welcomes the indeterminate other in the figure of the Malay than the chosen figure masks the abyss of indeterminacy opened. As an unknown gets substituted for an unknowable, an undetermined for indeterminacy, a new nature steps into the breech. This naturalization occurs by way of an anthropomorphizing figuration. The subject attempts to forget the threatening heterogeneity by putting a human face on it.

The name that De Quincey gives such scenes, where the origin is indeterminate and one puts a human face on an inhuman predicament is the Orient. It is, he says, an *officina gentium*, a factory of peoples. No doubt he gives it an Oriental face as an effect of the Anglocentrism announced in the title to his work and which he inherits from his place and time. But if we consider that the I does not so much espouse a received idea as stage its formation, we would have to nuance our condemnation of De Quincey as speaker for British imperialism somewhat. To stage the forming of an ideology is not to speak for it. If, moreover, we take into account the fact that the I is a participant in the scene that he, like the Malay, "assisted to frame," it becomes evident that De Quincey is pointing toward the conditions for the imposition and toppling of the idol of homogeneous Englishness (*OE* 57). And if we take seriously our earlier suggestion that the scene, as one about a language that "sounds like" Malay, may have been elaborated around rhyme words (One day a Malay . . . lay upon the floor) and homonyms (malady, *malaise*, and so on), we have to conclude that, while indeed about responsibility and ethics, the *Confessions* is very far from an expression of imperialist doctrine.

The scene of parting is illustrative of a new situation with respect to hospitality, for there we discover that the guest's departure does not mean that the house's purity will be reconstituted as before. The fantasy of English domination the neighborhood will have received binds the I guiltily and irrevocably to the determinate other he has made the placeholder for indeterminacy. The Malay steals off with more than the host's peace of mind; he has taken over a number of the latter's characteristics. Before, it was the host's house that was pure and inviolable; now, it is the guest's body that has to be treated as sacrosanct. Before it was the host who had the totalizing view—as witness his position as surveyor of the scene. But now it is the Malay who "bolts the whole." Worse still, the departed Malay carries off with him the secret of the I's identity: Is the hero a charitable English gentleman who has received his guest magnificently, or a murderer? We recall Levinas's insight that the subject is taken by the other, is "hostage" to the other. Certainly, the scene suggests that the host has indeed been delivered over to the determinate *peregrinus* as guarantee or hostage for the execution of a promise of absolute hospitality left unfulfilled.

Considered in terms of discourse, the scene exhibits an extreme case of the logic of the "incessant unsaying of the said" (*AE* 278), the Levinasian dictum that can be seen as stating that the undoing of ideology is the unfinished ethical task the subject takes on with respect to the other. Although it is radically fictional, the story of the Malay, insofar as it is taken up in a determinate context, reiterates the mastery that it questions. Because of their determinacy, De Quincey's fictions grant only a provisional and conditional welcome to the other, in every case under- or overshooting the open-armed welcome aimed at. Everything happens as if the I had to addict himself, had to bind himself over to having to bind himself over and over to the other; as if, in giving the Malay his opium supply, he had obligated himself to account for his repeated failure to complete the unsaying of the said of English mastery.[40]

And yet, in some respects De Quincey's tale seems to exceed and even belie Levinas's ethical account of the face to face between the subject and the human other. Despite his recognition that hospitality involves violence, Levinas would surely have looked in horror at what happens in the *Confessions* to his restrained formulation of the subject's openness to the other: "the subject is host." In De Quincey, an hour's hospitality opens the hero endlessly to visits by the other to whom he has entrusted himself: He has taken in an "incubus" (*OE* 67), who "fastened afterwards upon my dreams, and brought other Malays with him worse than himself, that ran 'a-muck' at me, and led me into a world of troubles" (*OE* 58). Judging by this statement, a permanent psychic disturbance affects the host in the exercise of absolute hospitality. We can measure the historical irrevocability of this disturbance by noting that the suspicion that the scene may be entirely fabricated does not affect its power to determine De Quincey's later thought and actions—as evidenced in his recurring violent dreams and his growing addiction. Hosting an alterity that puts the subject radically into question is understood by De Quincey to lead not or not only to transcendence, but also or else to a self-shattering unleashing of murderous impulses and to madness.

As for Levinas's other formulation—"the subject is hostage," whose truth we have seen confirmed by the fact that the Malay keeps the secret of the host's identity—that, too, takes an odd turn that can help us formulate a difference between the ethics of the two writers. The problem, simply put, is that hospitality as staged by De Quincey does not involve a face-to-face between humans so much as a face-to-mask encounter, a face-to-"face" with an anthropomorphism. Whereas the face for Levinas is emphatically not a figure or a prosopopeia or an anthropomorphism, the determinate human face of the Malay figures in the *Confessions* a suspicion concerning an irreducible fictional dimension plaguing autobiography.[41] Where there are masks, however, one has to ask what is being masked. Might a nonhuman face fit into the slot occupied by the Malay mask, say, the face of the animal, or even the face of death? While so far overlooked by our reading, there lurks an animal in the passage: the tiger-cat to which the Malay is likened (unless the household cat is rather anthropomorphized as the Malay?)[42] The later dream to which the story is key unleashes a proliferating host of animals: the crocodile, the ibis, parakeets, monkeys, cockatoos, birds, beasts, reptiles, snakes, and the fabulous sphinxes are all mentioned in a dream that threatens "innocent *human* natures" (*OE* 74, my emphasis). In short, Levinas's limitation of hospitality to the other with a human face does not take into account that the law of absolute hospitality, as De Quincey understands it, might require the subject to afford welcome and house space to the nonhuman.

Levinas's limitation on the inclusion of animals can be related to the host's language in the *Confessions*. As we have seen, the quotation from the *Iliad*, while it allows the production of a secret and thus a bond between Englishman and Malay, is also potentially just speech-like activity of the sort attributed to an animal capable of imitating speech like the parrot. A language that imitates and does not respond is spoken accusatorily in the later dream, where the I is "stared at, hooted at, grinned at, chattered at, by monkeys, by paroquets, by cockatoos" (*OE* 74). The dream expresses the subject's fear that he might have been just hooting and chattering as the animals do, rather than signifying a welcome to the *peregrinus*. Levinas's optimism concerning the progressive, ethically responsible undoing of ideology relies on an ability, put into question by the scene, to know when language is responsive and responsible and when it is jabbering gibberish.

The iterability of language means that the masterful, staged performative that unsays the said and allows one to enter into inaugural, heartfelt dialogue with the human other, may not be distinguishable from repetition. Or, to put it another way, the house of language is always open to visitation by a poetic spirit, which spirit allows consideration of the potential meaning of patterns that language has as a written language. Those patterns don't just gainsay the said; they also gainsay saying, and with it the scene of ethical relation and dialogue as implicating only humans. Language, too—or, perhaps one should say, language above all—is hospitable, and it is ultimately the logic of its hospitalities (relative and absolute) that rules in the situations described by De Quincey. All this is as much as to say that De Quincey's *Confessions* is not, in the last analysis, a Levinasian autobiography. The story is indeed about encounters with the other in which the subject emerges in a community as an ethical being hostage and host to the human other, with attendant fears and violence. But it is also about an I who speculates on a forgetting of the animal as the bearer of our inability to tell the difference between our language at its most and its least responsible.

Whereas Levinas helps us to read the crisis in the subject in autobiographical language insofar as it implies the human other, he does not tell us about the extreme responsibility we find in De Quincey. With absolute hospitality, De Quincey gives his I over to alterity without limitation or reserve, in a scene of swearing away or addiction (*OED*: "Addict, [*addictus* . . . from *ad* to plus *dicere*, to say, pronounce] formally made over or bound [to another]; attached by restraint or obligation; obliged, bound, devoted, consecrated.") The I as addict to the other, even to the point where the other is the other of the human—that is the extra-Levinasian message of the *Confessions of the English Opium-Eater* to which we have gained access, thanks to Levinas.

CHAPTER 5

Eating with the Other in *Les Paradis artificiels*

Some books are to be tasted, others to be swallowed,
and some few to be chewed and digested.

FRANCIS BACON, *Of Studies*

Critics of autobiography who have cut their teeth on Rousseau's *Confessions* cannot help but be sensible to numerous differences when they begin reading De Quincey and Baudelaire. One of those differences, at first little more than a direction given a motif, is indicative of a shift in the strategies for responding to the other in Modernist texts, among whom—against the usual tendency to group him with the Romantics—I am counting De Quincey as an early prototype. Through its connection to aesthetics, this motif can let us consider what the Modernist autobiographer, writing in the wake of the *Rêveries*, gains for the expression of the subject's relation to the other from the preference over narrative autobiography for more digressive, fragmentary, or meditative discursive forms. For it is to Rousseau, the solitary walker, the autothanatographical writer, rather than to the moralizing Rousseau of the *Confessions* that the Modernists declare their allegiance, be it the De Quincey of the dream fugues, or the Baudelaire who singles out for admiration in De Quincey an "intellect marked by endless musings, an intellect 'touched with pensiveness'" (*un cerveau marquée par la rêverie fatale*, **touched with pensiveness**) and who hyperbolizes that tendency in his own writing.[1]

The motif in question is eating.

With eating, we are at the center of our concern. "One never eats entirely on one's own," says Derrida in "*'Il faut bien manger' ou le calcul du sujet.*"[2] That means, first of all, that eating is the act whereby a one subject aggressively appropriates the manifold alterity on which its life as self-conscious subject depends. The subject has to eat others, regardless: As Derrida's title states, "*il faut bien manger*," where *bien* can have the meaning of an intensifier like "really" or "anyway," and indicate consciousness of the necessity to eat any thing and any time that something can be transmuted to food. One has to eat anyway means that there isn't anything else but eating; the subject's activity of knowing the world consists in reducing every other to food. There is even a note of resigned despair in Derrida's title, as if in recognition of the impossibility—even where it might be advisable—of ceasing to eat. If one never eats alone, given this command to eat voraciously, many others will be jeopardized by one's eating. Readers of autobiography will recognize the autobiographical subject with its insatiable hunger for difference it can internalize and transform into mirrors whereby to know itself, as well as its perennial bad conscience.

But Derrida's aporetic title also says that a meal is always an ethico-political occasion. The subject has to manage its eating with respect to the other; or as Derrida says, "*il faut bien manger*," where *bien* means well, according to rules of conduct written with respect to the Good. It is impossible to eat without reference to dietary law. The subject always dines with others, giving, leaving, or accepting from the other whereof to eat. With eating well, one takes one's place in a scene of hospitality, as host, guest, or hostage of the other's eating. That can mean a set of conventions operative within a given group, or ethics more generally. It could entail a demand to eat responsibly where no rules and no schedule can be provided beforehand. For if one has to calculate with giving the other to eat, that means one must calculate with the incalculable, to prepare to leave remainders when everything will have been eaten, and even to bestow oneself ahead of time on the other to be eaten as corpse. One must hold oneself ready, whenever the other will have demanded it, to jeopardize eating anyway so that the other might eat.

As Derrida points out a little later in the same essay, while the double obligation to eat and eat well is binding, it does come with a freedom and a responsibility to choose *how* to acquit oneself of those inescapable obligations, the way to eat and give others to eat. Just so, Baudelaire's "*Enivrez-vous*" tells us, the whole of human freedom boils down to a choice of intoxicants: We aren't free to decide whether to get drunk but need to educate ourselves on the available intoxicants because we do get to decide how to do so (*OC* I, 337). The problem of aesthetics is this problem of manner that arises as the way one delivers oneself of the aporetic obligation regulating our eating with the other. In short, eating promises to bring together very nicely the subject's relations to the other with a reflection on the aesthetic mode of expression. But first, a preliminary consideration concerning the text to be treated.

I have chosen to look at the motif through Baudelaire's presentation of it in *Les Paradis artificiels*. The move has some advantages because Baudelaire has done much of the work in bringing together the problem of form and of internalization. One chapter, "Le Goût de l'infini," directly addresses internalization as man's appetite for what is not like himself, for the absolute Other that infinity represents. As for the drugs discussed, the term "taste" already signals that they are not simply literal pharmaceutical compounds, ingestion of which is dangerous for the health of the body and the body politic, but are also figures for distinct formal tendencies or tropes.[3] The text unites Baudelaire's reflections on the internalizing of the other with a consideration of artistic strategies and seems an excellent place to address our problem.[4]

A further critical advantage derives from the hyper-economy of *Les Paradis*. Baudelaire does not indulge in a confessional narrative in this text. Rather, he collects and comments on the drug testimonies of others, among whom are Rousseau and De Quincey, in what amounts to a meta-autobiographical essay. As Baudelaire weighs the modes subjects have chosen in eating with the other, he has himself made some decisive calculations which give the work a testimonial flavor, despite his eschewal of first-person narrative. The result is an excessive economy, a vertiginous text in which the I discusses and internalizes (with) others discussing and internalizing (with) others on the problem of having to eat anyway and well that concerns the autobiographical subject. Baudelaire's decision to treat drugs as the meal of choice adds a complication—the drug is a supplement and brings with it a train of consequences concerning how it is to be taken into the body, a set of preparations, rituals, observances, doses and timings of doses, paraphernalia—but the method of internalization remains the locus of concern. We could not hope for a better place to explore the various modes a self-critical autobiographical subject might have for internalizing with the other.[5]

I

Eating Hashish, Telling Stories with Rousseau: Time to Eat

The best stories are told at a certain hour, when we are all at table.
No one has ever told a story well standing up or fasting.

BALZAC, "Another Study of a Woman"

The Hashish-Eater's Testimonial Narrative: *Kief* on Schedule

One distinct feature of Baudelaire's discussion of the hashish experience is that it takes place against the background of a communal meal and is destined to wind up as a narrative.[6] The choice of the drug does not only have meaning for the subject with its egotistical aim of self-nourishment, but also for the culture with its drive to transport. The specific other the hashish-eater aims to appropriate by the drug is the infinite, what Levinas calls the absolute Other. At the end of his high, the hashish-eater is proclaimed a "god who has eaten badly . . . but a God nonetheless" (*AP*, 71; *OC* I, 437). In short, the hashish meal sacrifices eating well to satisfy the desire of each to consume everything so as to become God.

An important consideration in the method of eating hashish that directly pertains to narrative is the timing of the act of ingestion. One might think that the hashish meal would be secondary. The subject would meet its physical and social needs first and then add the fancy meal of the hashish feast, "feeding on infinity" as Joshua Wilner's apt title has it, only after having assured its temporal survival. Not so. To stomach the green jam, you have to start with the substitute, representative as it is of the appetite for the infinite; and only later, after its effects have declared themselves, venture to increase them by eating a proper meal. Baudelaire's observation alerts us to a minor upset in the natural order, which assumes that food precedes the drug as the thing its supplement and green nature any paste whose color is the product of industry.

This deferral establishes that the subject's plan in taking hashish is for a narrative solution to the contradictory imperatives of eating well and eating anyway. The first effect of starting with the supplement is to suspend the legal side of *"il faut bien manger,"* which becomes a matter of the subject's appetite. The subject acts as if setting the satisfaction of its own appetites first is a precondition for meeting its obligation to the other. It is as though it were saying, "Since I must eat anyway, let me take in the thing adapted to my highest desire, which is to transcend my animal nature to become like God. That way, when it comes time to leave others to eat, I'll make a worthy offering." The I feeds itself now so as to deliver itself at its most delectable later, when the communal meal finally begins.

The Poem of Hashish states unequivocally that the hashish-eater is mistaken at every level. Seeking to satisfy an insatiable appetite for knowledge, to internalize, which is to say to idealize, the subject ends by sinking to a beast ("he wished to be an angel and he has become a beast" [*AP*, 39; *OC* I, 409]) because it converts every other into an object of pleasure. This reduction of alterity to sensible objects that can serve as symbols of its inner being constitutes its chief creative ability and is what makes it a God to its own credulous eyes. The gluttonous hashish-eater transmutes everything to serve as "fodder, pabulum to (his) implacable appetite for emotion, knowledge, and beauty" (*AP*, 70; *OC* I, 437). The degradation of ethics to what Kant would call the eudaemonic level of pleasure and pain is another effect of the drug: "Benevolence plays a great role in the *sensations* caused by hashish" (*AP*, 45; *OC* I, 413). Socio-ethical obligations are interiorized as a "flaccid, indolent, and mute benevolence" (*AP*, 45; *OC* I, 413), with ethics making an appearance in the watered-down form of subjective pathos. For the space of the high, the hashish-eater acts as if he could reduce his obligation to eat well to a morality of good intention. It is an obligation he vaguely hopes to pay off but has effectively made impossible ever to meet since no object can resist his appropriation, and the possibility of a payment falling due recedes along with the disappearance of time: "all notion of time, all painful sensations, have vanished" (*AP*, 57; *OC* I, 425).

The model does prepare an eventual reckoning when the balance will have shifted and the demands of the forgotten other will have to be recognized. At length, the high reaches "the morrow, the terrible morrow" (*AP*, 71; *OC* I, 437) when the hashish-eater is subjected to a painful moral accounting. This is, of course, a familiar scheme in Baudelaire's work. In such poems as "Rêve parisien" or "La chambre double," a clock or a pounding on the door wakes the narcissistic dreamer from an atmosphere of pleasure to a reckoning. This moment arrives from the outside, as an inevitable accident, the automatic consequence of the initial inversion and delay, as the falling due of an adjourned obligation and the return of the other in an unsublatable, unpalatable form. Baudelaire describes it as the day after the feast, when "Hideous nature, stripped of the previous day's glowing raiment, resembles the dreary relics of last night's festival" (*AP*, 71; *OC* I, 437). The path the I thought so individual turns out to be as predictable as a railway journey in the inescapable logic of then and now that leads to the same spot. "In the very infallibility of the means lies its immorality," states Baudelaire (*AP*, 73; *OC* I, 439–40). One's decision to engage with the drug is a choice to traverse the sure-fire stages of a delusion, one of the most predictable of which turns out to be the belief that one has "returned to reason" at the moment of awakening. For Baudelaire, the thought that one has awakened from the dream still belongs to the dream:

> . . . when you are fully aware that a new day is dawning on your life's horizon, you experience a sense of well-being; you feel gifted with a marvelous lightness. But hardly have you risen to your feet when a lingering bout of intoxication chases and grips you, like the remaining trace of the ball and chain to which you had been bound. Your enfeebled legs carry you timidly, and you are in constant fear that you might shatter like some fragile object. Your senses at length begin to yield before the influences of a vast languor (there are those who find it not without charm) which spreads over your faculties like mist over a countryside. There you are, for a few hours more, incapable of work, action and energy. (*AP*, 58; *OC* I, 426)

Waking up to a new day is a further stage in the high. If Baudelaire is so interested in the predictability of these stages, it is because it indicates that the obligation to the other is being met in secret all along. The subject has been acting as a nonsubject, and the choice to put off the obligation to eat well with one's fellows turns out to have been a choice to eat with another other, the other as the I enslaved to a routine not its own.

The drug testimonies of *The Poem of Hashish* all follow this pattern of delusion and awakening, which sets the telling of the tale in a time after the last awakening as an act of reparation. Each teller uses confession as a means to acquit an ethical obligation, to excuse previous excesses and to show the I capable in speech of more than animal behavior. Each confessional narrative divides a past of subjective appropriation from a present of truth-telling as restitution. A diction of temptation overcome, of resolution never ever (or only at carefully measured intervals) to get high again, characterizes these first-person narratives,[7] which are offered to the public in acknowledgement of an obligation to alert them to their animal nature. The subject converts the results of its internalizing into a form that appropriately emerges from the same orifice that took everything in, and delivers them to others in a postprandial tale.

But perhaps the automaticity that affects the I's experience with hashish also characterizes, even derives from, the program set by testimonial narrative. Indeed, we may suspect that the cry Baudelaire makes escape from the hashish-eater's lips near the height of his folly—"I am the most virtuous of all men" (*AP*, 69; *OC* I, 436)—is actually an ironic statement of the

right-thinking he sees in the confessional posture. To understand whether
Baudelaire sees confessional language as an effective method of paying off
an ethical debt, we must turn to his discussion of Rousseau, the model of
such confessions.

The Self-Divided Moment of Rousseau's Cry

It is no surprise that the name of Rousseau should come up in a consideration of the supplement, the morality of good intention, and the confessional narrative.[8] In a key passage to be considered throughout the rest of
our discussion of "The Poem," Baudelaire presents him as one of a myriad
of hashish-eaters:

> (The man who has taken hashish) completely confounds dream and action,
> and his imagination burns ever brighter before the enchanting display of
> his own amended, idealized nature, substituting that fascinating image of
> himself for the real individual, so deficient in resolve, so rich in vanity. And
> so he ends by proclaiming his apotheosis in these clear and simple terms,
> which for him represent a whole world of abominable pleasures: 'I am the
> most virtuous of all men!'
>
> Does this not remind you of Jean-Jacques, who, after having confessed
> to the world, not without a certain pleasure, also dared to utter the same
> triumphant cry (or at least the difference is slight), with the same sincerity
> and conviction? The enthusiasm with which he admired virtue and the
> excess of nervous sensitivity which brought a tear to his eye at the sight of
> a worthy action or at the mere meditation on all of the worthy actions he
> would have liked to perform, endowed him with an exaggerated idea of his
> own moral worth. Jean-Jacques became intoxicated without hashish. (*AP*,
> 69–70; *OC* I, 436)

Baudelaire's evaluation of Rousseau is ambivalent. It is true that he
somewhat scornfully likens Rousseau to the hashish-eater. The name
Baudelaire uses to refer to Rousseau is the familiar one of Jean-Jacques,
and there is a condescension implicit in it that suggests he has in mind a
Rousseauism familiar to his time, which he elsewhere critiques as a doctrine of good intentions put forth by a "sentimental and revolting" (*OC*
II, 54) [*infâme*] Jean-Jacques "in whom a wounded sensibility prompt to
revolt takes the place of philosophy" (*OC* II, 325). *Infâme*, like *abominable*,
is a term often linked by Baudelaire with man's voracious, cannibalistic
tendencies, and Rousseau's self-aggrandizing indulgence of his grosser appetites under cloak of virtuous feeling is indicated. Baudelaire seems to be

saying that what nineteenth-century hashish-experimenters were doing was looking for an automatic track to reduce ethics to subjective pathos, along the model of the *Confessions*. His critique of the hashish-eater thus operates to some extent as a critique of the strategies of internalization of that autobiographical text.

Yet Baudelaire also credits Rousseau as an exception to the general run of hashish-eaters. Rousseau's internalization may resemble theirs in effect, but it is different in manner. One sign of that is Rousseau's singular practice of fasting. "Jean-Jacques," Baudelaire says, "became intoxicated *without* hashish" (my emphasis). It is hard not to hear a note of admiration creeping into Baudelaire's evaluation of one who can get high with a "without." Eating well presumably involves an askesis, not just saying yes to certain foods, preparations, quantities, places and times to eat, but also abstaining from others. Rousseau's choice to do without hashish is a sign he is set apart from his epigones.

Rousseau's strategy concerns the inversion of meal and supplement so critical for the hashish-eater's narrative. Rousseau was apparently able to get the effects of the inversion without having to use an artificial supplement, to incur its expenses, to submit to its protocols. That is as much as to say that, according to Baudelaire, Rousseau never has it any other way. For him, the choice is not: Will it be food or drugs first, but always both food and drugs. Food is a drug. Grass is grass. Rousseau's man does not browse on *l'herbe*, as Voltaire suggested, but on *l'herbe* (as Baudelaire notes, for the Arab, hashish was *l'herbe*: that is, nature, and also the essence of nature [*AP*, 36; *OC* I, 406]).[9] Rousseau found a way to transmute nature itself into a supplement. For Baudelaire's Rousseau, eating is not a natural process sustaining the biological life of the individual and comparable to the process of knowing the world. It is a psycho-social activity of taking into the body supplements to stand for the other that goes missing when the subject individuates in symbolization.

The point is one that Sigmund Freud helps elucidate. In his account of the child's oral phase, the normal part of the healthy ego's development and maintenance called "incorporation," food is a substitute.[10] In that phase, the child desires a lost other that it takes it into its mouth in the form of an object and destroys even as it assimilates it. That it is desire and not just need that drives incorporation means that the oral phase entails supplementarity, with the consumed object substituting for a beloved other. Incorporation is the means the subject has to reintegrate the separated other by way of an object that it destroys and assimilates to itself through a symbolic substitute. According to Jean Laplanche and J.-B. Pontalis, putting food symbols in the mouth satisfies three longings: "it means to obtain pleasure by making an object penetrate oneself; it means to destroy this object; and it means, by keeping it within oneself, to appropriate the object's qualities."[11] In their intelligent summary, the personality is produced by way of this process of identification: We become what we eat. We can already see that the other concerning Rousseau is defined in terms of a temporal situation, as lost other; or, to put it in terms familiar to Rousseau criticism, as the lost mother.

Baudelaire's characterization of Rousseauian eating, read through the Freudian account of incorporation represents the theme as it appears in Rousseau's autobiography aptly enough. Particularly the early books of the *Confessions* bear numerous scenes readable in terms of incorporation. Everywhere, we spy the young hero setting out to capture inaccessible others by swallowing tasty substitutes. Much more is wished for as the young hero ogles the inaccessible fruit presided over by shopgirls than the wherewithal to satisfy stomach pangs. Is Rousseau punished for some infraction by being sent away early from dinner? His "good-by roast" (*OC* I, 32) expresses the sadness of an exile sent away from a communal love feast. The piece of meat snatched out of the beloved Maman's mouth, only to be popped fetish-like into Rousseau's own;[12] the delicious spread with which a Catholic clergyman tempts the Protestant youth toward conversion; the golden apple whose capture is to secure imaginary access to the dessert table from which the apprentice is systematically sent away; the humble bread and cheese missing from the formal dinners to which he is regularly convoked—Rousseau rings all the changes on the topos of eating a lost or inaccessible other through an object made to stand for it. Think, for instance, of the lusty upstart raining cherries down on Mlle Galley, or the valet spilling water at dinner toward Mlle de Breil.[13] Rousseau seizes the fruits of nature to answer his longing for reintegration.

This is as much as to say that Rousseau's *Confessions* are motivated by the recognition that the I occupies its place in the world at the expense of the other as it steps into language. In the vision we can extrapolate from Baudelaire, what Rousseau wants is to return to before the logos divides things into subject and object, real and ideal, food and drugs. He gets his means in precisely the same place the hashish-eater thought would guarantee his return to reason, confessional language. A fresh look at the passage cited earlier confirms that, so far as Baudelaire is concerned, Rousseau gets high on language:

[Jean-Jacques] after having confessed to the world, not without a certain pleasure, also dared to utter the same triumphant cry (or at least the difference is slight), with the same sincerity and conviction. . . . Jean-Jacques became intoxicated without hashish. (*AP*, 69–70; *OC* I, 436)

Rousseau's green jam is confession. How he deals with it is the key to his resemblance to the hashish-eaters, and also what makes him their model. Hashish-eaters get high by annihilating the other in the natural object available to perception, and believe that storytelling allows them to repent their error. Rousseau's high is an effect of his practices with narrative. The supposedly rational act of confession is, for Rousseau, the source of libidinal pleasure. Rousseau does not confess as an act of repentance. Instead, he confesses to provide material for further internalizing. He annihilates linguistic alterity by means of a deferral, inversion and naturalization that show a structural resemblance to the hashish-eater's process, even while they intervene at a different level.

To confess is not to make restitution to the other by a verbal offering expelled from the I's body. Rather, the words of the hypocritical penitent turn around in the mouth, serving as matter for further chewing (as is indicated in Baudelaire's case by the false etymology with which he often plays that links remorse to biting or *re-mordre*). Language can be treated as a natural object perceptible by a subject, touched by the tongue, heard by the ear. It can make up for a lost world as a sensation on ear or tongue, beyond what it articulates. Rousseau's cry is the example of language successfully naturalized into a mouthful. Reminiscent of the cry in the mouth by which the infant consoles itself for the lost breast, uttered at the high point of inebriation, it is proof of his power to feed himself on his own substance.[14] Rousseau operates the same reduction of the other to a phenomenal object as the hashish-eater, the same deferral of any reckoning with the other. The difference is that the alterity he reduces is linguistic, and the reckoning he defers is with material language. In Baudelaire's account, Rousseau makes confessing an occasion to defer eating well, while prolonging eating anyway. For, whereas the hashish-eater's rare drug can be obtained only at considerable expense, Rousseau has nearly unlimited access to his homegrown drug. At any moment, a truth-telling language can be converted to an object of pleasure, a day of reckoning can turn out to be a day of deferral of reckoning, and the subject apparently engaged in telling his story to others can be discovered actually engaged in a complex recuperative strategy that opens onto further narration. Rousseau's narrative does not end the *kief*; it provides an inexhaustible supply of further narrative.

Yet Baudelaire does not entirely dismiss Rousseauian confession as inaugurating the scheduled stages of hashish-eating. The verb by which he describes Rousseau's final linguistic production goes far toward explaining why. Baudelaire does indeed say that Rousseau ends with a cry of *triumph* (*le même cri de triomphe*), which cry expresses and presumably models the apotheosis of the subject to be found in the *kief*. But in terming the act *daring* (*a osé pousser le même cri*), he also declares it exceptional. The cry brings Jean-Jacques into jeopardy, isolates and singularizes him. A cry may be language at its most sensuous and natural, but it is also a toxic language in which the Rousseauian subject risks itself to death. That is because the cry cries for the other. The I may be begging for succor; it may be crying out in agony; it could be inviting the other to table or calling out in welcome, as a host beckons a guest to enter the home. Whatever its meaning, the cry ruins the very autonomy it celebrates by delivering the subject over to an other noncontemporaneous with it, on whom it must rely for news of its act. Rousseau divides himself in uttering this cry. We can read in it a solution to the double obligation to eat and to give others to eat for it goes beyond a morality of good intention centered on the subject and reveals Rousseau's excessive response to the other in his self-constituting act.

With the cry, Rousseau also ruins narrative autobiography, inaugurates us into the discontinuities of an autothanatographical text like the *Rêveries*. The notion that the subject might manage its obligations by arranging them sequentially is in question because the cry establishing the subject's autonomy at one and the same self-divided time gives the subject to the other as corpse-like. The undoing of the narrative scheme that we earlier saw Rousseau modeling forces us wonder whether what has driven nineteenth-century hashish-eaters to drugs might be that, with Rousseau, they have lost consolatory narratives of repentance. If they take hashish, it is to dull momentarily the pain of having to do without narrative; or, what amounts to the same thing, to stimulate artificially their old belief in its virtue. In the end, for Baudelaire, Rousseau's *Confessions* is not a cautionary tale of error and repentance, but of the end of narrative autobiography and the beginning of a self-divided, ironic subject.

In this analysis, Rousseau meets Derrida's double imperative to eat anyway and well with a language redoubled at its inception, *cri* and *é-cri(t)*. Rousseau's language practice as Baudelaire filters it recognizes what he seemed initially to ward off: namely, that one cannot defer the obligation to obey the contradictory commands to eat and eat well. Freedom consists in assenting in one's verbal actions to the obligation always already to have been meeting both, never to have eaten alone, always to have been leaving an invitation for the other. The effect of the cry is at once, undecidably, to open onto further narratives sourced in language as natural object—a prediction borne out by the plethora of post-Rousseauian autobiographical narratives—and to close off autobiographical narrative as past, because able only to account for the subject's likeness to all other subjects, but not for its irreplaceable singularity or responsibility.

Time After Time: Baudelaire's Reminder of Rousseau's Cry

The memory is a sort of stomach for the mind . . .

AUGUSTINE, *Confessions* X, 14

What happens when Baudelaire answers Rousseau's invitation to internalize him? In the domain of autobiography, Baudelaire's situation is that of a crow picking over the broken meats of the Rousseauian feast. How does he negotiate with the double command to eat and eat well from his position as belated autobiographer? As latecomer, his calculations with eating well are cast in terms of memory and a lost other. In a question that is not only rhetorical, Baudelaire asks: "Doesn't that *remind* you of Jean-Jacques?" (my emphasis). Baudelaire's strategy in *The Poem* of substituting the intoxications of others for his own drug narrative shows him engaged with the problem of remembering the others lost in the subject's eating fest. This goes along with an emphasis placed on fasting; Baudelaire's poet deplores the multitude of hashish-eaters who do not follow the procedures of eating well as "poor souls who have neither fasted nor prayed" (*AP*, 76; *OC* I, 441).

The memorializing gesture suggests that "*Il faut bien manger*" is not an either/or proposition for Baudelaire, but rather a both/and, with any act always a decision as to how to eat well and anyway the most economically. His calculation is that in remembering Rousseau, he will also be feeding himself.[15] And indeed, so unavoidable is internalization, it is not right to say that remembering others first means the subject will fast. "We might say that the memory is a sort of stomach for the mind," Augustine tells us,[16] and Baudelaire shows the memory accomplishing a work of annihilating difference similar to the operation of the sensuous imagination as it reduces language to an object, or the digestive system as it gives the manifold of experience the same treatment. The particular difference being annihilated can be understood if we recall that in the passage under examination, Baudelaire compares the cry of the hashish-eater with Rousseau's.

If Baudelaire is reminded of Rousseau's text by the cry he has made up for the ideal hashish-eater, it is because the ideas he has acquired of hashish-eating through all sorts of contemporary testimony, including observation, discussion, personal experience, and written anecdotes; and the ideas of Jean-Jacques for which he only has the evidence of the *Confessions*, are comparable in the memory as ideas. To interiorizing memory, there is no difference between the works left behind as testaments and objects met with in experience.[17]

The particular operation with language that corresponds to interiorizing memory is translation, understood as the commemoration of a previous language by another one. The kind of translation we are discussing can be termed "cultural" because Baudelaire has found the equivalent in contemporary cultural practices for Rousseau's literary *Confessions*. When describing the stages of the typical hashish high, he has sought synonyms by way of the shared content of a morality of good intention. The system of the one is convertible into the system of the other because of the shared meaning; terms found in the "living" present remind of the bookish original.

It is significant that Baudelaire should betray the Rousseau he has identified as self-divided by not distinguishing between experience and traces, between the cry as object of knowledge and as text. The betrayal allows us to link memory and translation with another important aspect of Baudelaire's manner of internalizing in *Le Poème du hachisch*: namely, "irony," a term I have already used to describe Rousseau's self-division. In his analysis of irony in *De l'essence du rire*, Baudelaire explores the laughter of superiority as a situation in which mockery of the other's fall goes along with an ignorance of one's own collapse; likewise in *Les Paradis*, the first sign of the hashish-eater's high is laughter, as evidence of the persuasion of a superior subject that he is not experiencing the delusions that transport his fellows. Baudelaire's translation of Rousseau exhibits such irony: He engages in doing exactly what he mocks: that is, reducing Rousseau to a consumable object by forgetting about the self-differing uniqueness of the cry he wants to translate. We can see a consequence of this forgetting in Baudelaire's gesture of setting up a kind of literary genealogy or narrative linking him to Rousseau.[18] Baudelaire's self-conscious belatedness is not enough to preserve him from the same naturalizing, the same cry of triumph, the same inauguration of a master narrative that he mocks in Rousseau. We might generalize our point and say that translation itself is ironic. It tries to get across the irreducible singularity of an original by an operation that assumes equivalents across the array of languages. It does the opposite of what it says by translating the difference between saying and meaning that the original says one-sidedly into meaning as doctrine.

Baudelaire is not blind to his inscription in this problematic. In the last lines of *De l'essence du rire*, Baudelaire tells us that it is the artist's duty to ignore no phenomenon of man's double nature (*OC* II, 543). His aesthetic choices have to be made in consequence. Only an artist "on condition of being double" (*OC* II, 543) [*à la condition d'etre double*] on condition that he foreknow his fall, Baudelaire has to offer up the equivalent of a remainder, and thus the equivalent in his own discourse of a daring singularity. In the case of Baudelaire's translation of Rousseau's cry, that means he has to look for a synonym in the target language of the exception, the self-differing "power to be at once oneself and another" (*OC* II, 543) that he has made an expressive utterance like any other through his translation of it into a cultural phenomenon.

Baudelaire provides evidence of a search for such an equivalent in the afterthought registered in the very sentence in which he is gleefully celebrating his successful translation. In an aside, a parabasis, the translator steps out of the shadows to interrupt his own moment of triumph. Baudelaire says: "Does this not remind you of Jean-Jacques, who also dared to utter the same triumphant cry (or at least the difference is slight) with the same sincerity and conviction?" (*AP*, 69; *OC* I, 436) [*Cela ne vous fait-il pas vous souvenir de Jean-Jacques, qui, lui aussi, a osé pousser le même cri (du moins la différence est bien petite) avec la même sincérité et la même conviction.*] The parentheses signal the interruption of interiorizing memory and the emergence of another facet of memory, the non-interiorizing memory of signs. Baudelaire's sudden qualms about his translation may have been awakened by a recollection of Rousseau's actual words; perhaps he has even gone to look them up. In any event, a memory of signs has been consulted and has indicated an inadequacy to the synonym offered. Only because he has consulted a memory held as writing can he confess that a slight difference has been lost.[19]

We can perhaps think of Baudelaire's parabasis as an approximate equivalent of Rousseau's cry. On the one side, the parabasis registers the paroxystic vanity of a triumphant translator affirming that he has effectively made Rousseau's text obsolete. On the other side, we can see Baudelaire's discourse beginning to divide itself, with the translator interrupting his process of a remembering as eating to recall a difference that has fallen outside his translation. Yet an incompleteness to this self-division has to be noted, given that the actual material difference of Rousseau's cry has been translated into a reflective statement concerning translation as practice of loss. Baudelaire's strategy of cultural translation makes everything intelligible, including the "little difference" that Rousseau's language in its materiality might have introduced had he quoted it, which he does not do, in a signal doing without.

However, Baudelaire does not simply comment on his own practice; he also seeks a material equivalent for the difference lost. In the passage under discussion, that equivalent is the mark, which Baudelaire makes critical at least twice. In one instance, a dash joins and divides Rousseau's baptismal name of Jean-Jacques. It was mentioned previously that calling the author by his first name could signify Baudelaire's disdain for Rousseau's morality of good intention. But the compound name is also a nod of recognition toward Rousseau's own signature difference. It is not simply that the latter often called himself by his first name, notably in *Rousseau juge de Jean-Jacques* or that the -Jacques part of his name was all that distinguished our Rousseau from the writer the eighteenth century called "Le Grand Rousseau," Jean-Baptiste, the poet. The dash introduces a break. For Poe, it "represents a *second thought*—an *emendation*."[20] It marks off thought considered as continuous from a thought after thought: the living, thinking subject from the survivor that has anticipated its death in an act of self-reading. Considered through Poe, Jean Rousseau would be the name of a subject like any other, caught up in the continuous process of identity building. But with -Jacques, Rousseau's name dares self-difference. The dash marks off the other-annihilating Rousseau of the confessional narrative from the other Rousseau as he will have been delivered to posterity in a text. By the compound name, Baudelaire recalls the written side of Rousseau's cry otherwise than as the content to which interiorizing memory reduces it.

The point is further borne out by a second mark, the parentheses that open Baudelaire's parabasis on difference within his own text. The parentheses delineate the border between the text construed spatially, according to an inside/outside distinction, and the same text as it exists in history: They indicate an artist stepping "out" of the narrative to consider the text's chances of success, in an intrusive thought that will have been possible only after the storytelling is done and the text has been offered as remains to the other. The parenthetical marks give evidence of self-irony, of a self-doubling that knows itself to be one. Not only do they re-mark the duplicity we saw in Rousseau's cry and name, but they do so inimitably, as the bite-print left by a pair of incisors, upended into a monument to the self-ironical subject [ ]. They are the marks by which Baudelaire shows himself to be more than just a victim of "voracious Irony / That shakes and bites me" (*OC* I, 78). The parentheses make the *Poem* a one-time text, a singular calculation with the demand to eat and to give others to eat. In staging his translator's discourse as self-ironical, Baudelaire's parentheses disrupt the narrative of transmission and represent in the target language the moment of self-division in Rousseau.

The logic followed by Baudelairian internalization here is a logic of time after time. On the one side, it is the time after time of repetition, of the repeated collapse into narrative, of irony striking a blind subject as it falls into narrative patterns to which it thinks itself superior. On the other, it is the time after time of a post-narrative economy, an accounting for the discontinuous time after when second thoughts strike and the writer becomes reader of his own text. In terms of our question of how Baudelairian self-irony responds to the imperative of eating anyway and eating well, this double logic of time after time is distinct from the decision to meet one's obligations "at one and the same self-differing time" characterizing Rousseau's last daring cry of triumph. With the logic of time after time, the problem is when and how often to interrupt an ongoing narrative to restage the inclusion of the framing discourse in the problematic and to mark its difference from mere repetition. As Baudelaire puts it: "I assume you have taken every precaution to choose the best moment for this adventurous expedition" (*AP* 40; *OC* I, 410) [*je présume que vous avez eu la précaution de bien choisir votre moment pour cette aventureuse expédition*]. It's all a matter of good timing, of choosing well one's moment to interrupt eating regardless by a reminder of the remainder.[21]

For Baudelaire, calculating with *"Il faut bien manger"* comes down to choosing one's time. The hashish-eaters pick a given moment of the day to eat the substitute first and tell tales after. Rousseau chooses the moment of telling and leaves writing for remembering after. Baudelaire's chosen moment is the time of memory and of translation as repetition, which is to say, both a punctual time of collapse back into narrative, and a time marked off for the after-thought. The self-division that Rousseau has capitalized on in a single moment is dispersed by Baudelaire throughout *Les Paradis* by a strategy with the writing system of dashes and parentheses that deliver his text repeatedly as a reminder of the remainder to be left the other, and thus of eating well.

II
Eating Opium with De Quincey: Allegory and the Addiction to Narrative

In the second part of *Les Paradis*, *Un Mangeur d'opium*, the translator does not look for equivalents to relate literature to cultural forms, but to relate text to text. Already in the opening pages of the *Le Poème du hashisch*, Baudelaire has told us that he can add nothing to De Quincey's "incomparable book" (*AP*, 34; *OC* I, 404). Instead, he presents himself as a translator facing an irreplaceable original and forced to summarize more than he likes of a text "which has not yet been translated into French in its entirety" (*AP*, 34; *OC* I, 404). In *The Poem*, translation has to do with individual symbols and their ironic duplicity; it promises an end to narrative autobiography. In contrast, as Alan Astro suggests in a short essay on translation in *Un Mangeur d'opium*, the trope corresponding to internalization in that text is allegory.[22] The outlook is correspondingly melancholic and invokes narrative as unfinished. What happens to the double obligation to eat anyway and to eat well in that text that makes allegory the trope of choice and pushes narrative, albeit curiously foreshortened, digressively extended, or open ones? We begin with a look at De Quincey, before looking at the transformations Baudelaire effects in De Quinceyan allegory through his translation.

De Quincey's Deranged Stomach

The title of De Quincey's book, *Confessions of an English Opium-Eater*, signals the importance of the eating motif. Yet the title is a strange one because it is literally inaccurate and contradicts what is said in the body of the text where it is abundantly established that De Quincey drank his opium in a preparation called *laudanum*. The only character who eats literal opium in the book, in fact, is the Malay. From the very beginning, we have to deal with a gap between the insistence with which the book thrusts the figure of the eater at us and the overall lack of literal eating in the book. The various motives the critics have devised to explain the mystery, while often ingenious, are generally unpersuasive.[23] Baudelaire has, if anything, accentuated the problem by his bold translation of the title as *Un Mangeur d'opium*, which centers on the eater.

As it turns out, De Quincey has made the subject's unmet hunger an important theme of his book. Very early in the *Opium Confessions*, the famished protagonist develops stomach troubles that both lead to the opium addiction and result from it. The process of internalization is under attack from the start by a stomach so quickly deranged by starvation that it soon rejects all nourishment. Obedience to the rules of eating changes meaning in the face of the impossibility of engaging in normal internalizing and affects the place of the supplement. In no way can De Quincey be said to

have elected to defer a meal for reasons of taste. If he has to find a substitute to eat, it is out of dire necessity because otherwise, the organ of digestion will turn and digest itself. A feeling of rats abrading the stomach (*OE*
3), a hunger so great that it turns around and bites a child (*OE* 17), a
stomach that rejects food and will accept only coffee, tea, wine, spirits,
opium—these are forms of the situation with respect to internalization
that determines De Quincey's drug taking. Eventually, the stomach becomes so habituated to the substitute as to protest at its absence. Necessity, not desire, drives the user to opium, which is thus not supplementary
at all, and the fact that the drug used to soothe the stomach at the last
redoubles its pains reinforces the general mood of hopeless melancholy.
The problem becomes to manage even a semblance of freedom for the
subject where necessity rules. The subject may have to eat anyway, but
that is definitely not a happy prospect for someone suffering from hunger
in so roiled an organ of internalization.[24]

It is to be expected that a protagonist whose experience is of shortage
in "esculent *matériel*" (*OE* 18) will make an unsatisfactory hero for an
autobiographical narrative. There can be no long tales of formation where
the opportunities for internalization are rare and sporadic. Out of a sort
of solidarity with his hero, the narrator seeks a mode of narration adequate
to the latter's starvation, even extending hunger to encompass the deprivation of the whole field of sensible objects, which he rejects together with
the "spurious and defective sensibility of the French" (*OE* 1), chief among
them, the French-speaking Rousseau. De Quincey's task is simplified
somewhat by a self-reflexivity that makes each anecdote abyssal and keeps
the story going by anecdotes of surviving deprivation. Such anecdotes as
he does tell will be blown up disproportionately by piled-on commentary
to encompass far more space than they warrant. In one instance of hyper-
bole, the narrator will dwell on an inconsequential accident when a trunk
fell against a door. Or, he will expend nearly six pages pinpointing the
exact moment when happiness appears: 4:00, on a stormy day in the winter
of 1816, "a parenthesis between years of a gloomier character" (*OE* 55) is
the "period during which happiness is in season, which, in my judgment,
enters the room with the tea-tray" (*OE* 60). In other cases, anecdotes that
might well have provided long developments are ostentatiously dropped
as celebratory of sensibility, with the narrator then bloating the narrative
by an inserted commentary. In one example of "draw(ing) a decent drapery" (*OE* 1) over demonstrations of feeling, he will jump over a period of
suffering (*OE* 52–3). In another, he will elide the circumstances of a voyage
that might have shown the hero's powers of improvisation, filling in with

an editorial comment that considers instead the authorial problem of the book's conditions of production: "Soon after this, I contrived, by means which I must omit for want of room, to transfer myself to London" (*OE* 16). Distensions and ellipses are the consequence on the level of the narrative of starvation on the level of theme.

With its fits and starts, gaps and spun out moments, the narrative signals not only the loss of the normal field of experience, but also its new field of time. Everything happens in De Quincey as if "to eat" were synonymous with "to corrode." Eating regulates the relations of the subject to itself and the other as rust eats metal, in time: which is to say, as it corrupts it with respect to an earlier state. It is as if a crisis in the stomach had been provoked by the undoing of the inside-outside metaphor that regulates internalization as ingestion. Both in its "unreasonable length" (*OE* 77) and in its failing to be quite long enough ("Within more spacious limits, the materials which I have used might have been better unfolded. . . ."[*OE* 77]), the narrative reflects that shift. It, too, is measured against some earlier model with respect to which it has fallen away.

Given this insistence on time and loss, it is not surprising to find that the others with respect to whom De Quincey eats are in no wise present. That is literally stated to be the case at the lawyer's house, where the protagonist observes that the several members of any party invited to table must stand with each other in a relation "of succession . . . and not of co-existence; in the relation of the parts of time, and not of the parts of space" (*OE* 18). In the mouth of the hero, the comment concerns the lack of sufficient dinnerware to serve more than one person at a time, but it also describes the discoursing subject's predicament with respect to its interlocutors. The De Quinceyan subject's choices are made with respect to an other absent from the scene where it is acting. His guests are not yet or no longer present. Any news the runaway gets of them comes from intermediaries, which explains why his pockets are less loaded with money, which would only engage him in commerce with contemporaries, than with books.

Among the far-reaching consequences of making this noncontemporaneity of host and guests the prototypical eating situation, we can count De Quincey's aforementioned preference for the literary mode of allegory. With the symbol, consciousness invests with meaning what is present to perception, making the sensible appearance of nature reflective of an idea. But allegory picks up and assigns meaning to matter left unattended to by the representational field of the symbol. Allegory involves the ascription by the intellect of meaning to a material that can be thought of as fecal in having been refused significance by the context in which it appears. That material has been variously theorized—as experience not yet received by consciousness (Benjamin), as the detail (Schor), as the materiality of language (de Man), among other related characterizations, whose differences can be neglected for our present objective of establishing that allegory ascribes meaning to an accident registered but gone unnoticed by the perceiving subject.[25] Thus, for instance, De Quincey's apprentice allegorist does not consort with others provided by nature, but by accident: "from my earliest youth it has been my pride to converse familiarly, *more Socratico*, with all human beings, man, woman and child, that chance might fling my way" (*OE* 20). De Quincey's tears as a runaway adolescent, shed while he takes leave of "chair, hearth, writing-table and other familiar objects" (*OE* 10), are made to stand for all leave-takings past and future (the dead father, the all-too-quiet schoolmaster insensible to a crashing trunk, the lost siblings, the removed mother, the disappeared Ann, the absent wife, the children who inhabit another world than their opium-addled father) and is the more affecting for showing a child momentarily arrested, as if dimly aware that the event will have had significance, but still unaware of what he is weeping about. The choice of this particular moment of loss over all others is explained by a decisive detail: The lost *familiar objects* tells us that it is the loss of the process of objectification and consumption, and consequently the I's death as desiring subject that is at stake. Allegory—"hieroglyphics" in De Quincey's word for it—is the literary mode by which the I foreknows itself as other and its autobiography as autothanatography.

The internalization process associated with allegory cannot be called eating if by eating, we mean the literal annihilation and assimilation of food objects to the subject through digestion. With this kind of eating, if the I takes in things, it is without submitting them to that natural process. The words De Quincey uses to describe his vision of the Malay's action with respect to opium are apposite here. He sees the latter "bolt the whole" (*OE* 57).[26] To "bolt" means to swallow whole and without chewing and connotes what lies under lock and key, encrypted, just as the Malay figure lies dormant in the I's memory until recalled by the opium dreams. A hero who collects material for later allegorization plunges it into a darkness from which it may never reemerge, unless, as De Quincey speculates about the Malay, the being carrying it be "drenched with an emetic" (*OE* 57) so that it can resurface as it does later in his opium dreams in a still-to-be-decrypted form. In any event, its meaning cannot be referred to the subject who ignores its significance. Eating in the senses De Quincey gives it is not the pleasurable process identified by Laplanche and Pontalis. It is a psychic mechanism for coping with loss, and it is to a discussion like that of Nicolas Abraham and Maria Torok that we must go to find an idea of eating that does not understand it as a metaphor for knowing. Their consideration of introjection, contrasted with incorporation, is revelatory.

Let's recall briefly the difference between the terms. In "Mourning or Melancholia," Abraham terms incorporation a "fantasy" that expresses the subject's ego-conserving and deluded relation to the other as an object to be eaten.[27] It has a "preventative and conservative function . . . fantasy is essentially narcissistic: it tends to transform the world rather than inflict injury on the subject" (*Shell* 125). Incorporation is a strategy the subject adopts to maintain unchanged its attachment to a single lost other it eats over and over in the variety of objects presented to it. As for the more difficult introjection, it is a "process" (*Shell* 125). More specifically, it is the process by which the I expresses its real relation to the lost other, accepting it as lost and giving up in consequence its own policy of self-conservation. In one dense passage, Abraham speaks about eating as it is understood in both operations:

> If accepted and worked through, the loss would require major readjustment [*un remaniement profond*]. But the fantasy of incorporation merely simulates profound psychic transformation through magic; it does so by implement-ing literally something that has only figurative meaning [*au propre ce qui n'a de sens qu'au figuré*]. So in order not to have to "swallow" a loss we fantasize swallowing (or having swallowed) that which has been lost, as if it were some kind of thing. Two interrelated procedures constitute the magic of incorporation: *demetaphorization* (taking literally what is meant figuratively) and *objectivation* (pretending that the suffering is not an injury to the subject but instead a loss sustained by the love object). The magical "cure" by incorporation exempts the subject from the painful process of reorganiza-tion [*travail douloureux du remaniement*]. When, in the form of imaginary or real nourishment, we ingest the love-object we miss, this means that *we refuse to mourn* and that we shun the consequences of mourning even though our psyche is fully bereaved. Incorporation is the refusal to reclaim as our own the part of ourselves that we placed in what we lost; incorpora-tion is the refusal to acknowledge the full import of the loss, a loss that, if recognized as such, would effectively transform us [*le vrai sens de la perte, celui qui ferait qu'en le sachant on serait autre*]. In fine, incorporation is the refusal to introject loss. The fantasy of incorporation reveals a gap [*une lacune*] within the psyche; it points to something that is missing just where the introjection should have occurred. (*Shell* 126–7)

The author gets at the difference between incorporation and introjection by showing the differing interpretations each gives the figure of eating. When we try to swallow a loss by eating it in a determinate object, we are taking a referent to be the proper meaning of a metaphor. Eating involves a demetaphorization or a literalization; it uses words such "that their very capacity for figurative representation [*figurabilité*] is destroyed" (*Shell* 132). The fact that it is a fantasy is clear after we understand that it is precisely reference, precisely the stability of the objective world that has been put into question with the loss of the other. Incorporation lets us believe that the objective world is not lost, that the subject has not been wounded but still has access to objects as the referents of figures in the "things" eaten. In incorporation, the threat to narcissism is dealt with by refusing "the full import of the loss, a loss that, if recognized as such, would effectively transform us." In short, incorporation converts a linguistic problem: the problem of substitution, of saying yes to the reconfiguration (*remaniement*) of everything; to a problem of cognition, the problem of what and how to eat in view of what is. With introjection, however, figures are not referred to objects but are allowed to remain what they are: replaceable figures. The subject swallows the other's loss figuratively; it takes in the substitute without assimilating it, accepts it without digesting it, knows its own death without understanding it, allows for its own heterogeneity to itself, accepts it is dealing in substitutes—opium-eating rather than eating, figures and letters rather than objects, consolatory narratives rather than true ones.

This territory, familiar through critical assessments of mourning and melancholy though still difficult and productive, is suggestive of a reason for De Quincey's paradoxical insistence on the figure of opium-eating in a book from which literal eating is all but absent. De Quincey centers his book on the difference between the letter and the figure, and more especially on the struggle between taking the eating motif literally by means of a defensive fantasy of incorporation and taking it figuratively, by an introjection that recognizes it as one determinate figure among others for "figurability" or substitution.

As Abraham and Torok explain, there are historical stakes involved. With incorporation, time passes but no transformation in the subject occurs. With introjection, the I transforms itself through its acceptance of loss and interruption. It has the chance to recognize the fantasy of incorporation for what it is, to accept its death, and thus to transform the very notion of what a subject is, from consumer of objects desperately holding onto a past ego ideal, to survivor. The injection of historical stakes lets us see that De Quincey requires us to reorient our discussion of "*il faut bien manger*" away from the discussion of how to answer the command as if it were a given, which we can now see is a matter of conserving the subject as it is, frozen in its position of obeisance to a threatened authority figure, toward the question of the authority attributed the command. Indeed, with De Quincey, we learn to read Derrida's phrase not as a command but an acknowledgment of a lacuna that is the condition for the supplementing fantasy in the first place: "there is indeed lacking whereof to eat" (the *il faut* of "*il faut bien manger*" comes from *falloir*, to lack). A behavior like De Quincey's where the subject obeys protocols for eating as a means to avoid swallowing its utter deprivation, is rightly called a "fantasy." Such a fantasy is not just protective; in Abraham's account, it involves a partial recognition that the ground itself is gone missing:

> It seems certain to me that the interlocutors aimed at by the fantasy, how-
> ever imaginary they may appear in the demands and attributes loaned to
> them, belong to another order of reality, to precisely that order of reality
> thanks to which language and fantasy are possible [*les interlocuteurs qu(e le
> fantasme) . . . relèvent d'un autre ordre de réalité, de l'ordre de cette réalité
> précisément grâce à laquelle le langage et le fantasme sont possibles*]. (*Shell* 124)

According to this passage, the fantasizing patient explains its behavior by reference to an imaginary interlocutor. The analyst does not simply see the explanation offered as an indication of a delusive wish to hold onto an already lost organization of reality. He also considers that it tells the truth in pointing away from the present to the order of reality that conditions language and fantasy. "*Il faut bien manger*" is not simply a matter of choosing a method to obey a command—that's incorporation, what the subject does when it wants to hold onto the God with which it identifies. Instead, it involves deciding whether the command is sourced in one sort of reality (the reality of the determinate fantasy) or another (the reality of the conditions under which determinate fantasies are possible.) The decisive move is to attend to the figurative status of the command, which allows the subject to divest itself of past beliefs. The decision to incorporate literalizes and refuses change; the decision to introject chooses the figure, swallows the lost ideal, and so gains access to what language and the fantasy are all about, which is the communion of empty mouths and filling the mouth with words (*Shell* 127), as Abraham explains.

Among the vistas opened for work on De Quincey by Abraham and Torok's work is the question of the success of the De Quinceyan subject at giving up the authority in which it has sourced its commands for living.[28] J. H. Miller's classic essay on De Quincey's response to the death of God is apposite.[29] If the subject on opium is understood as the subject confronting figurability and having to choose between incorporation and introjection, then the problem is no longer what gods does the I obey, but rather, which gods does it swallow as lost and what changes in subjectivity result. The struggle to maintain narrative coherency is one place where the crisis would surface.

It is worth noting that Baudelaire's discussion of the allegorical dream with De Quincey in mind is concerned with an epochal shift in the way humanity has sourced the dreams it has accorded allegorical, premonitory status:

> But that other type of dream! the absurd and unpredictable dream, which has no bearing on, or connection to, the character, life and passions of the dreamer! This dream, which I shall term hieroglyphic, evidently represents the supernatural side of life, and it is precisely because of its absurdity that the ancients thought it of divine origin. As this dream cannot be explained by any known cause, they attributed it to a cause external to man; and today, without mentioning oneiromancers, there is still a philosophic school which sees some sort of criticism or counsel in dreams of this nature, a symbolic and moral representation engendered in the very mind of the sleeping man. Such a dream is a dictionary to be studied, a language to which only the wise hold the key. (*AP*, 38–9; *OC* I, 408–9)

This passage confirms Baudelaire's interest in a difference between the dreams themselves, which are fixed if unreadable hieroglyphs, and the shifting explanations humanity has evolved to define the "supernatural side of life" they represent. Earlier ages made them derive from the gods; prefiguring psychoanalysis, he sees modern man as sourcing them in the self. While skeptical that such dreams do enjoin behavior as from the gods, Baudelaire considers that explanations of their source and discursive status can let us measure epochal transformations in the idea of the subject. The value of De Quincey's dreams for Baudelaire is that seismic changes can occur in subjectivity through a decisive rereading—as it does when we read "*Il faut bien manger*" not as a command but as a recognition of the need for supplementation. The problem is whether a given autobiography provides testimony of a past culture or a chance for the reconfiguration of subjectivity.

To see how De Quincey deals with introjection, we now turn to an exemplary passage from the *Confessions* about a crisis in internalization. De Quincey's hero is in a losing struggle to maintain its fantasy that all is well with the patriarchal structures in which he seeks refuge, with the command to eat with the other as the central place of struggle. The scene comes from the narrative of the genesis of De Quincey's addiction, and concerns the period when the hero resides part-time in the lawyer's house:

But I found, on taking possession of my new quarters, that the house already
contained one single inmate, a poor friendless child, apparently ten years
old; but she seemed hunger-bitten; and sufferings of that sort often make
children look older than they are. From this forlorn child I learned that she
had slept and lived there alone, for some time before I came: and great joy
the poor creature expressed, when she found that I was, in future, to be her
companion through the hours of darkness. The house was large; and, from
the want of furniture, *the noise of the rats made a prodigious echoing on the
spacious stair-case and hall; and, amidst the real fleshly ills of cold, and, I fear,
hunger, the forsaken child had found leisure to suffer still more (it appeared) from
the self-created one of ghosts. I promised her protection against all ghosts whatsoever: but, alas! I could offer her no other assistance.* We lay upon the floor, with
a bundle of cursed law papers for a pillow; but with no other covering than
a sort of large horseman's cloak: afterwards, however, we discovered, in a
garret, an old sopha-cover, a small piece of rug, and some other fragments
of other articles, which added a little to our warmth. The poor child crept
close to me for warmth, and for security against her ghostly enemies. When
I was not more than usually ill, I took her in my arms, so that, in general,
she was tolerably warm, and often slept when I could not: for, during the
last two months of my sufferings, I slept much in the daytime, and was apt
to fall into transient dozings at all hours. But my sleep distressed me more
than my watching: for, besides the tumultuousness of my dreams (which
were only not so awful as those which I shall have to describe hereafter as
produced by opium), my sleep was never more than what it called *dog-sleep*;
so that I could hear myself *moaning*, and was often, as it seemed to me,
wakened suddenly by my own voice; and, about his time, a *hideous* sensation
began to *haunt* me as soon as I fell into a slumber which has since *returned*
upon me, at different periods of my life, viz. *a sort of twitching (I know not
where, but apparently about the region of my stomach)*, which compelled me
violently to throw out my feet for the sake of relieving it. This sensation
coming on as soon as I began to sleep, and the effort to relieve it constantly
awaking me, at length I slept only from exhaustion and from increasing
weakness (as I said before) I was constantly falling asleep, and constantly
awaking. (*OE* 16–17, my emphasis)

A fine example of De Quincey's allegorical treatment, the passage gives us
the subject in uneasy slumber, his stomach in turmoil, and in communion
with another whose mouth is as empty as his own. Each detail has a purport far greater than the actors understand; the scene is thus an excellent
place to look at De Quincey's attempt to draw out the "hieroglyphic
meaning of human sufferings" (*OE* 23).

Note the several fantasies. The girl is deluded in thinking that the house is haunted by ghosts. The young hero does not destroy her fantasy—he promises to protect her from ghosts—even while he suggests it has a physical cause in the echoes of the shuffling rats. Meanwhile, he labors under a fantasy of his own. A penniless parasite, a virtual squatter nighttimes in a house rented by a shady lawyer, he acts as if he were an Englishman settling into his castle, "taking possession of (his) new quarters," vowing paternalistically to protect the girl, pillowing her fatherless head beside his on legal papers, despite her outsider status as unnamed and probably illegitimate child. The covenant he makes to hold her safe from all ghosts whatsoever is a parody of God's promise through Moses to shelter a people with a code of laws. Her belief in ghosts mirrors his equally deluded faith that playing the part of master will see them through.

Both fantasies involve incorporation, and indeed are the equivalent of fantasmatic attempts on the part of the stomach to eat anyway even where there is nothing to internalize. The ideal to which the children are tenaciously holding is that of the body as temple of the spirit and the head as seat of reason, which is the interpretative system associated with incorporation. Take the case of the girl's fantasy. She hears unexplained sounds echoing through the house and incorporates in that she takes those noises to be the perceptible form in which spirits are manifesting themselves.[30] As for the I's triumphant possession, its nature as fantasy is evidenced by his body become prey to outside forces. Its motion is not explainable by reference to consciousness and challenges his meaning system. As expressed in the language of the passage, the explanation given is magical, the jerks and twitches of his nether parts the expressions of visiting spirits: He hears himself moaning, he wakes to the sound of a voice that turns out to be his; he is haunted by a hideous sensation (from *hisde*, in old French, terror or fear) that returns upon him, just as ghosts are wont to do. Far from the healthy body of a mastering subject, his is compelled to action by visiting forces, but it is still moved by spirits. Like the girl, who assumes the stray sounds she hears must have been caused by an intentional being, he finds a reason to lie behind his movements: He has incorporated the girl's ghosts. The scene is about two desperate children trying to hold fast to the authority of reason and the law, even where that authority is under attack. As figured by the twitching stomach that keeps on working in the void, what eating anyway means is incorporation at any price.

However, the nightmarish struggle in which the terrified players are engaged suggests an introjection in the offing. And indeed, the long night of eating anyway comes to an end as the scene shifts to daylight, to a room and a moment when some "eating well" occurs. Now the lawyer is present, and the I lounges into the study, to take up such "fragments as he had left," and also—as it happens—to keep his promise to the girl and start laying ghosts. The study is a very significant room, not simply because it is a makeshift dining room, but also because it is the "Blue-beard room," the room that the "poor child believed to be haunted" (*OE* 19) because

> she was never admitted into his study (if I may give that name to his chief depositary of parchments, law writings, &c.); that room was to her the Blue-beard room of the house, being regularly locked on his departure to dinner, about six o'clock. (*OE* 18)

The room is secret to the child and yet is the source of her fears, the reality her fantasies point to allegorically yet hide from her understanding, so as to allow her to maintain partially her belief in the system that oppresses her. To recall Abraham's language, the room opens onto "another order of reality, precisely the order of reality thanks to which language and fantasy are possible" (*Shell* 124). While deluded in her belief that there were ghosts in the room capable of moaning, the child was not wrong to think that the dead were trying to get in touch from that room. For what is a depository of books if not a set of still undecrypted messages from the dead? Her error was to have believed a figure for books to refer to literal beings, phenomenally perceivable. Similarly the young hero, while wrong to think his body possessed by spirits, would have been on the mark had he only understood the allegorical meaning of his torments and seen the self-dispossessed body as a prefiguration of his writing career. The hidden meaning of the passage is found in the secret depository: Writing is what the subject defends against in its fantasies and also what lets it lay to rest and survive those fantasies.

Now the point is not to discover, yet again, that texts are about writing. It is rather that such a discovery here has to do with introjection, with freeing oneself from the naturalized commands of past authorities through a recognition of an open figurability to the world in its legal texts. Daytimes, De Quincey's hero answers the command to eat well and anyway by reading it as one among other possible figures for the law. That move entails a displacement of the proprietary paternal figure presiding over the house of law by a new ideal of the subject as squatter on the earth, having a meaning outside its present knowledge, capable of historical transformation because capable of accepting its death ahead of time. By considering things not from the present but as they will have appeared to readers, De Quincey gets access to the conditions for fantasy production and can substitute a new figure for an old one, laying to rest a past, ghostly paternal figure in an exorbitant response to the promise that linked him to the long-gone girl. For De Quincey, the condition for any literal eating as for the survival of subjectivity and the transformation in the ethico-political situation of eating, it is necessary to read the authority of a law like "*Il faut bien manger*" as problematic. In his foreshortened and digressive narratives, where the end of narrative is in question, allegory is a means of access to the conditions of experience; it opens onto the history of subjectivity as an unfinished procession of figures.

De Quincey's allegories are markedly ethical in tenor, unsurprisingly given his by no-means uncritical interest in Kant. Yet, ultimately, his ethics tends to take on the dogmatic cast of a right-thinking morality that didn't escape Baudelaire, who criticizes it as "British cant" (*AP*, 131; *OE* I, 491). In Baudelaire's view, De Quincey was a remarkable analyst of the opium of his time, but his own last delusion is to have claimed to have undone the chains of addiction and to have put fantasy behind him once and for all. Instead of recognizing the open, unfinished character of the process in the *Confessions*—imposed by the fact that any determinate supplement is only an example of a general figurability—De Quincey behaves as if a single successful introjection could get rid of them all.[31] In the end, then, De Quincey reverses his important point that the situation of infinite substitution is irremediable—which ought to have meant he would leave his story one of a process, says Baudelaire, "without denouement" (*AP*, 130; *OC* I, 490)—as if one could give up figurability as easily as opium, as if the subject as squatter on the earth were *the* moral subject. What about Baudelaire? As he translates De Quincey's *English Opium-eater* into the French context, does he seek to dispel the atmosphere of British cant criticized? What is the effect on allegory, which already in De Quincey takes authority as its problematic question? This brings us back again to our starting point, to the last response *Les Paradis* offers to the command to eat and eat well.

The Translator's Economies: The Speed of Eating in *Un Mangeur*

> . . . he has that set to his lips which indicates a mouth
> accustomed to chewing only ashes.
>
> FRANÇOIS PORCHÉ, describing Baudelaire;
> as quoted in Benjamin's *Arcades Project*

For Baudelaire, too, eating is corrosion and figures the process of history as it corrupts and renders past. Think of the vermin feeding on beggars in "Au lecteur;" worms and maggots eating the corpses of "Remords posthume," "Je t'aime à l'égal de la voûte nocturne . . ." and "Une charogne;" crows picking away at the dead in "Le Mort joyeux" or "Voyage à Cythère"; or vampires and other succubi and incubi—women, time, irony, the irremediable, and so on, in "Sed non satiata," "L'irrémédiable," "Le vampire," "Le poison," "L'horloge," "Une martyre," "Héautontimorouménos," and "Les métamorphoses du vampire." Everywhere something lies in wait to "Steal from Man what he eats" (*OC* I, 95) [*Dérobe(r) à l'Homme ce qu'il mange*] and "eats us as the worm does the corpse" (*OC* I, 54) [*se nourrit de nous comme le ver des morts*]. But the theme works somewhat differently than it does in De Quincey where the stomach, even as it hungrily turns its acid juices against itself, keeps alive incorporative fantasies. Baudelaire uses the motif chiefly as an allegory for reading as an internalization performed on a prior text.[32]

That it is a reader's action is already evident in the way that in *Les Fleurs* Baudelaire depicts eating as the necrophiliac action of worms, maggots, crows, or dogs on carrion. The attention is on the matter being eaten, the corpse left behind when the animating spirit has departed, and thus on something that resembles a text. These flesh-pickers are recognizable updates on the flower-plucking readers of the Renaissance *florilegia* to which the title *Les Fleurs du mal* pays allegiance. Baudelaire's eaters are doubly evaluated: parasites who prey on corpses; they also do the corpse a service by revealing its structure. In "Une charogne," the point is made at some length. There, the dog that grabs a morsel is helping to finish the "slow-to-come sketch" (*OC* I, 32) that the carrion represents, removing from it the organic bits that obscure its mineral-like textual features. The eater speeds along a process of decomposition already at work in the original.

Citing Benjamin in discussions of Baudelaire is so common a gesture these days as almost to require an apology. But Benjamin's notion of allegory is too helpful to pass over when it comes to considering *Un Mangeur*. In *The Origins of German Tragic Drama*, Benjamin notes that Baroque writers viewed history as a process of decay:

> In the ruin history has physically merged into the setting. And in this guise history does not assume the form of the process of an eternal life so much as that of irresistible decay. Allegory thereby declares itself to be beyond beauty. Allegories are, in the realm of thoughts, what ruins are in the realm of things.[33]

Benjamin will also say of nature what he says of architecture. The *Trauerspiel* seizes nature not "in bud and bloom, but in the over-ripeness and decay of her creations" (*Origins* 179). As a corpse offered to the voracity of worms, subject to what Benjamin calls an "afterlife," the text enters history. The process of allegorization, the process of entering history, the process of the corpse's consumption—these are synonymous. Benjamin observes that corpses are valuable in that nothing in them impedes allegorizing:

> For this much is self-evident: the allegorization of the physis can only be carried through in all its vigour in respect of the corpse. And the characters of the Trauerspiel die, because it is only thus, as corpses, that they can enter into the homeland of allegory. It is not for the sake of immortality that they meet their end, but for the sake of the corpse. . . . Seen from the point of view of death, the product of the corpse is life. It is not only in the loss of limbs, not only in the changes of the aging body, but in all the processes of elimination and purification that everything corpse-like falls away from the body piece by piece. (*Origins* 217–18)

"The destruction of the organic so that the true meaning, as it as written up and ordained, might be picked up from its fragments" (*Origins* 216)—that is what makes corpse-eating so valuable. In setting aside the symbol, the tragic drama interests itself in the body purified of the organic, as the dead thing it is when it enters its second, historical life. All this is well known. Less understood, however, is what Benjamin means in saying that a predilection for corpses is a consequence of the decision to give allegorizing "all its vigour," thus making energy key. He seems to say that there are degrees of energy in allegorizing and even that allegorizing is a matter of energizing a system: Corpse-eating short-circuits the fantasy of immortality and accelerates "life," defined here as the process of elimination Benjamin associates with history.[34]

In turning to *Un Mangeur* to consider Baudelaire's operations as translator on De Quincey's text, it seems right to think of them in terms of Benjaminian allegorizing. Translating is also a corpse-eating, with eating a figure for the linguistic act of bringing a foreign text into the inside space of a familiar language, and the worm living on the corpse a figure for the parasitical dependency of the translation. As we can surmise from various statements in "The Task of Translator," which emphasize translation's role in causing the original to rise "into a higher and purer linguistic air,"[35] it is moreover a corpse-eating that makes available a process begun in the original. Because the translator is concerned above all with representing the language of a text, and not the content of experience, the allegorical elements present in the first text come more quickly into view. The title of Baudelaire's translation, *Un Mangeur d'opium*, which represents the title of the original text, bears out the point by introducing a second referent in Baudelaire, as the eater responsible for divesting *The Confessions of an English Opium-Eater* of any residual nationalism or moralism. It is thus already an indicator of the *Un Mangeur*'s problematic originality. The struggle we saw enacted in De Quincey's new quarters between an ego under threat, attempting to conserve a decrepit power structure, and a transformative tendency is restaged in Baudelaire's text as the struggle within the translation between derivative, authority-conserving and inventive, authority-replacing aspects. The ground covered by such a conflict is very broad, including as it does both pragmatic translation decisions as well as more theoretical issues, among which the difference between allegory, "where history has physically merged into the setting," as Benjamin puts it, and allegorizing, where that merger is still in process. We will choose as our example Baudelaire's translation of the short passage just read in De Quincey as a convenient spot to center the problem, not only because Baudelaire makes a number of strong moves in rendering De Quincey, but also because the eating motif is an apposite place to study translation's effects on narrative economy.

First, however, it's worth recalling the paradoxical circumstances under which Baudelaire worked, where emerge several strategies for intervening in the economy of De Quincey's text. Baudelaire seems to have started with the idea of countering Musset's Romantic translation of *The Opium Confessions* with a version of his own, conceived like his Poe translations to respect the economy of the original, along the accepted idea that translation seeks to substitute a unit in one language for a unit in another in a one to one correspondence. Turned down by a first editor who apparently found the text too bizarre for French taste, Baudelaire then submitted the idea to Calonne, the director of *La Revue contemporaine*, who was willing to publish on condition that the poet provide a schematic summary, what the French call an *analyse*, of De Quincey's luxuriant and digressive prose. So instead of a translation respecting the economy of the original, that is what Baudelaire undertook, a summary, which would by definition obey a different, and presumably more "French" discursive economy—in brief, more Cartesian in its organization and concision.[36] The digest also pays homage to De Quincey's method of making excisions and digressive additions to Rousseauian-style autobiography, in keeping with the English suspicion of "spurious sentimentality" and preference for "decent drapery" (*OE* 1).

One important consequence of Baudelaire's procedure is what it did to the text's autobiographical dimension. In a typical translation of an autobiography, the first-person discourse of the original is represented by a first-person discourse in the target language, with the consequence that the relation of the translating, parasitical voice to the original voice is fixed. With a digest in mind, however, Baudelaire could not make use of the first-person because to do so would be to make the lying claim that he was translating De Quincey according to the ideal of a word for word translation. Instead, he introduces an omniscient narrator in charge of the summary, with the effect that the text's confessional force disappears and that he is free to reorganize the material and adopt the shifting perspectives that are typical of a third-person narrative. As one consequence, the material in De Quincey's story appears entirely disconnected from the present and utterly unresistant to allegorization, thereby resolving De Quincey's incomplete break with fantasies of incorporation. Benveniste says of the historical past used by the historian, that "truly, there is no longer even a narrator. Events are posed as they are produced, in the process of appearing on the horizon of history. No one is speaking here; events seem to tell themselves."[37] That is the case here. In Baudelaire's text, the De Quinceyan narrator is no longer with us: Events appear in their historical light, and *Un Mangeur* represents how De Quincey's life and dreams were already written—that is, how they were worded, but also how each event was foreordained and allegorical.

Into this third-person plot summary, Baudelaire has occasionally inserted first-person passages translated *tel quel* from the English, respecting the economy of the original. They are perhaps meant to provide a taste of De Quinceyan subjectivity, but again, it is of the subject allegorized for they have the status of museum pieces, bits of Romantic rhetoric drenched in formaldehyde, surrounded as they are by quotation marks. Baudelaire's procedure can be considered to complete that of the summary in terms of remembering De Quincey. He sorts and shares a literary inheritance, separating what is mannered (*AP* 82; *OC* I, 447), dead—the Romantic voice, the original's florid style—from the subject as undergoing allegorizing, which is a trait that lets De Quincey's text reverberate still in the modern French context. Although the excisions divest the original of its confessional armature and make its allegorical dimension accessible, they also bring up for discussion the taste of the French reading public and Baudelaire's competence as French digester of the English digester of Rousseau.

To make the transitions between summary and translation less awkward and to start fleshing out this portrait of the French reader, the translator introduced a first-person discourse of his own. These transitions are elongating, and are another instance of the transformations made with the economy of the original that respect its digressiveness. In the interstices between summary and translation, Baudelaire interjects confessional comments concerning his procedures like: "I will, I shall venture to say, summarize extensively" (*AP* 79; *OC* I, 444), "I could not bring myself to abridge" (*AP* 82; *OC* I, 447), "I cannot help but give the floor to the author himself" (*AP* 106; *OC* I, 468), "I can honestly state that" (*AP* 130; *OC* I, 490) [*j'avouerai franchement que*], "I rely on his text" (*AP* 131; *OC* I, 491), and so on. The interruptive first-person with its subjective slant once introduced, it proved unmanageable. Or so we may infer from its effect on the summaries, which often swell with insertions that a careful reading easily attributes to Baudelaire and that express the wishes, judgments, and obligations of the translator. When the third-person impersonal style resonates with a personal meditation and plot summary is suddenly distorted by the translator's self-statement, we are faced with the diffuse and fragmented subjectivity associated with Flaubertian free indirect style.

In these strategies of elongation, Baudelaire may seem to be primarily occupied with portraying himself. Yet, his confessions concern acts and obligations related to his parasitical existence on De Quincey's corpse, and as such, belong with the translation that initiates the text's second life. Indeed, Baudelaire several times offers himself up as the continuator of the original, continuator it needed because it was open ended in principle, just as the history of substitutions it considers is unfinished.[38] Baudelaire's additions are thus undertaken in the spirit of De Quincey, and can be thought as extensions of the latter's ethical allegories to encompass the reader-translator. They are comparable with the periphrases by which a translator is forced to render expressions for which there is no equivalent of similar economy in the translating tongue. Both the summarizing and elongating aspects, while no doubt more pronounced in Baudelaire's text than is usual, may be considered as the extremes between which any translation moves as it struggles to achieve the ideal of a one to one correspondence.

Viewed as an autobiography of the translator, *Un Mangeur* strips away the seductions of the De Quinceyan confessional subject to bring out the allegorical dimension more quickly. It then replaces the lost subject and story by the abbreviated confessions of the translator, who consequently appears as the legitimate inheritor of the first text. De Quincey's corpse feeds Baudelaire's emergent subject, and if the latter uses De Quincey's procedures of foreshortening and distending on De Quincey, it is to write the story of that emergent filial subject. The second text bears a resemblance to the first in the peculiar mix of self-symbolizing and allegory, of summary and elongation. It is not so new as to challenge the line of intergenerational transmission—differences of taste, time and context notwithstanding.

However, the description just provided of Baudelaire's procedures is inadequate to establish his inventiveness. To the extent that the methods Baudelaire uses are methods he has learned from De Quincey, they locate a command in the other's corpse, in a source-text as authority to which the translator owes fidelity. The translator in effect holds fast to an orthodox belief in the power of the original to determine the translation, in a command to translate (*"Il faut bien manger"*) sourced in the original. With translation, Baudelaire apparently attaches himself to a crumbling ego ideal he is occupied with maintaining. Because it is by De Quincey's strategies of distension and foreshortening that Baudelaire maintains his dependency, to show his text to be inventive, we have to show that he has transformed those economizing strategies.

With the context sketched within which Baudelaire's version of De Quincey's passage on starvation appears, we can now proceed to ask whether Baudelaire has indeed practiced translation according to a model set down in his source or, breaking radically with his author, has, as he puts it in similar circumstances, "made something . . . singularly different" (*OC* I, 276). Here is the English of Baudelaire's French version:

> In the midst of this desolation, however, there lived a poor little girl, not an idiot, but more than simple, certainly not pretty and about ten years old, unless the hunger that gnawed at her had prematurely aged her face. Whether she was simply a servant or the natural daughter of the man in question the author never learned. This poor abandoned child was very happy when she learned that she would henceforth have a companion during the dark hours of the night. The house was vast, and the absence of furniture and of wall-hangings made it more sonorous: the swarming rats filled the rooms and stairs with noise. In the midst of her physical sufferings of cold and hunger, the unhappy child had created for herself an imaginary ill: she was afraid of ghosts. The young man promised to protect her against them and, he adds rather humorously, *"that was the only aid I could offer her."* These two poor beings, thin, starving, freezing, slept on the floor with bundles of law papers for a pillow, without any other covering than an old horseman's cloak. Later, however, they discovered in the attic an old

sofa cover, a small piece of rug, and several other articles of clothing that gave them a bit more warmth. The poor child huddled together with him to keep warm and secure from her enemies from the other world. When he was no more than usually ill, he took her into his arms and the child, warmed by this fraternal contact, often slept while he could not. For during his last two months of suffering, he slept a lot during the day, or rather, he fell into sudden dozing; bad sleep haunted by tumultuous dreams; ceaselessly he woke up and ceaselessly he went back to sleep, pain and anguish violently interrupting his sleep, and exhaustion bringing it back. *What man of nervous temperament does not know this dog sleep, as the English language, in its elliptical energy, puts it? For moral pain produces effects analogous to those of physical sufferings like hunger. One hears oneself moaning; one is sometimes awoken by one's own voice; the stomach grows hollow and contracts like a sponge squeezed by a vigorous hand; convulsively the diaphragm constricts and rises; the breath grows short and anguish increases until, finding a remedy in the very intensity of pain, human nature explodes with a great cry and a bodily spasm that brings at last a violent deliverance.* (AP 89–90; OC I, 453–4, my emphasis)

Baudelaire has made the normal decisions of word choice and organization that are imposed by his task, all of which would be evident in a point-by-point comparison of the passage to the original.[39] But more important transformations interfere with De Quincey's narrative economy and possibly break with his program, never mind compromising Baudelaire's declared object of writing a less-digressive text.[40] Consider as an instance of Baudelaire's bizarre economizing the fact that, despite deep cuts in De Quincey's description of his broken sleep, the French passage contains 431 words and occupies 34 lines on a manuscript page, compared with the 453 words and 32 lines of the English—hardly a clear reduction. Let's look at the first of three significant instances of Baudelairian elongation, found in a sentence translated from the original and inserted in the summary with a bridging commentary: "The young man promised to protect her against them and, he adds rather humorously, *that was the only aid I could offer her.*" (*Le jeune homme lui promit de la protéger contre eux, et, ajoute-t-il assez drôlement, c'était tout le secours que je pouvais lui offrir.*)

The quoted sentence is an example of heightened allegorizing. It focuses the scene around the problems posed for a reader by what Baudelaire rightly identifies in his inserted comment as an aside. What did De Quincey mean by his witty addition to his sincere promise? Was he laughing at the irony of trying to save a starving child by providing her metaphysical reassurance? Was his point that his promise was useless because the ghosts plaguing the child were resident in the patriarchal laws that made her a pariah? Was he laughing sardonically at the thought that the promise of protection would entail taking the ghosts into his own body? The move sidelines the ethical pathos of the original scene, with its focus on charity and the promise, and makes the extraneous comment into the key. It is informative with respect to De Quincey, and, in a subsidiary way, to the translator. De Quincey's shift from fantasies of patriarchal power to a diffuse and self-directed irony signals that he has made himself a reader of his own text, as it were, already an inhabitant of the "Blue-beard room" of the study, and it is around that reader that Baudelaire unerringly recenters and elongates the translation. The added phrase serves Baudelaire's purpose of speeding up allegorizing De Quincey in keeping with the latter's "wishes." Because he sets the reader at the scene's center so quickly, Baudelaire does not need to explore the study as the source of ghosts and can cut that part of De Quincey's discussion.

In a second example of elongation, found in the part of the passage where we saw De Quincey struggling with defensive fantasies, the situation is made to cover the translator by means of some judicious additions. The example is provided by a comment on an English expression:

> What man of excitable and sensitive temperament has never known this dog-sleep, as the English language in its elliptical energy terms it? [*Quel est l'homme nerveux qui ne connaît pas ce sommeil de chien, comme dit la langue anglaise dans son elliptique énergie?*] For moral pain produces effects analogous to those of physical suffering like hunger.

The apotropaic maneuvers of incorporation we saw in De Quincey are at work in Baudelaire's version, where an anxiety can be heard in the comment on the wonders of English. The anxiety concerns the hypothesis that it is possible to bring a text into a target language without loss or excess so as to make the body of the one equivalent to that of the other. That hypothesis informs Baudelaire's admiration of the energetically elliptical English compound (dog-sleep) and his implicit judgment of slackness in the French prepositional phrase (*sommeil de chien*) that translates the same idea. The one for one equivalency between source and translation is endangered by the differing grammars and orthographic systems of the two languages, as exemplified in the extra word and letters of the French expression. Of course, the difference is minimal in a sense, and one would hardly expect even an editor demanding succinctness to reproach Baudelaire for an excess owed to standard French grammar and orthography. But it is not small in another, in that it concentrates at least two anxieties. In the first place, there is the fear that the exigencies of the French language system might determine the text's economy, and not the translator.

And then there are the fears of the post-Waterloo speaker of French concerning the relative health of the two nations as exemplified in the relative "energy" of their respective languages.[41] Baudelaire compounds things by adding a further sentence stating that moral suffering produces effects in the body that are similar to those of physical pain. That statement doesn't just give resonance to De Quincey's tormented physical twitches as an allegory for moral sufferings, now extended to cover anxious translators who lie awake worrying over the word *dog-sleep*. It also works as a statement of belief that the shrinkage or extension produced in the body of a prior text by grammar or spelling is expressive of the national genius of the translating language. In short, the passage partially reveals and partially wards off an anxiety concerning the mechanical aspect of language production, with the means of defense again an incorporation, exemplified in the understanding of English compound terms as manifestations of a lively English spirit. It is thus entirely fair to say that Baudelaire is indeed continuing in the wake of De Quincey, as he internalizes the consequences for translation of De Quincey's suffering. The idea of a genius to the language that can be divined from the operations of grammar is the "ghost" raised in the original that continues to haunt the translation.

The comment on the compound term has the second effect of suggesting that Baudelaire has identified as the particular strategy that De Quincey has used to energize English the technique of the compound term. Baudelaire's own compound—the text that mixes his bones with De Quincey's—can be understood as theorized in this aside, which then seems less an indication of anxiety than a gage of a successful struggle on Baudelaire's part to render De Quincey's compound in a French equivalent.

So far we have seen Baudelaire completing and extending the *Confessions* according to commands sourced in that text that let him express his own fantasy as faithful translator. He seems to have reached a convenient resting point in this particular passage: He has done what he needs to do to render De Quincey and make the latter's story echo in the translator's own situation; now his duty of succinctness suggests he should stop. Why then expand the sequence by a last long sentence, almost entirely Baudelaire's own? In that final sentence, we're going to have to ask about Baudelaire's idea of poetic invention and confront his cuts and elongations more directly, in terms of the amalgam.[42] Here it is again, along with the French:

> One hears oneself moaning; one is sometimes awoken by one's own voice; the stomach grows hollow and contracts like a sponge squeezed by a vigorous hand; convulsively the diaphragm constricts and rises; the breath grows

short and anguish increases until, finding a remedy in the very intensity of
pain, human nature explodes with a great cry and a bodily spasm that brings
at last a violent deliverance.

> [*On s'entend soi-même gémir; on est quelquefois réveillé par sa propre voix;
> l'estomac va se creusant sans cesse et se contractant comme une éponge opprimée
> par une main vigoureuse; le diaphragme se rétrécit et se soulève; la respiration
> manque, et l'angoisse va toujours croissant jusqu'à ce que, trouvant un remède
> dans l'intensité même de la douleur, la nature humaine fasse explosion dans un
> grand cri et dans un bondissement de tout le corps qui amène enfin une violent
> délivrance.*]

Signs of invention are present throughout. The point of departure of
the expansion, Baudelaire's translation of De Quincey's "my own voice"
by *sa propre voix*, is one. The invention lies in a twist Baudelaire gives the
by now-mechanical operation of transposing De Quincey's first-person
discourse into the indirect discourse of the third-person when he makes
sa depend not upon the third-person singular masculine pronoun *il* (he,
presumably De Quincey) but on *on* (one), a pronoun which in French
regularly replaces first- and second-person cases. The one awakened by
the sound of his own voice, in short, is quite plausibly the translator—and
that precisely despite the fact that as parasitical instance a translation is
not supposed to possess an "own" voice. The self-reflective turn of his
text goes along with an accumulation of characteristically Baudelairian
terms, among which "cry" and "explosion," both absent from De
Quincey—as though Baudelaire had suddenly realized that the translation were reverberating with his own poetic vocabulary. They thus indicate the translator reflective about the status of this translation among
his works. Waking or sleeping to hear "one's own voice," Baudelaire
enters a creative laboratory.

What are the implications of the scene for De Quincey's narrative
economy, and in what way does the emergence of a self-reflective poet on
the scene represent a significant mutation in the mode of meaning? To put
the question another way: Has Baudelaire introjected the text he is mourning here, transforming it in some fundamental way? A change in the way
the passage understands internalization can start to answer these questions. In De Quincey, the subject's sufferings are related to the stomach's
unfinished toil of digestion, to its inability either to give up incorporating
others or to cease tormenting itself that it is eating badly by engaging in
it.[43] But Baudelaire's vocabulary transforms the figure. *Creuser*, to "hollow
out," from *l'estomac va se creusant*, is a favorite Baudelairian word that

comes spontaneously to his pen wherever graves are being dug. In "L'en-nemi," for instance, "water hollows out [*creuse*] great holes like tombs" (*OC* I, 16); and in "Le mort joyeux," a skeleton sings: "I want to hollow out [*creuser*] a deep grave / Where I can spread out my old bones at lei-sure" (*OC* I, 70). De Quincey's critical relation to fantasy is accelerated and carried forward to its conclusion. Baudelaire refigures the stomach as grave-digger and crypt where is laid to rest the late stomach of De Quincey, as seat of the incorporative fantasies that kept narrative going. Similarly, the wrung-out sponge, reminiscent of the withered orange squeezed in "Au lecteur," figures a last-ditch effort to press meaning from a drying-up source, in a further indication that Baudelaire is using up the original and its dominant metaphor. These allegories are possible only because Baudelaire has cast himself forward to the end of the history con-ditioned by the stomach. His claim that the destruction of human nature will result from the stomach's activity (*jusqu'à ce que la nature humaine fasse explosion dans un grand cri . . . qui amène une violente délivrance*) bears that out. What lets him abridge the stages of suffering—in De Quincey and in human history in general—is a prolepsis or anticipation.[44] Unlike earlier cuts, each of which only momentarily disrupted the flow of De Quincey's narrative, Baudelaire's apocalyptic prolepsis goes straight to the end; it draws an internal line in the text that says that all narratives of suffering nature are over and from here on, the problem will be of what comes after. Anticipation is elliptical; it leaves out every moment intervening between now, the moment of revelation, and the end, to persuade that the an-nouncement is the end predicted: As the song has it, that "this is the end."

The prolepsis differs in another way from De Quincey's foreshortening techniques because it also acts to provide for endless elongation. To un-derstand this, it helps to consider that Baudelaire's added sentence can be read very differently, although still in a way that breaks significantly with De Quincey's text. We have only to consider the signs of increased vitality, be it in the assertion that the stomach lives by digging graves—one way to understand the expression *va se creusant*—or in the epithet of "vigorous" describing the active hand as it works the sponge. By the end of the pas-sage, absurdly, the stomach is about to become the site of a "delivery" (*délivrance*). If the belly has been suffering, it will have been from labor pangs. Nor is that emerging model treated unambiguously, for it is quite possible to understand the passage to be asserting not nature's demise but its triumph: *La nature humaine fa(it) explosion dans un grand cri et un bondis-sement de tout le corps* may be translated as "human nature explodes into, emerges into a great cry and a leap of the whole body." Now Baudelaire would be asserting not our transcendence of natural appetite but our *delivery* from a relatively circumscribed fantasy about human nature into more pervasive and disseminated fantasies, where the entire body comes into view as consumer. It is as though the single stomach had exploded into many stomachs, each attached to a different sense, with the body electrified by becoming the site of multiple appetites. This emergence of a more diffuse ideal of the stomach as authority to which to attribute commands is not necessarily a matter for celebration. Baudelaire is always willing to suspect that the leaps of historical process might as easily be relapses as moves forward: "universal ruin or universal progress, for the name matters little to me" (*OC* I, 666), he says in one important fragment of *Fusées*. In the reading proposed here, Baudelaire anticipates that De Quincey will have been anticipatory. Baudelaire's prolepsis exhumes the past otherwise, as a forecast of the explosion of hungers associated with capitalist consumerism. In this, Baudelaire's anticipation prolongs the life of De Quincey's master metaphor past the limit accorded it in De Quincey to give it a problematic contemporaneity with modern France. It makes as much sense to say that the prolepsis defers indefinitely the encounter with the limit, now become multiple, as it does to say that it reveals the end as imminent.

Baudelaire has incontestably transformed De Quincey's eating scene by staging it as a scene of burial and birth. He has precipitated the outcomes of the double command *"Il faut bien manger"* as it concerns history. "The world is going to end" (*OC* I, 665), he tells us in the *Fusées* fragment, and here, it is the how of that apocalyptic ending that he is considering. He can do that only because he has positioned himself outside the history of the natural stomach, considering it from the allegorist's perspective of what it will have meant. On the one side, he has cast himself forward past the end of the world dominated by appetite to consider our deliverance from notions of nature and our entrance into a time of eating well that Samuel Kramer and his adored La Fanfarlo typify in their dream of subordinating the organic process of digestion itself to the codes of love:

> It is to be deplored that the chefs of today are not constrained by a special voluptuary law to know the chemical properties of materials and obliged to discover where necessary, as for a love feast, culinary elements that are almost inflammable, quick to run through the organic system like prussic acid, to vaporize like ether. (*OC* I, 575)

The couple defines eating well as the project of destroying the organic system, and with it, the ideal of the unitary ego. The annihilation of the human race in the name of love is the outcome of carrying the command to eat well to its conclusion. On the other side, the prolepsis treats the future as a time already with us, a time dominated by the incorporating stomach, where there will be no remainders and no eating well, but only narcissistic consumers everywhere. This involves a fallen future where we return, as Baudelaire says in the *Fusées* fragment, not to a nature where "we will go looking, gun in hand, through the grassy ruins of our civilization for our feed" (*OC* I, 665), but to one better assorted to our modern day, a nature where bourgeois capitalism dominates, and everyone can be treated the same because everyone has been converted by capitalism into a consumable commodity (*OC* I, 665–6). *Americanization* is the term he gives to the new idea of "nature:" a dystopic future where animal appetites, wolves in the bonnets of bourgeois grandmothers, rule.

The two futures concerning the explosion of human nature at first appear quite different. Considered more closely, however, they have become indistinct: Both are written from the outside perspective of a survivor; both head inexorably to the same point of annihilation. If the aim is the destruction of humanity, one may prefer the flames of desire to askesis, but—as Frost tersely put it in similar dilemma—"ice / Is also great, / And would suffice." What this means in terms of the question of how to calculate with "*Il faut bien manger*" is first that any solution that reads the aporetic command as a choice between two possibles is a false solution. Viewed from the endpoint, where the subject and the other with which it eats have become contemporaries, eating well collapses into eating anyway; swallowing prussic acid in the name of love or devouring everything in sight both lead to the annihilation of the human, the sacrifice of the process for the sake of the outcome. In short, each solution entails a one-sided destruction of the other with whom to eat, which is not—in Baudelaire's last analysis—the other as animal or God or fellow-consumer, but the other as the human to come, and subjectivity as an ongoing project.[45] In a sense, then, Baudelaire's apocalyptic view of the stomach shows that the project of eating well as the project of giving, offering, leaving the other to eat, will have always been being bypassed in the present by the calculations of the appropriative subject, with its taste for the infinite, its corresponding bestiality and its neglect of its own historical character.

What to do if the project is not annihilation but survival, how to choose in view of the leftover, in view of starting at last to learn to eat well? Baudelaire's text constitutes a response to the dilemma it proposes. It chooses to delay the end it anticipates by relaunching the aporia of the impossible obligations within which the subject must negotiate with the other. For all the codes for eating well are not stored up in the lawyer's study, ready for the reading. They lie ahead, are still be written. *"Il faut bien manger"* means just what it says, "there is absolutely lacking good eating," which is why it is so necessary to write: The rules for eating well are still to come, laws still need to supply the framework so that eating well might at last be undertaken. To write them is to observe them in that it is to offer the chance for survival, to leave the other to come the where-withal for decisive calculations. Here the double value of Baudelaire's amalgamating prolepsis becomes apparent: To anticipate is to provide speedily, at the outset, an allegory of the stomach as crypt that sums up and renders past a process; at the same time, a prolepsis is a beginning like any other, and it delays the end of the process by opening an interstitial narrative within an already written history. There is an odd open-endedness as to where De Quincey's narrative is going under Baudelaire's pen. That can only be because Baudelaire has translated it into French in a way that does not simply produce on French the estranging effect De Quincey has on English, but does so through an inventive transformation in the economizing means. Whereas De Quincey uses foreshortening and distending as part of a strategy that lets him replace a discredited authority by another, for Baudelaire, prolepsis is the control dial of the historical process, and how we read it a means to accelerate or delay.

Baudelaire's text is not structured as an opposition between eating anyway (as with an animal) and well (as with a God) because from the end point, both come down to the same thing. Rather, it is structured in terms of the open question as to whether it is translating (that is, assimilating a text already written to a present context) or rather, rewriting (that is, encrypting an old fantasy through a new figuration that supplies the codes for subjectivity to come). It is structured by a set of procedures for economizing that learns everything from De Quincey except what could not be predicted: that is, the amalgam of opposing narrative tendencies in a same prolepsis. If we consider Baudelaire's sentence on the explosion of human nature in the light of this understanding, not as meaning the destruction of desire or its apotheosis but rather in the cryptic, enigmatic, and untranslatable aspect it would wear for his future translator, we could say that it looks like a reconfiguring of its dilemma for that subject to come, as the aporia with which it will calculate. The importance of the passage about human nature is that in yoking more than one future in an energetic compound of his own manufacture, Baudelaire's text actively cries out to the other to come for the decisive intervention of a translator. It calls out to the translator to say what he cannot: "how big a dose of my personality I have introduced into the original author is what I am presently unable to say" (*OC* I, 669).

Now the transformations that Baudelaire has wrought in the passage by forging anticipation into a strategy that abridges and elongates have consequences for the larger narrative of *Un Mangeur* and how we are to read it. If we step back from the passage to consider its place in the larger sequence of the lawyer's house, it becomes evident that Baudelaire's section on the encrypting-inventing stomach has a critical role. It has an effect on the literal economy of the text, lengthening the story of the hungry, dispossessed children while making most of De Quincey's description of the Blue-beard room superfluous since the stomach is now a figure for reading and writing. It also has an effect on the economy in a figurative sense because the childhood scene now has reverberations that it did not have in the original. Stepping back even further to survey the economy of the whole of *Un Mangeur*, we can conjecture that such cryptic passages allow Baudelaire to shorten dramatically the dream sequences, particularly those of the *Suspiria de Profundis*.[46] What need to describe dreams in a narrative including passages so hieroglyphical, written anecdotes more prophetic than the dream sequences themselves? The obscure anecdotes from childhood are the passages that the later dreams revisit to try to unpack.[47] Where a narrative of childhood proves more riddling than the language of a dream, we are in a transformed aesthetic landscape, in which the collapse of the distinction between poetic and prosaic language can also be detected.[48]

With the prolepses Baudelaire practices on De Quincey, more is at stake than aesthetics or the translator's desire to echo in his own language the effect of the original. It is a matter of writing the laws of eating well and anyway as a project ahead. Through prolepsis—among others, the prolepsis that sets a translation before an original—leaving a remains for the other becomes with Baudelaire the condition on which eating anyway, the future of subjectivity, depends. Anticipation thus throws the process of interiorization open for work, and so effectuates a delay in the end it predicts. It is in the transformations in the economy of narrative, in the amalgam that does not know the extent to which it is a translation or an invention, in the transformation of the means of saying to affect the speed of access to the conditions of eating that Baudelaire inaugurates.

In following out the various calculations made with the command "*Il faut bien manger,*" as represented in and by the two parts of *Les Paradis*, our long analysis has had to change focus, from a discussion of the forms and methods adopted in calculating with the eating command, to an examination of its source and authority. The shift corresponded to a shift from the natural dreams of hashish, which mirror the subject's failed self-transcendence and its collapse into animality, to the hieroglyphic dreams of opium, where the I is found to hold secret within itself, a noncontemporaneity with itself, an alterity that constitutes an important reserve for subjectivity. Irony and allegory act differently on autobiographical narrative to represent the feast it leaves for the other. With irony, narrative is the target of critique as the linguistic equivalent of the organ of digestion through which the self-satisfied subject processes everything. The problem is to seize the instant as the chance for self-doubling, to leave a second thought exorbitant to and interruptive of narrative. As for allegory, which returns to narrative as a dead form it must introject to regenerate, it gives history as an open, unfinished process in which the problem is whether we are following blindly the commands of the past, or whether its lessons rather constitute chances for further transformations in subjectivity.

In the case of both figures, however, we have to speak of a seismic shift in the way of conceiving what autobiographical narrative is about with Baudelaire, be it in terms of irony's rapid, punctual collapses and redoublings, or in allegory's more deliberate crumbling of figures once deemed authoritative. The effects on what autobiographical narrative looks like are profound—with irony's disruption and fragmentation, with allegory's foreshortening and distension. But more critical still is the effect on the way we are being asked to read autobiography. What Baudelaire does for us is identify the autobiographer's primary responsibility as to calculate with the incalculability of *"il faut bien manger"* in view of the other. The struggle to meet this responsibility is undertaken in autobiography as the privileged place where the subject learns of the other encrypted within it through allegory and irony. It seems that, where the other and the subject are not conceived as coexisting in a struggle over resources, but stand in a relation to one another of noncontemporaneity, it becomes possible to read and write rules for internalization that do not end in annihilation. If one conceives of autobiography not as first and foremost a problem of self-identification through appropriation, but in its address to the other lost to the self in its constitutive act, one comes closest to what *"il faut bien manger"* might mean for the genre. That is what Derrida seems to indicate when he says, at first translatably enough, that, *"Il faut bien manger ne veut pas d'abord dire prendre et comprendre en soi"* (*One must eat well anyway does not mean first to take and understand in oneself*); and then untranslatably, *"mais apprendre et donner à manger, apprendre à donner à manger à l'autre"* (*but to teach [or learn] and give to eat, to learn to give the other to eat [or to teach the other to give to eat]*.)[49] The subordination of the project of subject formation—that is, of how one internalizes—to the question of teaching, learning, giving, transmission, and legacy—that is, of writing the laws of eating for the other to come—has been somewhat neglected in recent studies of autobiography. Yet autobiography's true ethico-political thrust—as distinct from its morality of good intentions and its modeling of future subjects—depends upon it. It is through the insistent ironic and allegorical dimensions of autobiography that we understand the other to be its fundamental and long-term priority.

CHAPTER 6

Secrets Can Be Murder: How to Write the Secret in *De Profundis*

The egoistic note is, of course, and has always been to me, the primal and ultimate note of modern art, but *to be an Egoist one must have an Ego.* It is not everyone who says 'I, I' who can enter into the Kingdom of Art.

WILDE, Letter to Alfred Douglas

Yes, autobiography is irresistible.

WILDE, *The Critic as Artist*

Sorting Secrets

De Profundis, Wilde's autobiographical letter, is motivated by a double silence, and with it, a double secret and a double responsibility that say much about Wilde's concept of the I in its relation to the other. As we shall see, these two silences, which bring us into the arena of autobiography yet also bar entrance to it because muteness threatens to make confession problematic, are divided over whether that relation is under the aegis of conditional or unconditional laws, repeating the same division found in the discussion of hospitality in De Quincey. There, I discussed the two cases in isolation; here, we will be looking ultimately to consider them together in Wilde's foray into "the egoistic note" he associates with modern art.[1] The discussion of hospitality in De Quincey touched briefly on violence, and more especially, murder as an underside of hospitality in both its forms. In this chapter, murder and violence—what Derrida calls in a book on the secret, "the giving of death"—will surface as an important connecting thread because the secrets that silence portends in Wilde are generally lurid. A content withheld may be a violent past deed: say, Dorian's murder of Basil Hallward in *The Picture of Dorian Gray*, the killing of Podgers in "Lord Arthur Saville's Crime," the unconfessed murders of the poisoner Thomas Wainewright, or the clandestine execution of the condemned man in the "Ballad." In each case, the secret consists in withholding knowledge of a violent death from others. But even the apparently anodyne secrets of the inhabitants of Wilde's late-Victorian drawing rooms entail violence through their performative force: To possess oneself of a secret is to turn language from a tool into a veil, to void words of their agreed-upon communicativeness, and to choose them with reference to maintaining power over the content. The secret keeper infringes upon the social space by hollowing out the message-bearing potential of language, creating pockets of silence in the public sharing of information, holding out the promise of something to be known by withholding it.

There is benefit in such secrecy. Through the establishing of a formal reserve, the subject symbolizes herself and her right to an intact privacy and freedom. She puts forward appearances, signifiers as masks, as just that. As D. A. Miller puts it, secrecy's "ultimate meaning lies in the subject's formal insistence that he is radically inaccessible to the culture that would otherwise entirely determine him."[2] One might think that the move to bring a secret out in the open would reclaim meaning for the social space. But paradoxically—and Wilde is nothing if not a miner of such paradoxes—the restoration is also felt as a violence because the individual subject symbolized by the secret appears violated when that secret is exposed. One cannot divulge a secret and restore meaning without also exposing the repressiveness of the accepted meaning system and the violence of society in having imposed it. In the dynamics of the secret, there is a pressure to keeping it, given that it is through its reserve that the subject has constituted itself. It is presumably in establishing and drawing upon just such a reserve that the autobiographer is involved in confessing.

One of the recent influential works treating the secret in Wilde, Eve Sedgwick's remarkable *Epistemology of the Closet*, goes far toward exploring such a social understanding.[3] Indeed, for Sedgwick, the closet is above all a social, cultural problem. With the homosexual closet, a cultural construction of gender identification is replaced by a sexual identification that captures the body as a free signifier open to new determinations, thereby transgressing "an entire cultural network of normative definitions."[4] It is worth looking at Sedgwick's argument in closer detail to uncover the stakes of the social account of the secret, as well as what, if anything, might be missing for an understanding of autobiographical discourse in *De Profundis* from such an account.

Her argument would bear looking into for its own sake. A groundbreaking account for Wilde studies, Sedgwick rejuvenated almost singlehandedly a field that was stuck in moral disapproval of Wilde's life or in belittling Wilde's work. In one of his *boutades*, Wilde said that he reserved his genius for his life and his talent for his work, and most critics before Sedgwick have tended to agree with him, judging his work brittle and stylishly superficial in its aestheticist pose.[5] But Sedgwick found the homosexual secret could provide a transition between the biographical Wilde and the fictional Dorian that unlocked a new dimension to the text: It was to the staging of the structure of the closet and a homosexual subject producing itself as such that both fictional character and real-life author were devoted.

The homosexual secret could link life to art because it was a secret that disclosed a knowledge that does not exist prior to its disclosure, while yet having an empirical equivalent through the fixing of the knowledge structure to sexual identity. In this sense, Sedgwick agrees with such historians of sexuality as Foucault who make homosexual identity—although not same sex relations—a relatively modern phenomenon.[6] Through her insistence on performativity, Sedgwick provides a hermeneutics in which the speaking subject stages as the disconcealment of a hitherto unknown form of the secret the audience recognizes as its own. The closet is not a prefabricated structure in which something is hidden away, but rather comes into existence by the act of withdrawing something from view. Through it, a situation presumed natural—heterosexual identity—is undone; and a second situation—the chosen homosexual identity signaled by the decisive resignifying—takes its place. Wilde's flamboyant life provides examples of such an emergence; so also do the secrets that recur throughout Wilde's work. This story among men can be seen as a situation prototypical for autobiography where the confessional subject constitutes itself the holder of a secret. As such, it may have something to confess to an authority, along the Augustinian model, because it has stolen power by appropriating and hiding knowledge. But it also has something to confess to another subject, a brother from whom it has kept the mechanism of its access to power secret.

For Sedgwick, the individual homosexual's proliferation of effects of style is the inventive side of the closet structure. A plethora of details, all of which serve to foreground appearance as such, announce a thing to be known. They point to an artifice injected at the level of nature, stiffening it into a pose.[7] Such a strategy brings out the freedom of the signifier against the conventional relation between sign and thing. As transgressive performatives, moreover, the gestures elevate the dandy-like subject above the crowd as the master of individuality itself, one who anticipates a meaning experience may not bring: "Ordinary people waited till life disclosed to them secrets, but to the few, to the elect, the mysteries of life were revealed before the veil was drawn away."[8]

Sedgwick comments that next to the creativity of producing a secret, the act of emerging from the closet in a confession is disappointingly blank and self contradictory. To tell the homosexual secret is to make the signifier, so powerful and infinitely suggestive of the individual's freedom when reserved, into a label attached to a set of beings sharing the same revealed secret; it is to flatten the secret into a content, emptying it of all meaning as act. In her shrewd analysis, the power flows to the original detainer; and if homosexual panic surfaces at disclosure, that is because in the disconcealment of the knowledge structure, as it catches more that one conforming face in its mirror, it disempowers the secret's sharers from self-elevation through similar acts of withholding. The identification of the individual detainer of the secret as a homosexual at the precise moment that uniformity shows up causes fear in the insecure onlooker, who, fascinated by the display of power over the signifying system, suddenly sees the identity form as encapsulating him. For Sedgwick, the closet structure contains "both the most generative and the most murderous plots of our culture" (*Epistemology* 90).[9]

The differences Sedgwick notes between the stylizing performatives of silence and spoken performatives notwithstanding, by understanding silence as a performative, she ultimately defines it as discourse; and more specifically, as part of a dialogue to be had in encounters with like subjects in the name of knowledge. It has been noted that the play of the signifier, while experienced as liberating with respect to the constraints of representation, in fact is powerfully stabilizing because it determines the knowable referent of all texts as language.[10] That appears to be the case here, with the subject becoming possessed of a determinate secret to which all its actions point. An example of this sort of secret would be the famous green carnation Wilde wore to the opening of *Lady Windermere's Fan*: The carnation signifies to others a secret which becomes, in Sedgwick's parlance, an open or empty secret, because the act of signaling a secret is sufficient to set into play the closet structure's "I know you know" structure of recognition among like subjects (*EC* 164).

We may wonder, however, whether silence is always to be understood as a moment in a discourse, and whether all secrets are knowable as contents by subjects. The subject's silence as designating the possession of a secret may be at odds, for instance, with another sort of silence: the sort we found exemplified in Rousseau, where the pressure to confess was felt as an outrage against the child's moral being. When Henry James, writing of Marcher in "The Beast in the Jungle," calls his secret "unspeakable," we can understand him to mean it is not a topic suitable for public discussion. However, we can equally well see James opposing speech to some other sort of language—writing, for example—where the problem is not the suitability of the topic for publicity but whether language is limited to the spoken utterance.[11] At the very least, the religious dimension to formulations such as the unspeakable, the unnameable, and so on suggests a need to consider the secret as defining the relations of the self to the absolute.[12] Silence and speech may indeed be conceived as belonging to the single "self-contradictory field of force" (*EC* 9) of knowledge and identity formation to which Sedgwick limits them. But according to another logic, incompatible with the first, silence is a caesura in discourse and it opens onto an ethico-religious logic where the secret is for the other with whom one does not share in a dialogue.

It is this possibility that Derrida addresses in the title essay of *Donner la mort*, in the context of a consideration of the history of the secret proposed by the Czech philosopher Jan Patočka. For Patočka, the heterodox Christian secret, unlike the Platonic secret, is not in the subject's keeping. It sets the I into a dissymmetrical relation to an other with whom no exchange is possible. It is ethical and religious in import and is not a matter of knowledge and stable identity:

> God sees me, he looks into me in secret, but I don't see him, I don't see him looking at me, even though he looks at me while facing me and not, like an analyst, from behind my back. Since I don't see him looking at me, I can, and must, only hear him. But most often I have to be led to hear or believe him [*on doit me le donner à entendre*], I hear tell what he says, through the voice of another, another other, a messenger, an angel, a prophet, a messiah or postman, a bearer of tidings, an evangelist, an intermediary who speaks between God and myself. There is no face-to-face exchange of looks [*pas de face-à-face et de regard échangé*] between God and myself, between the other and myself. God looks at me [*me regarde*] and I don't see him and it is on the basis of this gaze that singles me out [*ce regard qui me regarde*] that my responsibility comes into being. Thus is instituted or revealed the "it concerns me" or "it's my lookout" [*ça me regarde*] that leads me to say "it is my business, my affair, my responsibility. . . .
>
> It is dissymmetrical: this gaze [*ce regard*] that sees me without my seeing it looking at me. It knows my very secret even when I myself don't see it and even though the Socratic "Know yourself" seems to install the philosophical within the lure of reflexivity, in the disavowal of a secret that is always *for me alone*, that is to say *for the other*: *for me* who never sees anything

in it, and hence *for the other* alone to whom, through the dissymmetry, a secret is revealed. For the other my secret will no longer be a secret. (*GD* 91)

Derrida insists that I bear a secret that pertains to me without being available to me. This secret is not one I keep from others, who share a language and a discursive situation—or what Derrida calls, following Levinas, the "face to face." It is a dissymmetrical secret, one that I do not even know I have, to which I have no direct access and that I have to hear about from an intermediary. It is certainly not one I can perform for others because it is not a secret I know anything about, and is indeed not really "my" secret at all if the I is thought as a sovereign subject, possessor of a knowledge it is free to reveal or conceal. It is more mine (*mon propre secret*) than any of the secrets I might possess or come to possess, but only insofar as *ça me regarde* (it looks at or concerns me) without my ever having a chance of knowing it, insofar as it remains a secret for me but not for the other. Derrida links this secret to the possibility of my own language becoming unintelligible to me, to the gap between signifier and signified that lets my words show patterns unrelated to what I say, and thus to reveal a hidden interiority. We cannot conflate the dissymmetrical secret with the homosexual secret, which is a secret that captures signifiers to refer to a single content and limits the open-ended indefiniteness of a "secret that is always for me . . . who will never see into it." The passage from Derrida suggests this by the differentiation between God's facing gaze and the analyst's look "from behind my back," in the position Derrida identifies in *La Carte postale* with homosexuality.

The dissymetrical secret seems to make autobiography conceived as a project of genuine self-revelation impossible. How am I to reveal the secret that I am for the other, a secret that I do not detain, with which I cannot identify? Yet how can an autobiography worthy of the name *not* seek to speak about it as central for understanding the I and its responsibility? *Donner la mort* is a critical text for us in locating and exploring in Wilde's autobiography its address to a silence where identity and subjecthood are endangered. For Derrida sees responsibility, ethics, starting here, where the I ceases to be a responsible subject: that is, one capable of performing its subjectivity as the constitution and revelation of a defined secret for others:

> How can another see into me, into my most secret self, without my being able to see in there myself and without my being able to see him in me? And if my secret self, that which can be revealed one to the other, to the

wholly other, to God if you wish [*Dieu si l'on veut*], is a secret that I will
never reflect on, that I will never know or experience or possess as my own,
then what sense is there in saying that it is "my" secret, or in saying more
generally that a secret belongs, that it is proper to or *belongs* to some "one,"
or to some *other* who remains some*one*? It is perhaps there that we find the
secret of secrecy, namely, that it is not a matter of knowing and that it is
there for no-one. A secret doesn't belong, it can never be said to be at home
or in its place [*un secret n'appartient pas, il n'est jamais accordé à un "chez soi"*].
(*GD* 92)

This notion of a secret that doesn't belong to me or to any subject, that is
available only to the other, that is not to be found anywhere "at home,"
and that is not an object of epistemological inquiry, brings us into the
neighborhood of the absolutely other, of "God if you wish," and thus of
the question of religion.

There is a potential for viewing the I as bearer of a secret for God in
Wilde, where we often find the term secret given an ethico-religious va-
lence. His heterodox insistence—Oxford interest in Catholicism and
deathbed conversion notwithstanding—that "my Gods dwell in temples
made with hands, and within the circle of actual experience is my creed
made perfect and complete" warns us that if this second secret is religious,
it is to at any rate not to be thought of in terms of metaphysics.[13]

For first evidence of such a secret in Wilde and one that can moreover
provide a glimpse of its interest for Wildean autobiography, consider the
picture guarded so jealously by Dorian and called the "mirror of his soul"
(*PDG* 169) and "his conscience" (*PDG* 169). By hiding the picture, Dorian
has acted in defiance of an injunction from God, who has "called upon
men to confess their sins to earth as well as to heaven" (*PDG* 169). The
injunction to confess, as revealed by Dorian's sinful act of locking up the
picture, in fact involves two contradictory logics. With respect to the confession owed men, Dorian fails to be autobiographical enough: His holding secret the portrait that registers his sins is tantamount to a refusal to
reveal himself to other subjects to whom the truth is owed. But, with respect to God, the same action has to be thought as too autobiographical.
By hiding the picture, he has read it as if it belonged to him and as if the
dissymmetrical secret, which Wilde elsewhere calls "his very secret" (*DP*
109), could be located in a determinate place. To appropriate the picture
as a portrait is a sin against the very secret, which belongs nowhere and to
no one and which has to be promiscuously available to the first comer (*un
secret n'appartient pas, il n'est jamais accordé à un "chez soi"*). In reading the

picture as a self-portrait, he has reduced the very secret to a piece of information and sinned against the soul. There is an aporetic logic in the relation between secrecy and confession: Secrecy sins against the openness of
the very secret, which commands confession; the identificatory moves of
confession denature or silence the very secret they purport to reveal by
locating it and treating it as determinate.

The Crisis in Telling the Secrets That One Knows:
Letters to Reading Gaol

In the autobiographical letter *De Profundis*, Wilde is concerning himself
with these paradoxes even as he meditates, as from one literary man to
another, on the problem of how to write the secrets one knows. There, he
lays out a version of the distinction between the secrets an I possesses and
its secret for the other in terms of the violences attendant upon silence.
The "strange silence" (*DP* 23) of Wilde's intimate and lover Lord Alfred
Douglas, familiarly called "Bosie," is the focal point. It was on account of
this love relation that Wilde was put on trial and landed in prison, where
he was finishing up to two years' of hard labor at the moment the letter
was written. Among the rare correspondence he had been allowed to receive in prison, nothing had come from Bosie. *De Profundis* is an accusa-
tory letter, meant to incite Douglas to break a silence that Wilde finds
personally painful—"your silence has been horrible," he says (*DP* 54).

It is significant that *De Profundis* was written in prison, where Wilde
was, as the French say, *mis au secret*, locked up with a little group away
from human society, where communication with the outside and with
other prisoners was all but forbidden. Wilde was allowed to receive and to
write one letter per quarter, with each letter having to be read and cleared
by the Governor of the prison. The prisoner thus had to decide which of
the various letters sent him over the course of a three-month period he
was to read during his sentence and which others would keep their secrets
until his release (*DP* 54). Prison exacerbates the paradoxes and demands
of secrecy. In prison, it seems that there can be no more secrets and, con-
versely, that there are only secrets and secret-keeping. There are meant to
be no secrets of the discursive sort among the prisoners, each of whom has
been de-individualized so far as possible. "I myself had no name at all. In
the great prison where I was then incarcerated I was merely the figure and
letter of a little cell in a long gallery, one of a thousand lifeless numbers, as
of a thousand lifeless lives" (*DP* 42). Each wears a uniform, has a number,

accomplishes a uniform set of tasks, eats a uniform meal at a uniform time, and retires to rest at a designated hour, "each dreadful day in the very minutest detail like its brother" (*DP* 46). There are to be no dandified subjects wearing green carnations in Wandsworth Prison or Reading Gaol. And yet if there is a disappearance of discursive secrecy, one can also say that that is because with the prison there is a hyperbolical secrecy, with the prisoners themselves become the content held secret by state, which manifests its power by withholding them from exchanges and effectively locking them into immobilized attitudes of assent to its power and their own disempowerment. The writer of a letter to prison faces a crisis: how to write secrets to a beloved other where the letter has to pass under the eyes of the Governor and the love for that other is the reason for incarceration?[14] It is significant that Wilde should have chosen to solicit an autobiographical letter from Douglas so close to the end of his stay, in circumstances where frank confession does not appear possible and the barest hint of a mystery would presumably raise concern in the authorities. It is all the more significant because he seems to see the situation as a proving ground that will force him to make strides in writing and that might help the apprentice poet Douglas as well. An examination of *De Profundis* lets us investigate the crisis in secrecy insofar as it uncovers responsibilities and provides new possibilities for the writer.

When it finally reached him, Bosie did not answer Wilde's letter and indeed later claimed never to have received it.[15] Yet, one has to feel for the unhappy Douglas because at the same time that it calls for an autobiographical response, Wilde's letter will already have stepped in to take responsibility for the interlocutor, to answer in advance, to witness for his secret in his place, and therefore, violently, unpardonably to silence him anew. As in any system of exchange where substitution rules, Wilde's accusation of Bosie for his withdrawal can be quickly turned into an accusation against Wilde for his usurping of the interlocutor's position. This is established right away in the paragraph of address, where a strange formulation makes the decision to write a letter *to* Bosie all but synonymous with the reception of a letter *from* him:

> Dear Bosie, After long and fruitless waiting *I have determined to write to you myself*, as much for your sake as for mine, as I would not like to think that I had passed through two long years of imprisonment *without ever having received a single line from you*, or any news or message even, except such as gave me pain. (*DP* 3, my emphasis)

By writing to Bosie, as Wilde anticipates, he will have received a line from him, Bosie will have said what he would have said in response, even to the point that Wilde claims to have written Bosie's life story in his place: "You see that I have to write your life to you" (*DP* 35); "if you have read this letter as carefully as you should have done you have met yourself face to face" (*DP* 105). Part of what makes the letter so self-laceratingly terrible can be traced to its tendency to bring about the very situation of silence and abdication of responsibility it finds so painful. Not only are the charges so overwhelming as to make an adequate response difficult but also, should Bosie respond, he could only repeat the confessions Wilde has made for him. Through the performative, Wilde takes over the scene of language, which is the scene of responsibility in his text, and silences his lover by seemingly speaking his secret "for" him. The ethical implications of the act of assuming the I in discourse, implications discussed in earlier chapters in connection with Benveniste and Levinas, are worked out by Wilde in his relationship with Bosie. As I, as subject of discourse, he speaks for Bosie and for every subject; in doing so, he does violence to the other as subject, reducing all to silence by taking over the scene of language and responsibility. The usurping violence entailed by this mastering is very near the surface in *De Profundis* in the violence against the other as potential subject deprived of speech (*tu tu*) by the speaking I. It should be noted that Wilde is not interested in bringing Bosie to account only: The structure is specular; and in accusing Bosie of irresponsibility, Wilde calls himself to account for his own responsibility for the other to whom as for whom he speaks.

Richard Ellmann has rightly called *De Profundis* a love letter, however, and despite the panoply of strategies it deploys to reduce Bosie to an echo, an almost unbearable note of urgency and longing indicates another dimension to silence, also Levinasian, with implications for the very secret.[16] Even with all that Wilde has done to "[take] into account the silent recipient's supposed responses" (*DP* xi), as Ellmann puts it, the speaker still cannot explain "the secret of your strange silence" (*DP* 23): "What I must know from you is why you have never made any attempt to write to me" (*DP* 116). After 100 pages of hearing about Bosie's irresponsibility, we are right where we started, still waiting to hear the reasons for his non-responsiveness. In the end, no one but Bosie can answer for Bosie. This gap between Wilde's tortured attempt to anticipate Bosie's responses and his ultimate failure ever to speak for the other constitutes, as Ellmann says, an avowal of love. The other is loved as bearer of a secret that remains secret against all the I's proleptic thinking and discursive prowess. In Ellmann's reading, Bosie's silence has a function disparate to the exchanges of dialogue, as an index of the solitude of each one and of the infinitely unknowable and desirable very secret for which a given other stands, and which can only be read in the gap between what is said and what is meant that the silence represents.

Wilde's request for an answer to the letter is thus tantamount to a prayer that the other share the secret of its reserve as other with the I: "Remember that I have yet to know you" (*DP* 117). The secret of the other as defined here is his irreplaceability, what makes it that no one can respond for him. Wilde has much at stake in Bosie's silence. No one can speak for Bosie means also that no one can speak for Wilde. The intimation of the uniqueness of each one comes through the mediating silence or reserve of the other, which is not a matter of a determinate content withheld but of death anticipated through the sacrifice of discourse as the scene of subjective triumph.[17]

Wilde's letter thus has a double aim, in keeping with the aporia of the secret and responsibility Derrida discusses in *Donner la mort*. On the one side, Wilde wants to persuade Bosie to confess his secrets so as to resume their neo-Platonic dialogue in an atmosphere of openness; on the other hand, Wilde wants to bring him news of Patočka's heterodox Christian secret to inspire the neophyte writer to a similar effort. Recognized as well is a double obligation, taken up as such, with respect to the interlocutor's silence in *De Profundis*. On the one side, the other's silence must be respected because it is through a silence significant of the other's solitude that the news of irreplaceability emerges. On the other side, the other must be made to break his silence and to give his reasons because until he does, the I will be speaking for him, with the universality of the I's discourse silencing all other subjects, taking over the dialogue and eradicating the possibility of exchange. Responsibility and the secret play out between the two in a paradoxical injunction:

> Each must respond to the other and, addressing the other, explain himself as subject by making his secrets known, even at the price of taking over the scene of language and occupying it entirely so that the other cannot respond.
> Each one must respond for himself and for himself only, as before God, in the name of the irreplaceable uniqueness of each one.

Still to be considered, however, is the relationship between these injunctions and how to write them in a letter. Here, the lack of a letter from Bosie represents a particular problem. Is the missing letter the equivalent of a silence in an ongoing conversation? Is it rather a sign of a writer shrinking from dealing in the deeper silence that writing brings, and not

knowing how to manage his dissymmetrical secret without confessing it as
the secret of a forbidden love? Wilde investigates Bosie's unresponsiveness
as a means to get at the writer's responsibilities in saying the secrets one
knows, looking to Bosie's parents for the models from which the latter has
learned his bad writing habits.

One responsibility concerns the decision of when to write, given that
writing imports its nonresponsiveness into discourse. Consider the letters
of Lady Queensberry whose fault is to have written to Wilde when she
ought to have spoken to Bosie:

> Instead of speaking to you about your life, as a mother should, she always
> wrote privately to me with earnest, frightened entreaties not let you know
> that she was writing to me. You see the position in which I was placed
> between you and your mother. It was one as false, absurd, and as tragic as
> the one in which I was placed between you and your father. . . . All the
> underhand and secret communications with me were wrong. What was the
> use of our mother sending me endless little notes, marked "Private" on the
> envelope, begging me not to ask you so often to dinner, and not to give
> you any money, each note ending with an earnest postscript *"On no account
> let Alfred know that I have written to you"*? What good could there be from
> letters such as your mother used to send me, except that which did occur,
> a foolish and fatal shifting of the moral responsibility on to my shoulders?
> (*DP* 97–8)

Lady Queensberry writes when duty dictates that she speak her message
in a maternal discourse of counsel to her son. "The first duty of a mother
is not to be afraid of speaking to her son" (*DP* 98), and Lady Queensberry
has not only neglected that duty but has shifted responsibility for speaking
to the writer Wilde.[18] From the examples, we can deduce that writing where
speaking is an obligation falsifies intersubjective commerce: The mother's
intimate dialogue with her son takes place through an intermediary; Wilde's
love for Bosie is falsified by his role as parental counselor; their shared homosexual secret will be masked by the heterosexual secret introduced by the
private correspondence between a man and a woman; *De Profundis* itself is
ventriloquized, appearing as a parental discourse of admonishment. What
is more, Lady Queensberry traduces and trivializes the very secret whose
paraphernalia she adopts. Notice the indications of a simulated very secret:
Lady Queensberry fears an encounter with her son as Kierkegaard's Abraham trembles before the absolute; she chooses an intermediary to deliver
news of her wishes for Bosie's conduct; she writes postscripts recommending a supplementary secrecy where writing is concerned, as if to say that a
letter is more than a mere accessory. Although her actual dealings are with

a spoiled and wayward son, in Wilde's account, Lady Queensberry's way of writing treats them as dealings with a god. Where intersubjective communication is at stake, responsibility is a matter of choosing whether writing is the appropriate mode of communication.

The writer's responsibility is also to decide how to write. Lord Queensberry sets a bad example here. Bosie descends from violent stock: "Through your father, you come of a race, marriage with whom is horrible, friendship fatal, and that lays violent hands either on its own life or on the lives of others" (*DP* 25).[19] Bosie's threat of suicide (*DP* 17), even murder (*DP* 22), and his eldest brother's suspected suicide are of a piece with the particular irresponsibility with which the father's side of the family approaches letter writing. Consider the abusive letters and telegrams exchanged between Bosie and his father or sent to Wilde, as pawn in their struggle with one another. These letters are not simply full of terms that violate social codes; they also violate the reserve of letters by going public indiscriminately. Bosie and his father send telegrams and postcards without envelopes; they leave cards about in public places, and otherwise invite spectators in on their private affairs,[20] with a "passion for notoriety (that) was not merely individual but racial" (*DP* 34). Father and son delight in one-upping one another: The father sends a letter with a violent content ("with its obscene threats and violences" [*DP* 32]); the son answers with "a pert telegram" (*DP* 32) that bruits the quarrel. The father responds to the limited publicity of the telegram by public attacks, and the son ripostes by firing off a pistol in a public place. The course staked out is a spiraling increase of publicity:

> All you could think of (besides of course writing to him insulting letters and telegrams) was to buy a ridiculous pistol that goes off in the Berkeley under circumstances that create a worse scandal than ever came to *your* ears. . . . You scented the public scandal and flew to it. . . . You saw the immense opportunities afforded by the open postcard, and availed yourself of them to the full. (*DP* 33)

The genius of the male Queensberrys is to violate the border between public and private through an exploitation of the "immense opportunities" the letter provides as system of iterable marks for reaching beyond the single addressee to a broader public. To take the quarrel between Bosie and his father onto the stage, by way of the trials, was to play out a private dispute that

> should obviously have remained a question entirely between the two of you. It should have been carried on in a backyard. Your mistake was in

insisting on its being played as a tragic-comedy on a high stage in History, with the whole world as the audience, and myself as the prize for the victor in the contemptible contest. The fact that your father loathed you, and that you loathed your father was not a matter of any interest to the English public. Such feelings are very common in English domestic life and should be confined in the place they characterize: the home. Away from the home-circle they are quite out of place. To translate them is an offence. Family-life is not to be treated as a red flag to be flaunted in the streets, or a horn to be blown hoarsely on the house-tops. You took Domesticity out of its proper sphere, just as you took yourself out of your proper sphere. (*DP* 107)

The term "translation" that Wilde uses to characterize the male Queensberrys' acts of writing indicates that on the paternal side of the family writing substitutes for a previous text. The problem is not whether to write or speak but to find a method of translation adequate to its origi-nal (the sacred text of the *Old Testament* on which the father-son writings are modeled in *De Profundis*).[21] The translations offend as translations. What seems to make them so bad is their coarseness and unidirectionality. In every case, they glorify the act of writing while providing scandalous publicity to a single feature of the text, its ability to overreach or fall short of reaching its intended addressee. The Queensberrys believe themselves disengaged of responsibility to anything but the intentional act; the text itself need never reach its destination. The crypts of writing, its "strange silence," are lost in their translations.

   Although writing that refers to earlier writing is primarily concerned with the how, the how also involves a "when," a matter of timing with respect to the arrival of a text in a context. For Bosie and his father, letters arrive whenever and wherever they pitch up. The writer's responsibility ends with the act of sending them off, and they deliver their entire charge immediately. One anecdote Wilde recounts illustrates the difference be-tween the treatment Wilde and Bosie accord the timing of the secret's arrival. Bosie has sent a violent letter of abuse that arrives soon after the guests have gathered at a luxurious lunch that Bosie has requested Wilde to offer him. Wilde invents an excuse for Bosie's non-appearance and puts the letter in his pocket, to be read later. When, at last alone, he pulls the letter out, Bosie arrives with a request for advice and assistance, without any reference to the lunch he had missed or apology for the letter (*DP* 94–5). To Douglas, a letter is a bomb that explodes to divulge everything upon arrival. To Wilde, it can have more than one referent and need not arrive all at once; in the anecdote, he delays reception of the physical let-ter, secreting it in his pocket and hiding its contents with a fiction about its referent, "explain(ing) to your friends that you were suddenly taken ill, and that the rest of the letter referred to your symptoms" (*DP* 94–5). A letter may not reveal everything at once; after reading the entire letter, Wilde corrects his first metaphor by reflecting that Bosie's letters "were really like the froth and foam on the lips of an epileptic" (*DP* 95). Wilde does his authoring where the letter touches the context. A letter may be a self-referential fiction, but it will reverberate in a way that not only reveals and transforms something about the context where it arrives but that requires a new act of writing. Bosie's letters neglect the timing related to the secrecy of what is never at home: a timing internal to writing that goes off in little charges with delays and reserves in a reader the text has had to ready to receive it. Through his discussion of Bosie's father, Wilde defines the writer's responsibility to calculate with the incalculable—the speed of the letter's arrival, the accidents of its delivery, and the logic of its secrecy, which is always both to manifest and to carry reserves for the context in which it arrives.

Opposing explanations for Bosie's silence emerge from the discussion of his parents. Anyone writing to a prisoner must calculate with the conditions regulating the reception of letters. A letter sent to prison will receive no publicity beyond its two predetermined readers, each of whom will chew it over looking for suspicious utterances (the Governor) or messages of love (the prisoner); it can make no splash and get no immediate response. How is Bosie's father's son to write such a letter, which would have to have calculated with its reception ahead of time?

The protocols for sending a letter to a prisoner are regulated and demand openness. Wilde explains, it must be sent in an envelope addressed to "'The Governor, H. M. Prison, Reading.' Inside, in another, and an open envelope, place your own letter to me: if your paper is very thin do not write on both sides, as it makes it hard for others to read" (*DP* 116). The letter is not only to be as legible as possible, but must be written with "perfect freedom" (*DP* 116), "with full frankness" and "without fear;" it should contain nothing "false or counterfeit;" Bosie should not write what he doesn't mean (*DP* 117). It has to accept to be open, to obey rules; Douglas has to give up the idea of writing a letter where speech would be sufficient because with a prisoner, only letters are possible. It has to be a letter such as one trained by Lady Queensberry could not write.

The prison situation brings out quite graphically the writer's obligations through the failures of Bosie's parents to meet them: to write where writing is necessary because there is no other chance of access and to write calculating with the text's reception. Bosie's silence is partly a signal of his irresponsibility as a writer to the obligations of his craft, and Wilde's call for a response reads like a challenge from a teacher to a student writer to leave off his inherited writing practices to explore a new vein more attentive to the complexity and relativity of modern life (*DP* 50).

And yet, paradoxically, the assignment is made easy by prison rules. Bosie does not have to decide whether to write because only by writing can he reach the prisoner. He doesn't have to decide how to write, either. Not only are the mode and addressees prescribed in writing to prison, but an accident has made a calculation with the letter's reception inevitable: Any letter bearing the address of Reading Gaol, which is the condition of its reaching its literal destination, secretly talks about reading as reception. It will, therefore, send an allegorical message the Governor cannot stop; and in doing so, testify to a regard for the other addressed. The prison conditions that would keep a Queensberry son from writing to Wilde are, when seen from another perspective, the perfect conditions for an apprentice writer.

The analysis has established so far that Wilde does not construe the secret as content and the very secret along an oppositional logic, where one has to choose which of two modes is to be sacrificed. He hypothesizes that a same text can meet both the obligation to disclose hidden contents and to deliver a message to the loved other standing for the very secret. A letter from Bosie addressed to Reading Gaol would be a letter already resignified, Sedgwick's idea of the green carnation sent the reader-lover, even as it gives the censor-Governor to read a frank tale "about yourself: about your life: your friends: your occupations: your books (. . .) about your volume and its reception" (*DP* 117). The obligations to secrecy and openness in writing are not opposed but can be made to work together to smuggle a forbidden content into prison. Bosie's nonresponsiveness is that of an inexperienced writer missing a singular chance to meet those responsibilities, construed as responsibilities to another with whom one is in dialogue and who is starved for a discourse carrying through a detailed description of quotidian affairs, a private message of love and concern for its other as reader.

Telling Secrets One Doesn't Know: A Letter from Reading Gaol

But Wilde is not concerned only to educate a younger writer in how to write a love letter to a prisoner. *De Profundis* is also a meditation on how to write an autobiographical letter *from* Reading Gaol, complicated by several facts. In jail, there are no current doings to report; a letter sent out to the wider world, never mind to so negligent a recipient as Douglas, can have had few chances of being understood—besides, Wilde must be gloomy about the prospects of writing as a means of deliverance from a place with such a name. Critics of *De Profundis* have long been puzzled by a change in tone halfway through the letter, where the list of griefs against Bosie, already interrupted by an introspective turn that sets the burden for Wilde's ruined life "on my own shoulders" (*DP* 57), turns to a meditation on the religiously charged topics of consolation, humility, and sorrow.[22] In that section, too, silence and the writer's responsibility to the secret are addressed, but this time, Wilde manifests a skepticism concerning the value of articulate language to answer for the silence that isolates him: "I have grown tired of the articulate utterances of men and things. The Mystical in Life, the Mystical in Nature—this is what I am looking for, and in the great symphonies of Music, in the initiation of Sorrow, in the depths of the Sea I may find it" (*DP* 115). Here, silence is not indicative of withheld knowledge but of the gap earlier discussed between saying and meaning that allows for allegory. It may not even manifest itself as quiet but rather as inarticulateness in utterance. The aim is not to provide an explanatory account for the reasons for such silence, which could only transform it into a content, but an equivalent, what Baudelaire would have called a "correspondance," in one's own language. The "mystical" is a name for that gap and Wilde lists a set of equivalences for it—music, sorrow, and the sea.

A letter from July 1896 in which Wilde despairs of finding a literary solution for a prisoner's silence lays out the dimensions of the difficulty. In that letter, sent to the Home Secretary in unsuccessful appeal for the commutation of his sentence on the grounds of ill health, he speaks of being "condemned to absolute silence" (*CL* 658). Absolute silence is characterized as "this solitude, this isolation from all human and humane influences, this tomb for those who are not yet dead" (*CL* 658). Given the radical nature of absolute silence, the idea that allegory might reconcile the divergent demands of openness and secrecy is beside the point. Absolute silence is not a moment preceding speech but a dumbness indicating a violent deprivation, comparable to the premature encrypting of the living. Wilde's health concerns—in the letter he mentions madness, erotomania, deafness, and blindness—all indicate the disarticulating fragmentation of the body under the pressure of this silence. Literature is an important part of the problem of privation: "horrible as all the physical privations of

modern prison life are, they are as nothing compared to the entire privation of literature to one to whom Literature was once the first thing of
life, the mode by which perfection could be realized, by which, and by
which alone, the intellect could feel itself alive" (*CL* 657). Beyond the loss
of books and paper, Wilde mourns the loss of an ideal of Literature, a
Greek aesthetics in which beauty is defined as the form adequate to an
idea and acknowledged as the ideal best suited to the life of the mind.
The deprivation of this aesthetic ideal means Wilde will have to enlarge
Literature's scope in his letter to respond for an early descent into the
tomb.

In *De Profundis*, Wilde finds a sort of solution to say this radical deprivation in the figure of a heterodox and duplicitous Christ. Wilde's Christ
significantly speaks both Greek and Aramaic (*DP* 81). In him are associated without merging the languages of classical aesthetics and of a poetics
linked to Romanticism. That Christ's teachings are about art is stated at
the outset of the section where Wilde explains his long-held position on
religion: "while Metaphysics had but little real interest for me, and Morality absolutely none, there was nothing that either Plato or Christ had said
that could not be transferred immediately into the sphere of Art, and there
find its complete fulfillment" (*DP* 71). The specific region of art where
Christ operates is poetry: "Christ's place is indeed with the poets" (*DP*
72). In one passage where Wilde explains in terms pointing to the shift to
poetics that Christ made himself the mouthpiece of the dumb, he delin-
eates a form of mediation and responsibility quite different from that regulating his dialogue with Douglas:

> To the artist, expression is the only mode under which he can conceive life
> at all. To him what is dumb is dead. But to Christ it is not so. With a width
> and wonder of imagination that fills one almost with awe, he took the entire
> world of the inarticulate, the voiceless world of pain, as his kingdom, and
> made of himself its eternal mouthpiece. Those of whom I have spoken,
> who are dumb under oppression and 'whose silence is heard only of God,'
> he chose as his brothers. He sought to become eyes to the blind, ears to
> the deaf, and a cry on the lips of those whose tongue had been tied. His
> desire was to be to the myriads who had found no utterance a very trumpet
> through which they might call to Heaven. (*DP* 77)

This is most emphatically a Christ with a literary bent, the perfect me-
diator to make up for the silence, deafness, and blindness complained
about in the letter of appeal. The beings for whom Christ makes himself
a mouthpiece cannot not be silent; muteness is their defining trait. To say

this silence, which is the silence of death, Wilde's Christ does not speak to or about them, as a partner in dialogue. He has to invent a language enabling them to give speech to their voicelessness, to say not their Greek reasons for silence, but their pain at their exclusion from all discourse. The inarticulate cry that Christ invents can then bring to human ears this "silence . . . heard only of God."[23] For Wilde, Christ's cry is self-abnegating in a strong sense. When "he chose as his brothers" the speechless, he gave up speaking as a subject of discourse addressing other potential subjects. Wilde says this when he opposes Christ to the artist. The former does not express anything· that is, give outward, sensible form to inward thought or emotion. Instead, he makes sensible the pain of being without subjectivity, of being exiled outside the inside/outside distinction that ideas of expressive language assume. Christ can be called a mouthpiece or instrument because his words do not express his inner thoughts so much as translate the pain of inarticulacy into another medium.

Note the difference between the notion of responsibility that was to regulate the ideal letter from Bosie and the one associated with Christ. In the former case, responsibility engaged an autonomous subject possessed of secrets and capable of entering into exchange with other subjects. His responsibility was to render an account of his use of freedom in a candid language with reserves of secrecy. But as trumpet or mouthpiece, Christ has no human interlocutor and only a problematic freedom. Unconcerned with communicating content or accounting for motives and under no pre-existing contractual obligation, his imagination does not respect already established borders between inside and outside, speech and silence, private and public, life and death, but invents a hitherto unrecognized obligation with respect to the other lying outside of exchange. In this sense, his act of speaking can be called "inaugural." Note, however, that Wilde has identified as one characteristic of the inaugural performative that it is not a speech act in the usual sense of the word. Christ doesn't speak for the mute so much as fashion his life into a prosthesis they might use to speak the pain of their silence.[24] Such fashioning entails self-mutilation. In one particularly significant parable that Wilde retells from the Gospels, the prosthesis comes first as "the proper basis of actual life" and the "very keynote of romantic art:"

> That which is the very keynote of romantic art was to him the proper basis
> of actual life. He saw no other basis. And when they brought him one taken
> in the very act of sin and showed him her sentence written in the law and
> asked him what was to be done, he wrote with his finger on the ground as

though he did not hear them, and finally, when they pressed him again and again, looked up and said "Let him of you who has never sinned be the first to throw the stone at her." It was worthwhile living to have said that. (*DP* 83)

Christ, who speaks English here thanks to Wilde's translation of the Greek Testament rather than to the King James Version, is asked what to do in the case of an adulteress. The law sentences adulterers to death by stoning; as she was taken in the act, there can be no doubt of her guilt. Christ does not plead extenuating circumstances or argue for mercy. He does not answer the question of "what was to be done" by an interpretation or explanation of how to apply the text of the law. Instead, he provides two enigmatic responses to the single question. The first is remarkable in stopping discussion. The questioners point to a sentence in the written law that seems applicable and ask what to do: that is, whether and how to apply it. Christ answers by a doing that doesn't distinguish between writing and doing. His translation rewrites the problem of the sentence of the law into a new medium and makes the ground and finger into something quite different than they are for the questioners. To the questioners, action is determined by the will and takes place in a world where there are things evident to the senses like the woman's deed—a *ground*, which is to say a place of stability from which to decide a punishment, gather and launch stones—and bodies, whose fingers let one grasp and hurl them. But Christ treats the ground as though it were a page, the stones as traces thrown down, the finger as inscribing the relation of the body to the ground. In an act that is violent with respect to the law, he reconfigures the relation of body to world. This translates writing into a new arena, generalizing it, and raises the stakes because it requires the judges to consider the categories of their judgment. The equivalent he provides for the text of the law "rhymes" with it as another sort of writing.

The questioners apparently don't get this cryptic response for they ask the same question again and again. The second response, also enigmatic, consists in a translation of the question itself. What was to be done to apply the law is suspended by the law of who is to apply it and who is to recognize the who: "Let him of you who has never sinned be the first to throw the stone at her." We can imagine the listeners stopping nervously to take stock, each examining his conscience to ask whether he is the exceptional one, each covertly examining the others to determine who is to be given the chance to sin by being the first to throw the stone. Now the translation does not consist in seeking an equivalent for a signifier but a synonym for the signified of throwing stones, which is "killing." One word for killing is "casting stones;" another is "sinning." Whoever has never thrown a stone will throw the first stone; whoever has never sinned will commit the first sin. With this translation, Christ tells the woman's judges that each of them is at stake in the question, potentially to be elected to the role of murderer as innocent, potentially exempt from the ritual killing as having already sinned. The identity of each is uncertain, and that uncertainty repeats the uncertainty concerning the ground as stable basis.

Derrida sees what he calls an exorbitant responsibility arising where the dissymmetrical secret brings identity into question. It is the responsibility acknowledged by a self that finds itself interrogated by a question it has raised, by a *ça me regarde*. It is connected not to the will and to action as springing from personal decision, but to vocation and conscience as the recognition of a trembling identity:

> The question of the self: "who am I?" not in the sense of "who am I" but "who is this 'I'" that can say "who"? What is the "I," and what becomes of responsibility once the identity of the "I" trembles *in secret*? (*GD* 92)

Derrida's self-questioning I describes the case before us. Christ translates the woman's silent, off-stage trembling before the law first into the trembling of the ground and the writing finger and then into the trembling of you who must throw or decide who is to throw the first stone. The identities of those who judge her are concerned in the woman's case, and it is to that concern that Christ responds by a parable that—precisely because it sets aside the facts to ask about language—can solicit from its listeners their acknowledgement of a responsibility not defined in terms of the literal text of the law.

For Wilde, "the secret of Jesus" is participation: "whatever happens to another happens to oneself" (*DP* 72), "there is no difference at all between the lives of others and one's own life" (*DP* 76). Christ translates everything that happens to the other into what concerns me as what puts me into question. His extension of this rule of participation to everything makes him the great exception, for whom "there were no laws: there were exceptions merely" (*DP* 83). He is the great individualist, who hears in everything—including the death sentence passed against an adulteress—a *ça me regarde* that implicates its audience and invites inventive translation.

With these several characteristics in mind—Christ the great translator, Christ the great participator, Christ the great exceptionalist—we are in a position to understand what Wilde means when he says Christ is a poet, not an artist, the "precursor of the Romantic movement," and to identify the literary solution he brings to the problem of the absolute silence of prison. In this definition of poetry, language is not a form for representing ideas: It is a system of mute traces that by their indeterminacy testify chiefly to an uncertainty as to identity. Christ invents an interiority linked to the crypts of writing and unsuspected by the phonocentric Greeks with their rational division of things into mind and body, idea and form. Poetics rather than aesthetics is the problem because poetry invents faced with a language that is not representational or expressive but ungrounded at its source.

If Christ is specifically a Romantic, Wilde says, it is because "we can discern in Christ that close unity of personality with perfection which forms the real distinction between classical and romantic Art" (*DP* 71–2). What Christ has done is extend the problem of the cryptic language of poetry, with its indeterminacy, to the personality so that his life expresses that poetic principle: "His entire life also is the most wonderful of poems" (*DP* 73). This brings out an important difference between the letter Wilde wants the apprentice writer to write and Christ's writing. Bosie is to write literally about events in his life and give them an allegorical, secret meaning through the address to Reading Gaol. Those events are not in question, any more than the possibility of his ascribing figurative significance to them. But Christ does not ascribe meaning to his life as a strategy to get across a secret message of concern. He writes because life is already writing. There is no outside to figurative language, no literal language pointing to referents that can be given an allegorical address. Every supposed referent is already taken up in a more general situation of writing. Wilde's Christ runs a heterodox salvage operation. He does not redeem the sinner by reference to a God at the end of history as guarantor of meaning, but by means of new equivalents of linguistic indeterminacy showing that each referential story can be framed by a self-referential story.

The Christ figure, who in every gesture makes the radical ungroundedness of the world the condition for beauty as well as of suffering, thus provides the poetic model Wilde needs to make up for being deprived of tongue, ears, eyes, reason, phallic will, literature, and his identity as an aesthetic artist. Writing is a prosthetic device allowing *poesis*, the reinvention of the "proper basis of life" (*DP* 83). Even without a longer discussion of this Christ that owes more to poetry than to religion, it is possible to disagree with the judgment of Auden that Wildean discourse on Christ is "childish and boring" (*DP* 129). A discourse on "religion" as a godless Confraternity that sets aside morality and metaphysics in favor of poetics and a responsibility emerging where identity is in question is more interesting than such comments admit. We need to think of Christ in Wilde's text as a poet who does without an authoring instance and invents a responsibility exorbitant to Greek rationalism or to the believer's notion that man exists to interpret and apply God's law.

The Christ figure does not only present a redemptive solution, however. A victim of violence and even self-violence, his sayings sweep away the old order and, in imposing a new one, expose the arbitrariness of the law.[25] We will not find this darker side discussed in the section on Christ however, since, as Wilde tells us, "the whole life of Christ, so entirely may Sorrow and Beauty be made one in their meaning and manifestation, is really an idyll" (*DP* 74). Christ makes the terrible seem idyllic, which is as much as to say that he makes the very secret, which is not just a secret of love but also of violence, very secret indeed.[26]

Because Christ's life seems so idyllic, it will be rather in the anecdotes of life with the poet Douglas that Wilde will explore Christ's violence— what we might provisionally equate with his Aramaic rather than his Greek-speaking side. It is with Bosie that is manifested the devastating power of the idyll to work out its logic in human life. Wilde, who has been studying "the four prose-poems" (*DP* 80) of the Gospels with the idea of writing his own life as a dramatic parable, finds in his relations to Bosie the material to stage a conflict between the command to expose the very secret (represented by Bosie) and the effort to preserve it as secret (represented by Wilde).[27] That makes the anecdotes about life with Bosie the place to go to ask about Wilde's response to the twin logics of the very secret as pressing toward publicity and in need of reencryption.

The passage I want to consider comes toward the end of a longish anecdote revealing the lovers' relation in a state of unhealthiness that pop psychology would call "co-dependency." Wilde details a quarrel that reads like a choreographed action and reaction between Baudelaire's victim and executioner, cheek and slap, as recounted by the long-suffering cheek. Bosie has passed on his influenza to Wilde; bored with playing nursemaid, the former breaks various promises to cheer the sick man, and instead goes out in pursuit of pleasure. When Wilde's note of reproach reaches him, instead of apologizing, he angrily attacks. Bosie later repairs to the sick room, not to beg forgiveness but to renew the battle so vigorously as to persuade Wilde that his life is in danger. When the latter hurries to take refuge with the landlord, Bosie disappears. Although Bosie returns, it is only to pack his bags and pocket some money that Wilde has left lying about. The relation, Wilde concludes, is irrevocably over. Bosie then writes an abusive letter that arrives just in time for the birthday of the recovered Wilde. Wilde's letter of rupture is deferred when he reads a report in the newspapers of the death of Bosie's brother in a mysterious gun accident and Bosie reappears, his suffering effecting a temporary reconciliation.

Violence is a theme in the passage in the spoiled act of murder, the brother's death, the broken covenants, and the threat of ruptured relations. It is also to be found in Bosie's abusive language, his verbal repetition of the threatened act of violence against Wilde and his gesture of sending abuse to another. Wilde calls Bosie's letter a sort of death sentence, "a sin for which there is no pardon." As Bosie does it, writing one's life is killing to the soul. The passage that particularly concerns us occurs toward the end of the anecdote and features Wilde reading Bosie's birthday letter:

> Wednesday was my birthday. Amongst the telegrams and communications on my table was a letter in your handwriting. I opened it with a sense of sadness over me. I knew that the time had gone by when a pretty phrase, an expression of affection, a word of sorrow would make me take you back. But I was entirely deceived. I had underrated you. The letter you sent to me on my birthday was an elaborate repetition of the two scenes, cunningly and carefully set down in black and white! You mocked me with common jests. Your one satisfaction in the whole affair was, you said, that you retired to the Grand Hotel, and entered your luncheon to my account before you left for town. You congratulated me on my prudence in leaving my sick-bed, on my sudden flight downstairs. *"It was an ugly moment for you,"* you said, *"uglier than you imagine."* Ah! I felt it but too well. What it had really meant I did not know: whether you had with you the pistol you had bought to try and frighten your father with, and that, thinking it to be unloaded, you had once fired off in a public restaurant in my company: whether your hand was moving towards a common dinner-knife that by chance was lying on the table between us: whether, forgetting in your rage your low stature and inferior strength, you had thought of some specially personal insult, or attack even, as I lay ill there: I could not tell. I do not know to the present moment. All I know is that a feeling of utter horror had come over me, and that I had felt that unless I left the room at once, and got away, you would have done, or tried to do, something that would have been, even to you, a source of lifelong shame. (*DP* 22–3)

The passage takes up the problem of the quarrel between two writers over dramatic authorship, which has framed the longer anecdote. It is earlier established that Douglas has made scene after scene, and now he has written them down, his letter consisting of "an elaborate repetition of the two scenes, set down cunningly and carefully in black and white." Wilde, who has bogged down while working on *The Importance of Being Earnest*, has taken these lodgings in order to "try and finish my play" (*DP* 20), and now the letter remembering Bosie's letter is another scene-writing.

The original quarrel over broken promises thus concerns aesthetic matters in Wilde's text every bit as much as the love relation. It specifically addresses Wilde's declared aesthetic program, laid out tersely in *De Profundis* as the responsibility to find words that are "an absolute expression of my thoughts, and err neither through surplusage nor through being inadequate" (*DP* 105).[28] In this quest for a unity of form and meaning, he states a relation to a Greek-speaking Christ, for whom "Sorrow and Beauty (can) be made one in their meaning and manifestation." An art that seeks to find a form adequate to a meaning is one that can, even in saying a discrepancy, console by deferring the maximum exposure of the gap between meaning and manifestation. It is this program that is under attack by the poet Douglas as reiterator of disjunction. Douglas's letter, which arrives when Wilde is expecting "pretty phrases" and boasts of the threatened murder as "an ugly moment, uglier than you imagine," is a taunting affirmation of excess and inadequacy and seems to confirm at a deep level Wilde's statement that "while you were with me, you were the absolute ruin of my Art" (*DP* 7). Bosie boasts of an excess intention in the unexecuted murder threatened. His movement toward Wilde ("you moved suddenly toward me" [*DP* 21]) enacts the disjunction as an excessive form to which no certain meaning can be attached: "I felt it too well. What it really meant I did not know." The list of the possible modes of intended attack further confirms the hypothesis of inadequacy ("whether you had with you the pistol . . . whether your hand was moving towards a common dinner-knife, whether you had thought of some specially personal insult, or attack even") as does Bosie's proneness toward unfortunate accidents in intentional action ("the pistol you had bought to try and frighten your father with, and that, thinking it to be unloaded, you had once fired off in a public restaurant in my company"). The lack of adequacy of saying to meaning is the linguistic form of the contagious flu that has stalled Wilde's work on a play where "being earnest" is crucial.[29]

The conflict between Wilde's aesthetics, which requires secrecy about the difference between meaning and saying, and Bosie's insistent publicizing of that difference is focused first by Bosie's term for the intended murder—the "ugly moment," which in the *fin-de-siècle* speech of a fop means "dreadful, bad moment." Wilde's retrospective framing of the quarrel as a conflict over scene-writing restores the aesthetic meaning. With this in mind, we can see what the linguistic equivalent of Bosie's violence is. It consists in taking literally an act whose meaning lies suspended between the referential and the figurative. Like Christ's questioners in the parable, Bosie is concerned with deeds and their judgment. Wilde's reframing restores the lost figural dimension to which Bosie's word alerts him and asks the question of who is I in the scene. The power of a single sign to deliver first a literal meaning of murder and then the allegorical meaning of attack on aesthetics to the reflective narrative confirms the rule of finding words that are an "absolute expression of my thoughts" (*DP* 105). Wilde's action makes the gap to which Bosie calls attention appear reparable and its repair the aim of art.

The inadequacy of form to meaning affects semantics alone in the case of "ugly moment." Where it is a matter of semantics, it is always possible to construct a narrative leading from illusion to retrospective understanding. But what happens when disjunction instead affects the relation between the stated meaning of an event and the grammar in which that meaning is expressed? In one section where Wilde is anticipating the lovers' separation, a disjunction appears but this time not between one subject who is blind and another who is not, but within a single speaker, between what he "knew" and what his sentence organization knows for him:

> I knew that the time had gone by when a pretty phrase, an expression of affection, a word of sorrow would make me take you back. But I was entirely deceived. I had underrated you. The letter you sent to me on my birthday was an elaborate repetition of the two scenes, set cunningly and carefully down in black and white!

According to Wilde, Douglas has confirmed the sentence of separation by repeating again the fault that has led to it. The first injury was the injury of the broken promises of love. Now, breaking the larger promise of a conversion narrative expecting repentance for faults, he has followed one injury by another. Wilde's search for the saving figure as a means of keeping the secret and Bosie's compulsion to repeat the same gesture of literalizing and publicizing the gap are ever at odds.

However, by juxtaposition, the lines suggest another reading: Wilde has underrated Bosie in not thinking him capable of devising a new strategy for getting taken back; Bosie has cunningly heaped abuse on abuse as an unexpected means of reawakening love. Armed as he is against repentance, Wilde has no defense at all against further injury, which calls into question the outcome he has predicted. A text like this one does not just mean two irreconcilable things—melancholy and parting; surprise and love's renewal—but does so by way of differing strategies. On the one side, making use of expressive rhetoric, the I piles up evidence for separation; on the other side, the power of grammar is mobilized to say possible reconciliation. Because it is a function of Wilde's prose, we cannot attribute this meaning to Bosie; however, we can call it a "Bosie-effect" insofar as the text seems to deliver a secret without a subject's knowledge, and thus to publicize the lack and surplus associated with Bosie. The lapse indicates a doubleness within the I itself, who is suspended between a being striving for adequacy and one delighting in excess and inadequacy.

Circumstances can be imagined under which a gap between grammar and semantics could emerge that would be too great to bridge and would create a feeling closer to terror. The sublime is not a usual part of the Wildean vocabulary although we will see an example in a minute of a disjunction that has the potential to be read in that direction. But here, the frame Wilde has provided of love on the rocks tames its violence. When grammar says what remains hidden to the speaker, a blow is dealt the sovereign subject by a mechanical side to language. But that blow is partially parried by being read as from Cupid's arrow, with any trembling found in the speaker's discourse put down to love's bewilderment. To render the complexity of modern life, Wilde says the writer has to provide "atmosphere, with its subtlety of nuance, suggestion, of strange perspectives" (*DP* 50), and we can see that atmosphere as the diffuse note of love and longing provided by a gap manifested but not stated between semantics and grammar. We must emphasize that the secret one does not know is not allowed to emerge all at once, in a determinate place, as content. Instead, the instances of difference between the semantics and grammar are allowed to accumulate, providing the material for a possible revision of meaning.

In the case just discussed, the I's discourse is affected by a gap whose meaning remains unstated. In the other case to be considered, the gap again affects the saying of a same speaker, but it now shows up as an explicit theme to devastating effect. At the end of the passage, Wilde quotes Bosie's judgment on him as a failed artist:

> You concluded your letter by saying: "*When you are not on your pedestal you are not interesting. The next time you are ill I will go away at once.*" Ah! What coarseness of fibre does that reveal! What an entire lack of imagination! How callous, how common had the temperament by that time become! "*When you are not on your pedestal you are not interesting. The next time you*

are ill I will go away at once." How often have those words comes back to
me in the wretched solitary cell of the various prisons I have been sent to I
have said them to myself over and over again, and seen in them, I hope
unjustly, some of the secret of your strange silence. For you to write this to
me, when the very illness and fever from which I was suffering I had caught
from tending you, was of course revolting in its coarseness and crudity; but
for any human being in the whole world to write thus to another would be
a sin for which there is no pardon, were there any sin for which there is
none. (*DP* 23)

Bosie's judgment as quoted is identificatory. With it, Bosie arrogates to
himself the position of decider and judge as to what is to be done. He
accomplishes this by a literalization that makes the gap between saying
and meaning a theme, first in the theme of the aesthetic distance achieved
from real life by the successful artist set on his pedestal by making meaning
and form correspond, and then in his decision to distance himself whenever the artist fails. In exposing disjunction as theme, Bosie does violence
to the logic of the very secret, which wants further crypts and not their
one-sided, determinate divulgence. We can see the violence partly in the
way that Bosie's literalizing closes off debate and stabilizes the oscillations
of identity. Each figure is identified and given a prescribed set of actions
to perform: Wilde, the author-idol, stands on or falls off his pedestal; and
Bosie, I-the spectator, alternately fascinated and bored, approaches or dis-
tances himself from the idol. In either case, Douglas accepts the authority
of the classical aesthetic model, reproaching Wilde only when he fails to
live up to the ideal. Bosie's literalizing shifts an open-ended question as to
an authority toward a trial scene where authority is assumed, guilt is to be
ascertained in its exercise, and just punishment meted out for any failures.

Perhaps the most interesting thing about what Bosie writes is that it
quickly turns its violence against the self. His judgment exhibits a disjunction, inserting a mechanical, compulsive note into his discourse because it
occurs in the very sentence that condemns such disjunctions. What Douglas means to say is what we have just explained: So long as Wilde makes
form and meaning coincide, Bosie will worship at his altar, which is an
altar entirely compatible with his eudaemism and his cult of the will. But
as saying, Bosie's judgment has the force of a binding legal sentence, far
different from the expression of autonomy intended. The I is less a speaker
than a grammatical category that imposes its laws on all those who make
use of it. When Bosie says "I will go away," he means "I, Bosie, I intend,
I decide." But the auxiliary verb makes the sentence perfectly readable as

a statement of a programmed set of steps that will transpire each and every time the conditions stated are realized, without any reference to human decision or will. Whenever Wilde falls off his pedestal, whenever art fails to make meaning and form coincide, the I will go away as I, as intentional subject. The sentence sentences the I to death, which is to say, to a programmed dependence on a certain ideal of art, through the very statement meant to speak and assert independence. Bosie's statement is not so much a judgment on past events recommending what is to be done as a program setting his death into place, even to its location and time. Where structure commands events, the literal is not what precedes and is made sense of by allegory; rather, events occur as the literalizing of the possibilities of the story structure.[30]

It would be difficult to find a situation the phrase does not make sense of. It is sententious enough to be extended to every human being, each of whom is an I and an Idol, idealizing and idealized, having reposed an ego ideal in a love object and the object so idealized, sacrificing that object to ego and oneself so sacrificed, a semantic and a grammatical subject. Wilde's statement of the same point, which is less blinded about the universality of the situation of the I, says "each man kills the thing he loves." In Bosie's sentences, the grammatical category of I kills the sovereign subject that is the object of its cult. Bosie is a functionary of the egotism of a shifter-centered language; his strange silence is that of one who plays a role in the tragedy of a self-divided I and entirely fails to realize it is his own. His words make a far better description of the mechanical movement of a clock's hands than a subject's decision. The law he writes that sentences him to death is that of blind repetition.[31]

How is Wilde to save this situation, which is to say, to write so as to reencrypt the gap that Bosie has given an unbearable exposure by literalizing it in his letter? For it is to be noticed that Wilde reproaches Bosie with done the unpardonable thing of "writ(ing) thus to another human being." So far, Wilde's aesthetics have been equal to his task. He has been able to keep the destructiveness of language secret while yet harnessing its power. But how is Wilde to save a Bosie, including even the Bosie in himself, who, whenever he means I—I, the freedom and particularity of each one— says not-I—not-I, the condemnation of each to a same unquestioning obedience to the law of egotism—as a prisoner living "according to the inflexible laws of an iron formula" (*DP* 46)? What is the artist to do now that art itself stands indicted, its idealizing of the sovereign subject critical to the mechanism and its crypts revealed not a reserves of meaning for the future but as markers of self-murder?

Christ's actions in the parable of the adulteress provide a template for understanding Wilde's solution. Christ began by acting as if he did not hear his questioners and wrote with his finger in the sand. Wilde does something similar, rereading Bosie's judgment and quoting it twice.[32] The reasons for the importance of his gesture of rereading and rewriting are several: It brings out the repetition of writing as an unconsidered excess in Bosie's letter, to which Wilde gives full exposure in the theme of words returning in memory; it is also an instance of repetition and in a sense "responds" to the theme by acting to repeat; and finally, given Wilde's judgment that sending the sentence to anyone is unpardonable, to resend it twice as he does here is an assumption of the responsibility for that act, an "accept(ance) of everything" (*DP* 75), a "self-realisation" (*DP* 87)—to use the term in the sense Wilde gives it, that is, neither solely a cognition nor an action but a speculative actualization that makes the doer the stake of the action judged. From his response, it is already possible to suggest that while Wilde accepts that one has to submit to the tragedy of I, one doesn't have to submit unprotestingly, without calculation or response. Quoting Bosie's same sentence twice is to realize the duplicity of I in its self-sentencing saying, to coin a new equivalent for the secret and so to extend a chance of survival to the I's project of interiority. Quoting does that because it is itself split—a mere repetition that actualizes the problem of repetition as a rewriting of the same, it is also an acknowledgement of the excess to repetition with which new calculations will have been possible. Given repetition, Wilde asks, what is to be done? What are the chances it allows and in what hypotheses are they to be mobilized? That makes the question not what is to be done when the law commands violence, but rather, what is the status of the law? What can be done with the law itself? With the full exposure of repetition in both its aspects, the irremediable becomes an opportunity to reinvent things.

Following Wilde, we called this gesture of quoting or rewriting a self-realization. It is the nature of a realization that it be problematically act and idea, that it shape circumstances in no longer considering them as finished facts but as elements of a pattern still in formation. If one considers that writing is a content, we read its allegory where we arrive at the same point and fall into sterile repetition; but if it is considered as an opportunity to revise the conditions under which a given content has been produced and a judgment made, then getting access to allegorization is to open onto a fresh set of possibilities. The effect of Wilde's requoting on the plot is to start to open "strange perspectives" and new plot possibilities. The requoting can be thought as a symptom of the rippling shock waves sent through the artist-lover recognizing a Frankenstein of his own creation. Or it may be a representative of the way Bosie's words return to haunt the prisoner and say the truth of Wilde's own tragedy. Or it may be an example of the sin of sameness from which he, born antinomian and made for exceptions (*DP* 60), himself suffering "the paralyzing immobility of a life, every circumstance of which is regulated after an unchangeable pattern" (*DP* 46) wants to save the Bosie in himself. As realization of repetition that participates in the paradoxes of the situation, each single possibility is less interesting than the fact of their proliferation. Requoting is the source of no meaning and of proliferating meaning directions.

Now let's look more closely at what Wilde says in response. He does not try to attenuate things:

> For you to write this to me, when the very illness and fever from which I was suffering I had caught from tending you, was of course revolting in its coarseness and crudity; but for any human being in the whole world to write thus to another would be a sin for which there is no pardon, were there any sin for which there is none. (*DP* 23)

It is the worst, most inhuman, unpardonable sin to have addressed such a sentence to another human being. Christ did not try to save the adulteress by interpreting her meaning or excusing her in some way but accepted the worst-case scenario: There is the law, there the case made out, there the woman's guilt, and there the death sentence to be applied according to law. Wilde does not ask whether Douglas "deserves" the death his sentence delivers. No doubt he does, as much as anyone can be said to deserve it. Wilde presents the sin in its very worst light as the sin of despairing humanity and as his own sin. He delivers over the internal division of an I that must remain through and through, constitutively, the same, which is to say, irresponsible, split between a secret it knows through the Greeks and a very secret that demands to be re-presented in its unknowability:

> People whose desire is solely for self-realization never know where they are going. They can't know. In one sense of the word it is, of course, necessary, as the Greek oracle said, to know oneself. That is the first achievement of knowledge. But to recognize that the soul of a man is unknowable is the ultimate achievement of Wisdom. (*DP* 87)

Wilde goes even further than Bosie, however, in hypothesizing that the situation is hopeless, there where Bosie still places hope in a redeeming authority. No solution can be found to make meaning and form coincide; each new I-saying will repeat and remobilize the disjunction, and the aesthetics devised to repair the gap is part of the problem. It is impossible to catch up with and acknowledge meaningfully the gap between what your words say and mean because the saying can only repeat the disjunction. Hypothesizing that repetition of the same as the unforgivable realizes Bosie's death sentence as Wilde's own. In this sense, Wilde speaks not like the Greek-speaking Christ, who makes the terrible idyllic, but like the Aramaic-speaking Christ, who brings out the fragmentation and self-mutilation to which the idyll condemns us.[33]

But the actualization does not simply realize the impossibility of forgiveness. It also speculates in an exorbitant hypothesis on pardon and the impossibility of the unforgivable. There is no sin, no matter how horrific, that cannot be forgiven, no repetition that is not excepted from the law of the same because each can be rewritten as a parable. Wilde's response is similar to Christ's response when asked what was to be done. Both look to the exception. In Christ's case, the worst sin that requires the exceptional penalty of death allows him to speculate that there might be an exceptional being without sin; in Wilde's case, the worst sin gives a chance to posit that the story of each sinner can be re-read as exceptional. In aggravating Bosie's sin to the worst, Wilde forgives it by rewriting it as the exceptional.

Considered in terms of the secret, Wilde's strategy of realization differs in several important respects from his earlier strategy of making form and meaning coincide by resignification. Reframing muffled the violence of writing while exploiting its energy in figures of suspended meaning. Now, his hypothesis that Bosie's words are impossible to forgive and impossible not to forgive works against the secrecy of the secret, gives the broadest possible exposure to the gap as the theme of unforgivable repetition of the same. All texts are condemned for publicizing the gap, starting with his own. But the same realization rewrites things with a difference, framing the worst by way of an exorbitant, unprovable hypothesis that there may be no sins that cannot be otherwise rewritten, no instance of repetition and exposure that cannot be salvaged as exceptional and thus by opening onto an undetermined future where events are summoned to test the hypothesis. Taking the two sides of the realization together, we can say that Wilde reencrypts the secret by making each act of writing, starting with his own, enigmatic. This is the theme of rewriting the past as Wilde's future task which returns as a leitmotif in the letter: "what lies before me is my past, I have got to make myself look on that with different eyes, to make the world look on it with different eyes, to make God look on it with different eyes" (*DP* 117–8). The hypothesis that there is no such thing as an unforgivable sin is the most violent of hypotheses because although "just" a fiction, it posits that fiction cancels violence. At the same time, because the hypothesis reencrypts the secret and provides for an undisclosed future, it can be said to "redeem" as one token is redeemed by another, responding by a further equivalent of an open question. It does this without reference to a father at the end of history who might provide justice and reconcile actions and intentions at the end.

Wilde's transformation of the logic of Bosie's secret as content into that of the very secret confirms our statement that Wilde's letter from the tomb does not view the two modes of secrecy as opposed. His point is rather that they are mutually dependent, the one the truth of the other, and every decision has had to calculate with both. Bosie's decision is to transform the secret without a content, the undecidable, into a decidable content. This is felt as a violation of the logic of the very secret in favor of knowledge and action, but at the far end, the gap reemerges in the I itself. As for Wilde, his tendency is rather to transform every secret with a content into an undecidable text by realizing his life as a parable. His interest is the open question as a hypothesis generative of future interpretation, hypothesis that gives out onto epistemology without itself being knowable.

How does this relate to Sedgwick's account of the secret? The homosexual secret, insofar as it raises the question of identity as a crisis and calls upon the exorbitant responsibility of *ça me regarde* is a translation of the very secret. But the homosexual secret installs the secret as a closet containing an identity, a given content, and by a literalizing, one-sided translation, transforms the crisis in identity that is self reflexive, mobile, and inclusionary into a stable identity verifiable in terms of knowledge. *De Profundis* suggests that the mobile roles in a self-reflexive text like Baudelaire's "Héautontimorouménos" (the self-punisher) make a better model for the artist because there, the point is not the verification of a stable social pattern or the production of a model, but rather an accounting for the instability in the I itself that is at once condition for and obstacle to the process of identity formation.[34]

However, it is true that the homosexual secret was the specific secret with a content whose outing gave Wilde the opportunity to reinscribe his story as a parable, and as such, to make it the place of crisis, where he had a chance to question his identity and reshape his past. It is, therefore, all the more significant that Wilde should have chosen to recast the knowable secret of homosexuality in recognizably politico-theological terms as the "Confraternity of the fatherless." He and Bosie are exemplary as two brothers traversing a crisis in the very secret as a crisis in authority, with one holding onto the discredited God, a paternal figure against which he revolts, and the other accepting everything, even the loss of filiation in the loss of his first born son (*DP* 75) to rewrite Christ as a bilingual, agnostic, and Romantic poet-brother, a model for living on in an unstable and de-centered universe.[35] From this, we can conclude that for Wilde, the question of who must remain a question. The process of identification is ongoing and does not end with the confession of one identity or another.

It is also to be considered that Wilde's positioning of the secrecy of the secret as among brothers needs to be put in connection with an odd title which he several times in his work affixed to fictional and real-life women: "Sphinx" or "Sphinx without a secret."[36] The absence of sisters from the confraternity and womankind from the scene of the secret, or—to put it another way, the role of a who determined as not possessed of a secret—is worthy of further study. There is a question of evaluation raised by Wilde's characterization of woman with reverberations for what we have said: Is a "Sphinx without a secret" a false enigma, a mere appearance of secrecy, an inside lacking interiority, a closet without a secret, as was the case with Lady Queensberry's letters marked private? Or is it rather an enigma precious in telling the truth of secrecy, which is its openness, in saying that the secret is always realized in the open, in plain sight, if only we had developed the protocols to read it? The "Sphinx without a secret" may be the enigma that stands outside the hiding/revealing that the know-able secret installs, her dispossession a reminder that the very secret is not at home anywhere and does not belong to anyone including a given confraternity that thinks to have appropriated it. Given what we have said about Wilde's decision to put writing right out in the open as key—given, too, Derrida's formulation of the very secret as what is hidden from me but not from the other—it seems that the evaluation of the "Sphinx without a secret" might be critical. The Sphinx, it will be remembered, guards the gateway to the city. Wilde's parable of the fatherless brothers who have to live together in a world from which the discredited God has not quite finished departing may have to be reconsidered in terms of that Sphinx.

Over the course of this chapter and more broadly of the book, I have argued for the need to consider writing, here linked with the very secret, and the exorbitant responsibility associated with it in reading what autobiography has to say about the other. The very secret arises as the postulate of a disjunction, at the worst, as the disarticulation or death of the I. But it is also what allows Wilde to postulate beauty, love, the modulations of inner life and conscience, community, forgiveness, as he seeks to respond in advance for that death, and in doing so, to defer it. The subject's relation to the very secret of writing is often destructive, as is shown in Bosie's carelessness with letters that return to destroy their sender almost at life's beginning. On the positive side, the very secret allows the inventive search for equivalents enabling new calculations with writing's excesses as the place of the subject's survival.

It is finally the drive to keep identification open ended that characterizes the autobiographies we have read here. Writing about the self descends the I prematurely into the crypt; but through the writing of that crypt and its possibilities, it can speak for the project of the survival of subjectivity. At the very beginning of this book, I asked a two-part question: whether autobiography serves to produce identities; and, if so, whether that process is necessarily a process of liberation. Wilde's letter suggests in answer to the first that life-writing, as it is practiced by Bosie—that is, referential fictions rewriting the question of who as the history of an empirical subject—brings death mechanically. However, it also suggests that the same life story can be rewritten as a parable in which the I does not just foreknow its participation in the death scene but calculates with it and produces a text confirming that its past lies ahead, as what is to be written. As for the second part of the over-arching question, *De Profundis* confirms what we saw in earlier chapters; that an open-ended process is open ended in every sense. The most terrible can indeed turn idyllic, sorrow and beauty can indeed become one, but the idyll is also the most terrible, art turned injurious, in mechanically realizing its possibilities in our lives.

In the midst of modern struggles with identity in a globalized world, what makes autobiography so compelling is an indeterminacy that has to be read in its double aspect: as an I's acceptance of a limited responsibility to confess the secrets that it knows, in the name of truth; and, in its unlimited aspect, as the text's potential over and over to confess like Augustine, out of regard for the other, the secrets I do not know. Let's let Wilde sum up here: "Yes," he says, in a sentence that assumes responsibility in its double and divergent aspects for the letter from prison that is *De Profundis*: "autobiography is irresistible."

1. The double principle of verification and verisimilitude, historical truth and fictional consistency was at the center of many works on the question of genre and autobiography in the 1970s and 1980s. Besides a few early highlights—Roy Pascal (*Design and Truth in Autobiography* [Cambridge, MA: Harvard University Press, 1960]) and Georges Gusdorf (especially his early "Conditions et limites de l'autobiographie" in *Formen der Selbstdarstellung* [Berlin: Duncker & Humblot, 1956], 105–23)—never mind later work by such as Philippe Lejeune (*Le Pacte autobiographique* [Paris: Éditions du Seuil, 1975]) and Paul de Man ("Autobiography as De-Facement," in *The Rhetoric of Romanticism* [New York: Columbia University Press, 1984], 67–81)—one should not forget Gérard Genette's famous footnote in "Métonymie chez Proust," in *Figures III* (Paris: Éditions du Seuil, 1972), 50, which by itself spawned a generation.

2. Jean-Jacques Rousseau. *Oeuvres complètes*, vol. I (Paris: Éditions Gallimard, 1959), 1150. All further references to this and the other four volumes of the Pléiade edition will appear in the text. Unless otherwise noted, translations are my own.

3. Gusdorf, "Conditions et limites." In English in *Autobiography: Essays Theoretical and Critical*, ed. J. Olney (Princeton: Princeton University Press, 1980).

4. See Lejeune's famous definition of autobiography as retrospective narrative in *Le Pacte*, 14.

5. Jacques Derrida's "Signature, événement, contexte" in *Marges* (Paris: Éditions de Minuit, 1972), while published before Lejeune's texte, could be read as an extended critique of its premise.

6. de Man, "Autobiography," 70.

7. de Man, "Autobiography," 71.

8. Françoise Lionnet. *Autobiographical Voices: Race, Gender, Self-Portraiture* (Ithaca: Cornell University Press, 1989), 16.

9. The names to be associated with the exploration of autobiography in this direction are too many to count, starting with Michel Foucault's *Moi, Pierre Rivière* (Paris: Éditions Gallimard, 1973) and leading through Gayatri Spivak's important "Can the Subaltern Speak?" in *Marxism and the Interpretation of Culture*, eds. C. Nelson and L. Grossberg (Urbana: University of Illinois Press, 1988) on down to current-day investigations of post-colonial autobiography. Sidonie Smith and Julia Watson have edited a collection of articles, *De/Colonizing the Subject: The Politics of Gender in Women's Autobiography* (Minneapolis: University of Minnesota, 1992), that can serve as a useful introduction. Alice Kaplan's *French Lessons: A Memoir* (Chicago: University of Chicago Press, 1993) provides a notable early example of critical confession.

10. In some cases, the silence denotes a positive hostility. Debra Castillo's otherwise alert article on Latin-American women's autobiography ("Rosarios Castellanos: 'Ashes without a Face,'" in *De/Colonizing*, eds. Smith and Watson, 242–69) believes strongly that all testimony is of experience, which sets autothanatography out of court. She finds John Updike's musing that his autobiography is written in the face of death frankly self-indulgent next to the records of writers who have seen intellectuals disappear to "real" government forces (242–3). In what sense can a death by torture be termed "more real" or "worse" than a death from heart failure or old age? A comparison can be made only by a watching consciousness, which considers the spectacle provided by others' deaths, and compares them from a dramatic perspective. For the one contemplating a coming death, no comparison is possible. It's simply his or her singular, irreplaceable death that is on the way. The testimony as to its coming is the point.

Autothanatography is the bet of Jacques Derrida's "Circonfession," written in response to Geoffrey Bennington's systematizing "Derridabase," (both appearing in *Jacques Derrida* [Paris: Éditions du Seuil, 1991]), where it allows him to consider unprogrammed events and "what I might in the future think or write" (18).

11. For a discussion of the event in this sense, the reader is referred to Paul de Man's "Phenomenality and Materiality in Kant" (in his *Aesthetic Ideology*, ed. A. Warminski [Minneapolis: University of Minnesota Press, 1996]) as well as to his "Anthropomorphism and Trope in the Lyric" (*The Rhetoric of Romanticism* [New York: Columbia University Press, 1984], 239–62) where de Man is concerned with what he calls "*historical* modes of language power" (262).

12. Augustine, *Confessions*, trans. R. S. Pine-Coffin (Middlesex and New York: Penguin, 1961), X, 5.

13. Charles Baudelaire. *Oeuvres complètes*, ed. C. Pichois, vol. I (Paris: Éditions Gallimard, 1976), 699. Hereafter cited in the text.

14. See Jacques Derrida's discussion of the other's language in *Le Monolinguisme de l'autre* (Paris: Galilée, 1996).

15. de Man, "Autobiography," 70.

16. Paul de Man, "Lyric and Modernity," in *Blindness and Insight: Essays in the Rhetoric of Contemporary Criticism*, 2d ed. (Minneapolis: University of Minnesota Press, 1983), 166.

17. See Cynthia Chase's excellent essay on Baudelaire translating Rousseau in *Decomposing Figures: Rhetorical Readings in the Romantic Tradition* (Baltimore: The Johns Hopkins University Press, 1986). See Virginia Swain on Rousseau and Baudelaire in *Grotesque Figures: Baudelaire, Rousseau and the Aesthetics of Modernity* (Baltimore: The Johns Hopkins University Press, 2004). See also Pierre Pachet, *Le Premier venu* (Paris: Éditions Denoël, 1976) and Jean Starobinski's essays on Baudelaire's rewriting of Rousseauian scenes of gift giving, "Sur Rousseau et Baudelaire: Le dédommagement et l'irréparable" in *Le Lieu et la formule: Hommage a Marc Eigeldinger* (Neuchâtel: A la Baconnière, 1978), 47–59 and "Rousseau, Baudelaire, Huysmans (les pains d'épice, le gâteau et l'immonde tartine)" in *Baudelaire, Mallarmé, Valéry, New Essays in Honour of Lloyd Austin*, ed. M. Bowie et al., (Cambridge: Cambridge University Press, 1982), 185–200.

18. Jean Starobinski. *La Transparence et l'obstacle* (Paris: Éditions Gallimard, 1971), 9. *La Relation critique* (Paris: Éditions Gallimard, 1970).

19. Baudelaire and Rousseau were alike in this one thing: Each had an elder brother named François. In almost no other respect was Baudelaire's brother "like" Rousseau's, however, for François Baudelaire was a pillar of the community, a responsible, bourgeois elder brother who helped in the family decision to keep Charles Baudelaire's inheritance in trust so that the spendthrift poet could not touch the capital.

20. In covering François's back, Rousseau is not only defending him, but he is also covering the facelessness that characterizes François in this position, so as to defend us from that back and all that it might presage. An erotic charge is also discernible, particularly in the context of the homosexual episode in the hospice at Turin (*OC* I, 66–9).

21. See Jean-Jacques's discussion of François's pseudonym (*OC* I, 1215). See Geoffrey Bennington's book *Dudding: Des noms de Rousseau* (Paris: Galilée, 1991) for a reading of pseudonyms in Rousseau.

22. In Rousseau's descriptions of pity, the pitying subject is generally at a remove from the object pitied, and incapable of stepping in as he does in the *Confessions*. See, for instance, the *Second Discourse* in which Rousseau cites Mandeville's "pathetic image of a man shut in who watches outside a ferocious animal snatching a child from its mother's breast, crushing its weak limbs with murderous teeth, and tearing the living entrails of the child with its claws. What awful agitation is felt by one witnessing an event in which he bears no personal interest? What anguish does he not suffer at the sight, at not being

able to help either the fainting mother or the dying child?" (*OC* III, 154–5). The proximity of the I to the event and his interest in the scene complicate the story, making it something more and less than an example of pure pity.

23. Jacques Derrida. ". . . '*ce dangereux supplément*,' " in *De la grammatologie* (Paris: Éditions de Minuit, 1967), 203–234.

24. *Coup* is an important word in the early books of the *Confessions*.

25. In the *Confessions*, tears are shed whenever the mother is remembered or spoken about: "Whenever he said to me: 'Jean-Jacques, let's talk about your mother,' I would say to him, 'alright my father, then now we are going to cry,' and my words alone would already draw tears from him" (*OC* I, 7).

26. Emmanuel Levinas. *Alterity and Transcendence*, trans. Michael B. Smith (New York: Columbia University Press, 1999), 23.

27. Jacques Derrida, *Donner la mort* (Paris: Galilée, 1999), 127.

28. See note 3 (*OC* I, 1238).

29. Rousseau does not refer to his unsuccessful attempt to settle the inheritance question in the *Confessions* but does discuss on one occasion his father's financial interest in the trust (*OC* I, 55) and their long wait for news of François (*OC* I, 246). Isaac Rousseau continued to receive the interest from François's share until his death. The transformed relations of rivalry obtaining between Isaac and Jean-Jacques are suggested by the fact that both are equally François's inheritors.

30. "Suzanne Bernard my mother having left her two children, my elder brother François Rousseau and myself, the inheritors of a house near the City Hall, this house was sold upon my mother's death by my father to M. de Pélissari for 1500 écus, under the condition that M. de Pélissari, acting as the trustee of this money until the majority of the children, would pay the interest to my father" (*OC* I, 1214).

31. Rousseau comments in the *Dictionnaire de Botanique* on the development of a system of nomenclature for plants that allows people in more than one locale or time to talk about the same plant. The problem of plant nomenclature before the Bauhin brothers and Linnaeus shows parallels to the situation facing those who might have liked to remember François (*OC* IV, 1203–6).

32. Rousseau evinces the following points in proof of François's death: "so far as the death of my brother is concerned, here are the circumstances that establish its certainty: 1) My brother has been absent for 20 years; while we often received letters and news from him during the first year, he suddenly stopped sending any, and for 19 years we have heard nothing more of him. 2) A common rumor, whose source is a tale told by several people who had come back from Germany and had known my brother, is that he died in Brisgaw. Indeed, his last letter to my father was dated from Fribourg. If things are so

difficult to untangle today, it is easily seen that the causes are 1) the length of time that has passed since then 2) the uncertainty we are in as to the precise place where exactly he died 3) that he may well have changed his name, as it seems to me I have heard said he had done 4) finally, that my brother was not a very important man, and indeed was then very young and inexperienced. He had only to die suddenly, or to have neglected during his malady to inform his family of his situation, or not to have been able to do so—perhaps as a result of the kind of illness, perhaps because he was unable to make himself under-stood—in order for us not to have had and never to be able to have positive knowledge as to its time and place." A footnote then follows: "Add to this that the usage in Catholic countries is to accord funeral honors only to those who are dead in the arms of the Church, and it would then be useless to seek his name (*son non*) in the death registers" (*OC* I, 1215–16). In the imprecise spell-ing of the day, Jean-Jacques has made François's name (*nom*) into a negative (*non*), preceding Lacan.

33. It is worth noting that Jean-Jacques's father recommends the Genevans to his son as a "people of friends and brothers" in the *Lettre à d'Alembert* (*OC* V, 124).

34. In the *Mémoire*, Rousseau speculates that the untouched inheritance is a sign of his brother's having given his fortune to his father and brother. For in the event that François is still living, the fact that he has neglected to take steps to claim his inheritance shows that he has no need of it but has aban-doned it to his brother and his father: ". . . should my brother still be alive, by the most incredible of all fortunes, it is at any rate certain that he is in a situation in which he has no need to claim his rights and can indeed do without them without any pain, since he has neglected to make use of them" (*OC* I, 1216).

35. See Jacques Derrida on the double logic of the supplement articulated around the *plus* of metaphor in "La Mythologie blanche," in *Marges*, op. cit., 261–73.

36. Neil Hertz has suggested to me a further, very revealing instance of Rousseau's taking of responsibility for an exorbitant logic. In the *Second Prom-enade*, after a near death experience and in the midst of a deluge of false reports and premature obituaries, Rousseau receives a visit from a Mme Ormoy, whose name sounds just like *hors-moi*—outside myself—and thus belongs without belonging to the pattern as one in which the expropriating movement of death dominates.

37. See especially Paul de Man, "Kant's Materialism" and "Kant and Schiller," in *Aesthetic Ideology* (Minneapolis: University of Minnesota Press, 1996), 119–62. For readings of what de Man means by "materiality," see *Ma-terial Events: Paul de Man and the Afterlife of Theory*, eds. T. Cohen, B. Cohen, J. H. Miller, and A. Warminski (Minneapolis: University of Minnesota Press,

2001), particularly "As the Poets do it . . ." in the same volume, 3–31, where Warminski is concerned with discrepant logics of the event.

38. Philippe Lejeune. *Signes de vie: le pacte autobiographique 2* (Paris: Éditions du Seuil, 2005).

CHAPTER 1. DEVELOPMENTS IN CHARACTER:
"THE CHILDREN'S PUNISHMENT" AND "THE BROKEN COMB"

1. Paul de Man's description of autobiography by way of figures has made possible its analysis in other terms than the psychological and moral issues raised by a given individual's capacity for self-knowledge and self-deception. De Man shows that the logical tensions of autobiography do not spring from an individual subject's inadequacies but are the objective expression of a linguistic predicament. Because he not only described those tensions with theoretical precision but also pointed out the regular paths along which the understanding moves as it confronts its figurality, he can be said to have made it possible to study autobiography with the rigor of a critical method, cf. especially "Autobiography as De-Facement," in *The Rhetoric of Romanticism* (New York: Columbia University Press, 1984); and "Reading (Proust)" and "Excuses (Confessions)" in *Allegories of Reading* (New Haven: Yale University Press, 1979). That is not to say, however, that autobiographical texts do not reserve surprises. For de Man, the interest of literature, and—it's fair to say—autobiography, is as a "wild card" (*The Resistance to Theory* [Minneapolis: University of Minnesota Press, 1986], 6).

2. Andrzej Warminski. "Introduction" to *Readings in Interpretation: Hölderlin, Hegel, Heidegger* (Minneapolis: University of Minnesota Press, 1987), xxxi.

3. Warminski, op. cit. *Readings in Interpretation*, xxxii.

4. As one example of the mobilization of such a dialectic, we could cite Paul Ricoeur's comments in *Soi-même comme un autre* (Paris: Éditions du Seuil, 1990), which reconcile the notion of authoring a fictional book with the apparently heterogeneous insight of autobiographical texts that we are at best the "coauthors" of our lives. Says Ricoeur, "exchanges between the multiple meanings of the terms 'author' and 'position of author' (*authorship*) contribute to the richness in meaning of the notion of the power to act (*agency*)" (my translation, 191), and can thus be taken to converge in a fruitfully meaningful way. Not necessarily so, we would assume, for Warminski, who would certainly consider Ricoeur to have begged the question of reading by conflating the question of whether I am the author of *My Life* with the question of whether I am the agent of my life.

5. Ricoeur, *Soi-même*, 138. It will be obvious how much the following discussion of narrative owes to Jean Starobinski's analyses of Rousseau: particularly, for the first narrative scheme, to *La Transparence et l'obstacle* (Paris: Éditions Gallimard, 1971); and for the second, to "Le Progrès de l'interprète" in *La Relation critique* (Paris: Éditions Gallimard, 1970), 82–169.

6. Rousseau himself seems to have privileged the two scenes; the first draft of the *Confessions* recounts only those two anecdotes from early childhood. See *OC* I, 1155–8.

7. The *Ébauches* uses the term only once, but also pushes it toward the meaning of reward (for delaying the reception of rewards and punishments): "although it never happened that I did anything with the plan of deserving it" (*OC* I, 1155) [*à dessein de la mériter*].

8. See Gérard Genette, "Discours du récit" in *Figures III* (Paris: Éditions du Seuil, 1972), 72 for a definition.

9. Georges Gusdorf, "Conditions et limites de l'autobiographie" in *Formen der Selbstdarstellung* (Berlin: Duncker & Humblot, 1956), translated as "Conditions and Limits of Autobiography" in *Autobiography: Essays Theoretical and Critical*, ed. J. Olney (Princeton: Princeton University Press, 1980). See also Starobinski, op. cit., *La Relation*, for more explicit formulations of this position as they pertain to Rousseau.

10. Starobinski, *La Transparence*, 18–21.

11. Philippe Lejeune, "Le Peigne cassé," *Poétique*, 25 (1976); see also *Le Pacte autobiographique* (Paris: Éditions du Seuil, 1975), especially 22–6.

12. Lejeune's theory of a repression helps defend Rousseau against the accusation of a mere "womanish" slip in intention. It goes along with a construction of "male" virtue as the power to reveal the truth about the structure of intentionality in general.

13. One of the more apt crystallizations of this structure is Blanchot's brief tale of St. Bonaventure. God gives Bonaventure, who dies in the midst of writing his memoirs, the grace of returning to life in order to finish them. God thus condemns Bonaventure to repeated deaths. He comes back to write the end of his life and then to die again; but in doing so, he leaves the time of his last writing and agony unaccounted for, which necessitates a new return to write the time of writing and death. In the hermeneutical account, a single return would get across the point by revealing the structure of the interpreter's return. But God is more demanding: Bonaventure's responsibility is to write the time of writing as conditioning repeated deaths and survivals. It identifies an unfinished, infinite task for Bonaventure for which a single iteration will not suffice. See Maurice Blanchot's introduction to the French translation of Karl Jasper's *Strindberg et Van Gogh* ("La Folie par excellence" [Paris: Éditions de Minuit, 1953], 13). See also Paul de Man's "Excuses" (in *Allegories of Reading* [New Haven: Yale University Press, 1979]), 290, where the tendency of the confession as a performative to generate a supplementary series of confessions is taken as the source, among other things, of the *Rêveries*.

14. Lejeune, *Le Pacte*, 85.

15. See the introduction to *La Transparence* in which Starobinski asserts that Rousseau confused existence and idea, 9.

16. See *The Question of Jean-Jacques Rousseau*, trans. P. Gay (New York: Columbia University Press, 1954).

17. See Blanchot's review of Starobinski called "Rousseau," in *Le Livre à venir* (Paris: Éditions Gallimard, 1959), 63–74.

18. The question of a linguistic negative that cannot be reduced to the determinate negatives of philosophical texts is the question of reading for Warminski.

19. In eighteenth-century Swiss dialect, according to the Pléiade footnotes (*OC* I, 1243), a *plaque* is a kind of niche made in the wall of a chimney that opens out into a contiguous room. I know of no exact English equivalent.

20. In the *Profession*, inner assent is neither belief nor conviction, but designates an earlier stage in the formation of ideas when persuasion and logic have not yet been differentiated: the stage of examining opinions to decide which to reject as *invraisemblable* and which to investigate as the simplest and most reasonable. See *OC* IV, 569, and Paul de Man, "Allegories of Reading (Profession de foi)" in *Allegories*, 227–8: "The only claim made for the 'inner light' that the mind is able to throw upon its powers is a dubious, unfounded hope for a lesser evil, entirely unable to resolve the condition of uncertainty that engendered the mental activity in the first place."

21. The child might be studying a lesson from the *Méditations*. The rooms represent quite literally the Cartesian distinction between man's soul and body; the interpretative dilemma inherited from the scene of the children's punishment resembles Descartes's reasons for suspending judgment. The main problem of the narrator—the establishing of certainty—also alludes to the *Méditations*. The fiction of the *Malin Génie*, which allows Descartes to suspend his judgment, may here be serving the narrator as proof that the child has an alibi because until the cogito has been founded, it is impossible to state whether the senses or reason is responsible for our ideas, whether the will or a simple nervous mechanism is responsible for our actions. That fiction is extended by Rousseau to include the source of the memory, and finally the source of the *Confessions* in their entirety. See Henri Gouhier, "Ce que le Vicaire doit à Descartes" in *Les Méditations métaphysiques de Jean-Jacques Rousseau* (Paris: Vrin, 1970), 49–83, for a discussion of borrowed themes. That for Rousseau, judgment is always practical, will naturally imply differences from the Cartesian situation.

22. See, for example, Lejeune, "Le Peigne," 14: "The narrator has abandoned his position of adult observer situated next to the Lamberciers and pretending to observe the child. He lets the attitude of the narrator become expressed more and more as it can only be known from the inside, although he still does not provide all the information." My translation.

23. Lejeune, "Le Peigne," 29: "If external appearances condemned him, we have also to believe that internal appearances were at the very least ambiguous. It must indeed be a nightmarish situation to be wrongly accused of having

done what one had avoided doing precisely because one wanted to do it." My translation.

24. Note that the narrator appears to be concluding in this formulation, against the Vicar, that matter can sometimes destroy itself.

25. Rousseau tells us in the preamble that he may occasionally find himself using such fictions. What better ornament to represent both the cause (faulty memory) and effect (empty space in the narrative) than an ornamental comb with half its teeth missing? For the teeth of the comb are a catachresis, and as such, both substitute a figure for the missing proper term and are the proper term. The catachresis expresses very well the uncertainty in Rousseau's phrasing as to whether his faulty memory shows up in the substitution of fictions, like the fiction of the children's punishment, for actual events, or as literal holes (ranging from windows, missing teeth, to narrative sequences of uncertain origin).

26. To Dom Deschamps, September 12, 1761, *Correspondance générale*, ed. T. Dufour (Paris: Armand Colin, 1926), 209.

27. The phrase "sentiment of injustice and violence" has excited no comment. But the odd pairing under the term "sentiment" of a juridico-moral concept like injustice, and a concept of force like violence, is worthy of note. It would be difficult to say whether sentiment is an inner feeling or a sensation here.

28. The principle of constructing a text around an absent term is a familiar one in poetry. For instance, in Mallarmé's sonnet "Salut," the rhymes of the tercets (*m'engage, tangage*) point, as does the poem's subject matter, to the missing term, *langage*.

29. See, for instance, the scene of the stolen apple (*OC* I, 34) where the master's beating of the apprentice and the pen's beating out its author are equated.

30. The analysis owes much to Walter Benjamin's discussion of memory in "On Some Motifs in Baudelaire," and particularly to his description of an incompatibility between the process of laying down traces and functions of consciousness like memory. *Illuminations*, trans. Harry Zohn (New York: Schocken, 1973), 160.

CHAPTER 2. REGARD FOR THE OTHER: EMBARRASSMENT IN THE *QUATRIÈME PROMENADE*

1. See Paul de Man, "Excuses," in *Allegories of Reading* (New Haven: Yale University Press, 1979), 278–301. All further references to this work will appear in the text. The story is quickly told: Rousseau stole a ribbon and, when questioned, blamed the theft on another servant named Marion, to whom he confesses he wanted to give the ribbon. The head of the household could not

discover which party was guilty, and dismissed both with the comment that the guilty party would be punished by conscience. Rousseau claims the episode was at the source of the *Confessions*, and returns to it again in the *Rêveries*. For a recent discussion of the scene, see Jacques Derrida's "The Typewriter Ribbon: Limited Ink (2)" in *Material Events: Paul de Man and the Afterlife of Theory* (Minneapolis: University of Minnesota Press, 2001), 277–360.

2. The prefatory poem to *Les Fleurs du mal*, "Au lecteur," with its discussion of the economic benefits of the shameful act and its accompanying remorse, can be thought of as a reading of Rousseauian shame. In the poet's diagnosis, our preference for *le mal* comes down to a matter of doing more with less, of superior psychic economizing: Doing evil occupies us first in the shameful act and then, reflexively, in the remorse that works us over afterwards. Certain of the prose poems—for instance, "Le Mauvais vitrier" or "Assommons les pauvres"—have inherited the setup of a confession of shame from Rousseau, but again with the added twist given by the ironic understanding that the structure can serve as a mechanism for producing pleasure and profit. Baudelaire's discussion of Rousseau in "Le Poème du haschisch" puts the finger on the pleasures of remorse as part of a Rousseauian strategy of self-divinification. See *OC* I, 433–7.

3. The distinction between guilt and shame is not pertinent for our discussion, where the issue is not the self's guilt with respect to a victim or its shame with respect to the community but its role in the act of confession. In one typical situation outlined by Douglas Cairns, the embarrassed self is found on stage, speaking in public. The concern is with the act rather than the content of the speech: "One can be embarrassed to speak in public, and one's embarrassment may be adequately explained by the public nature of the action; but if one were ashamed to speak in public, people would naturally wish to discover the reason for one's shame, what it was one was ashamed *of*." *Aidos: The Psychology and Ethics of Honour and Shame in Ancient Greek Literature* (Oxford: Clarendon Press, 1993), 7.

4. English translations, sometimes slightly modified, are owed to Charles Butterworth, *The Reveries of the Solitary Walker* (Indianapolis: Hackett Publishing Co., 1992).

5. For Hans-Jost Frey, writing of embarrassment in *Interruptions*, "The embarrassed person . . . has nothing to say and knows only that there would be something to say and that he cannot say it. The embarrassed person has no inner wealth to which he is merely unable to give expression: he dries out where the paralysis of the tongue seizes him and he stutters himself away. There is nothing to expect from him; he does not have the depth of still waters. His failure is without reason, deep or otherwise, his falling silent not the silencing of anything. Embarrassment is flat, an emptiness without depth." Trans. G. Albert (Albany: State University of New York Press, 1996), 72–3.

6. In the *Second Discourse*, for instance, Rousseau sharply criticizes attempts to derive the relations of government to society from those of the father to the family. Not only can we not understand government by looking at the father of the family, but fatherhood itself is inconceivable without society:

> Instead of saying that civil Society derives from Paternal power, it should have been said on the contrary that the latter draws its principal strength from the former: an individual was only recognized as the Father of several when they remained assembled around him. (*OC* III, 182)

7. Peter Szondi, *Poésies et poétiques de la modernité* (Paris: Presses Universitaires de Lille, 1981), 85–91.

8. Cairns, 7.

9. As will become apparent, my difference with de Man is largely one over strategy. De Man himself relies heavily on the passage on the embarrassed lie to explain the metonymy that has Rousseau grabbing for the meaningless signifier Marion; it even models his discussion of anacoluthon and the text as machine. The interest of extending the discussion to consider embarrassment, however, is that it lets us consider the self's relation not to itself but to the other. Instead of the I turning to writing to get around embarrassment for self-presentation, embarrassment would be one of the signs whereby the writer's vocation as implying a regard for the other declares itself.

10. Jean Starobinski, *La Transparence et l'obstacle* (Paris: Éditions Gallimard, 1971), 243.

11. Such statements can be easily misread, as if Rousseau were remarking, either naively or contemptuously, that he wanted only to *appear* to be equitable in his account of others. His point is a more general investigation into what is involved in undertaking an explanation with others, understanding why they might have adopted a course of action he finds unjust.

12. Emmanuel Levinas, *Totalité et infini* (The Hague: Martinus Nijhoff, 1961), 41.

13. J. L. Austin, *Philosophical Papers* (Oxford: Oxford University Press, 1970), 115.

14. See Wendy Brown's "Freedom's Silences," in *Censorship and Silencing*, ed. R. Post (Los Angeles: The Getty Institute, 1998), 313–27, for a nuanced discussion of silence.

15. See Rousseau's fiction of an ideal world, *OC* I, 668–72. The two interlocutors on stage dialogue about an absent Jean-Jacques whose difference and isolation is explainable in terms of the hypothesis.

16. "What is even more fatal is that, instead of keeping silent when I have nothing to say, that is precisely when I have a raging desire to speak, so as to pay off my debt as quickly as possible. I hastily stammer out ill-considered

words [*des paroles sans idées*], and am only too happy when they mean nothing at all." (*OC* I, 115)

17. See, for instance, Emmanuel Levinas, *Autrement qu'être ou au-delà de l'essence* (The Hague: Martinus Nijhoff, 1974), 126.

18. The chief instance Rousseau quotes in the *Confessions* of having blundered is also a scene where he is joining a conversation in mixed company. See *OC* I, 113–17.

19. See the sometimes contradictory attitudes in the *Confessions* (*OC* I, 342–5; 356–8; 415–16).

20. It would not, however, have constituted anything like a tribute to Thérèse given that the joke turns on Rousseau's bachelor status during the time she bore the children.

21. The adjective *benoît* means "good, sweet" but also, "having a sweet appearance, ingratiating." The noun form, *un bénêt*, means a "simpleton, a silly person."

22. See the account of the misnaming provided in the notes to the *Rêveries* (*OC* I, 1791), and in Charles Butterworth's translation, op. cit., 60–1.

CHAPTER 3. THE SHAPE BEFORE THE MIRROR:
AUTOBIOGRAPHY AND THE DANDY IN BAUDELAIRE

1. *Correspondance*, ed. C. Pichois and J. Ziegler, vol. I (Paris: Éditions Gallimard, 1973), 610. All further references to the work will be cited in the text.

2. See the letter to his mother on January 11, 1858: "So then you haven't noticed that there are two pieces that concern you in *Les Fleurs du mal*, or at least that allude to some intimate details of our past life, from that period of widowhood that has left me such singular and sad memories—the one: I have not forgotten our suburban retreat . . . (Neuilly), and the other that follows it: The big-hearted servant of whom you were jealous . . . (Mariette)? I left these pieces without titles and without clear indications because I have a horror of prostituting intimate, family things" (*C* I, 445).

3. Charles Baudelaire. *Oeuvres complètes*, ed. C. Pichois, vol. I, Pléiade (Paris: Éditions Gallimard, 1975), 85. All further references to the two-volume work will be cited in the text. Unless otherwise indicated, translations of Baudelaire are my own.

4. Speaking of one letter to Baudelaire's mother, the authors complain: "The reader of such a letter is put in an awkward situation. Its rational and irrational arguments are so inextricably linked to one another, in it sincerity so easily becomes a mask, that one hesitates between sorrowful astonishment and admiration at a scenario so genially improvised." (Claude Pichois and Jean Ziegler, *Charles Baudelaire* (Paris: Fayard, 1996), 250. My translation.

5. "La Morale du joujou" might be thought the exception, yet it presents itself rather as an allegory in the form of a fairytale than a lived experience and

was destined by Baudelaire to appear in *Reflections on Some of My Contemporaries* as a critical essay.

6. See the letter to his mother, April 1, 1861, where he speaks of "a great book I have been dreaming about for two years: My Heart Laid Bare, where I'll pile up all my fits of anger. Oh! If it ever sees the light of day, the Confessions of J(ean)-J(acques) will seem pale" (*C* II, 141). In another letter to the same correspondent dated June 5, 1863, he is more precise about the form it will take: "Well yes! This book so much dreamt about will be a book of resentments. Certainly my mother and even my step-father will be respected. But while writing my education, the manner in which my ideas and my feelings were formed, I want to make it understood that I feel myself foreign to the world and its cults. I'll turn against *all of France* my real talent for impertinence. I have need of vengeance like a tired man has need of a bath." (*C* II, 305). The chosen mood of anger betrays a thirst for distinction. Instead of love—which tends to insist upon the self's appropriation of the other as the loved object—Baudelaire rings the changes on the self-portrait here; it is a self-portrait achieved by saying not what I am, in myself and in my relation to others, but, through what I think of others, what I am not.

7. In defining autobiography, Philippe Lejeune places narrative at the center of the genre (*Le Pacte autobiographique* [Paris: Éditions du Seuil, 1975]), 14.

8. See *OC* I, 667. There is, however, a dated fragment in *Hygiène*, ". . . today, January 23, 1862, I received a singular warning, I felt pass over me *the wind of imbecility's wing*" (*OC* I, 668) [. . . *aujourd'hui 23 janvier 1862, j'ai subi un singulier avertissement, j'ai senti passer sur moi **le vent de l'aile de l'imbécilité***], which fragment tends to get read as referring to symptoms of the syphilis that rendered Baudelaire speechless in 1866 and killed him in 1867. But the experience referred to is muddy, particularly given the presence of the poetic *topoi* of wind and wing, as if Baudelaire were boasting of having found a strong new inspiration in idiocy.

9. "We will know at last (following some research into the antecedents, of course) whether Fusée XII has an autobiographical value or whether it has to be added to the list of titles and sketches of novels and novellas," op. cit, *Baudelaire*, 18.

10. The actual terms capturing Sartre's attitude here are those of Michel Leiris, in his "Introduction" to J.-P. Sartre, *Baudelaire* (Paris: Éditions Gallimard, 1947). All further references will be cited in the text. Translations are mine.

11. Thus, for instance, Bernard Howells says about *My Heart Laid Bare*: "Self-portrayal is determined from the outset in terms of distinction from, and opposition to, others. It is the pretext for the expression of resentments, for a series of free-ranging acerbic observations and judgments of topical interest

in the personal, literary, social and moral spheres. The term *Journal* is appropriate enough for this reason at least, that it serves to distinguish Baudelaire's intentions from autobiography in the narrow sense and from those techniques of retrospection and anticipation which create the illusion of mastering the subject." In *Baudelaire: Individualism, Dandyism and the Philosophy of History* (Oxford: European Humanities Research Centre, 1996), 70. See also Didier Blonde's *Baudelaire en passant* (Paris: Éditions Gallimard, 2003) and André Hirt's *Il faut être absolument lyrique: une constellation de Baudelaire* (Paris: Éditions Kimé, 2000).

12. Georges Bataille, "Baudelaire," in *La Littérature et le mal* (Paris: Éditions Gallimard, 1957), 37–68. All further references will be cited in the text. Translations are mine.

13. There exists a large number of critical works on the Dandy. Besides Howells, Hirt, Sartre, and Bataille, the following works have been particularly helpful in the formulation of the problem in this essay: Roland Barthes ("Le Dandysme et la mode," in Émilien Carassus, *Le Mythe du dandy* [Paris: Armand Colin, 1971]), Benjamin Fondane (*Baudelaire et l'expérience du gouffre* [Paris: Éditions Complexe, 1994]), Michel Foucault ("Usage des plaisirs et techniques de soi" in *Dits et Écrits: 1954–1988*, vol. IV [Paris: Éditions Gallimard, 1994] 539–561), and Michel Lemaire (*Le Dandysme de Baudelaire à Mallarmé* [Paris: Klincksieck, 1978]).

14. As cited in Howells, op. cit., 33.

15. This point is borne out a little later in the *Salon* by a passage in which Baudelaire suggests that the adoption of the principle of individualism has led to the decline of art, in particular of Romantic art, and notes the early signs of a new tradition (*OC* II, 492–93).

16. For reasons that will become obvious over the course of this book, this is a central point of disagreement with Sartre. My claim is that poetry as Baudelaire practices it, responds beyond the notion of the responsible subject answering for an act, and engages a responsibility of an unlimited sort.

17. To Sartre, the ideal poet is better represented by Arthur Rimbaud (*Baudelaire* 146–7), or even by George Sand, Victor Hugo, or Pierre Leroux (*Baudelaire* 124), all of whom are engaged artists with new ideas about social forms to propagate.

18. In this statement about death, Sartre suggests that there is a parallel between the subject's attempt to understand itself as object, and its attempt to anticipate its death. It can be wondered whether those two attempts would indeed be parallel from a Hegelian perspective because the problem posed for dialectic by a consciousness that confronts its own death (in lieu of that of a slave consciousness) ultimately allows the question of a negation that is not determinate to be raised, which the subject considering itself as object does not do. Sartre's dialectic gets a certain slipperiness from this parallel.

19. Barbey d'Aurevilly, *Du Dandysme et de Georges Brummell* (Paris: Plein Chant, 1989), 99; Baudelaire pays tribute to Barbey's text as early as the *1846 Salon* (*OC* II, 494). The Dandy's work is with signs for Barbey, as is evident from the untranslatable "joke" that seems to motivate the style. *Râper* is a term used in woodworking and cooking, where it means "to grate or scrape." Only by extension does it come to designate clothing as an adjective and to mean "thread-bare." The Dandies have revealed the old metaphor at the source of the term as applied to clothing, and have furthermore provided a good metaphor for the work of metaphor itself as a wearing away of linguistic functionality by their scraping of the fabric until the suit almost ceases to serve.

20. For Foucault, the Dandy's job is the reevaluation of given values: "To be modern is not to accept oneself as one is in the flux of the passing moment; it is to make of oneself the object of a complex and difficult elaboration: what Baudelaire calls, in the vocabulary of the time, 'dandyism.'" op. cit., "Usage des plaisirs," 570.

21. Translations from *Le Peintre de la vie moderne* are by Jonathan Mayne, in *The Painter of Modern Life and Other Essays* (London: Phaidon Press, 1964), 22–3. I have occasionally modified them slightly.

22. In *A Concise History of Greece* (Cambridge: Cambridge University Press, 1992), 27, Richard Clogg says:

> Perhaps most important of all, during the last quarter of the eighteenth century, the subventions of merchants enabled young Greeks to study in the universities of western Europe and, in particular, those of the German states. Here they came into contact not only with the heady ideas of the Enlightenment, of the French Revolution and of romantic nationalism, but they were made aware of the extraordinary hold which the language and civilization of ancient Greece had over the minds of their educated European contemporaries.

23. Otho's move was doubly astute: for if, on the one side, "Otto" would have signaled European rule in Greece, through an accidental effect of the signifier, it was also have reminded of the earlier oppressor—the Ottoman Empire.

24. Honoré de Balzac, *Traité de la vie élégante* (Clermont-Ferrand: Presses Universitaires Blaise Pascal, 2000), 83.

25. Françoise Coblence reminds us that one etymology of "dandy" traces it back to "dandin," meaning "fool, simpleton, shifting from foot to foot" (*sot, niais, se balançant d'une jambe sur l'autre*). *Le Dandysme: Obligation d'incertitude* (Paris: Presses Universitaires de France, 1988), 14.

26. Mayne, op. cit., *The Painter of Modern Life and Other Essays*, 25.

27. Mayne's illustrations of the work of Constantin Guys feature many human figures depicted from the back, as if to confirm the point that this attitude often chosen by Guys especially interests Baudelaire.

28. The famous Dandy is supposed to have remarked apropos of the King: "I made him what he is, I can easily unmake him." Barbey, *Dandysme*, op. cit., 63 [*Je l'ai fait ce qu'il est, je peux bien le défaire*]. By this remark, George Brummell presumably meant that he had set the model of elegance and *bon ton* to which the other George aspired. But if we are right to see the Dandy's signifying gestures as important for the emerging nationalism of the nineteenth-century, it may be true in another sense.

29. "La Soupe et les nuages" contains a figure of the artist taken from the back. The poet is sitting dreaming of his ideal in the clouds when he awakened by a "muse" who strikes him from behind and, calling him away from his cloud architectures, reminds him of his soup and of his homosexual posture (*sacré bougre*). See on the problem of incorporation in the poem, Joshua Wilner's fine *Feeding on Infinity: Readings in the Romantic Rhetoric of Internalization* (Baltimore: The Johns Hopkins University Press, 2000).

30. See Neil Hertz's discussion of the apotropaic stiffening that parries the castration it fears in "Medusa's Head: Male Hysteria under Political Pressure," in *The End of the Line: Essays on Psychoanalysis and the Sublime* (New York: Columbia University Press, 1985), 161–215. The sudden concentration on the sounded signifier of the whistle as a phenomenal property to language that can make up for the disappeared visible world is another gesture of parrying.

31. The various commentators of the poem do not appear to have noticed that the poem is not about a hero's death, but rather about a "heroic death;" it is a death that requires an extraordinary feat to achieve.

32. See Andrzej Warminski's "Dreadful Reading: Blanchot on Hegel" in *Readings in Interpretation: Hölderlin, Hegel, Heidegger* (Minneapolis: University of Minnesota press, 1987), 183–191, for a discussion of "linguistic death."

33. What makes Fancioulle's acting out of death different from Sartre's idea of Baudelaire attempting to seize himself as object is that it is not a problem of vision but of reading, and thus not one of objects and subjects, but of readers and texts.

34. The double for the Dandy is: the reality of the idea doubled by the phenomenal appearance that represents it. The double nature of the artist is as symbolist who finds forms to represent invisible ideas; and as symbolist who finds synonyms, chosen for sound or rhyming properties, for length of line—in short, for literal and material reasons.

35. The book on literary Dandyism that Baudelaire wanted to write would no doubt have brought forward the relation, particularly in Chateaubriand, the author of an autobiography written from the perspective of death, *Mémoires d'outre tombe*.

36. According to Anne Martin-Fugier *in La Vie élégante ou la formation du Tout-Paris 1815–1848* (Paris: Fayard, 1990), Dandyism is over by 1840. In her

mind, that makes Barbey's treatise on Brummell possibly "an attempt to return to the source that is aimed at regenerating a compromised value" (384–5). From the perspective considered here, however, the point is to note that the figure heading up the cult of regenerating value has become a victim of its own cult. Dandies are "at once priests and victims," says Baudelaire (*OC* II, 711).

37. This is borne out by the fact that, with the exception of one letter, itself ambiguous, (and the previously cited notice in *Fusées*, where Baudelaire is recalling a past precocity), it is not Baudelaire who calls himself Dandy, but always his biographers who do so. In a letter to Sainte-Beuve on February 21, 1859, Baudelaire says that he has chosen to publish a poem with an out-of-favor editor "by a dandyism of heroism" (*C* I, 554) [*par un dandysme d'héroisme*]. The Dandy is a biographer's figure in this case, too.

CHAPTER 4. HOSPITALITY IN AUTOBIOGRAPHY: LEVINAS *CHEZ* DE QUINCEY

1. Thomas De Quincey, *Confessions of an English Opium-Eater* (1856), in De Quincey, *Collected Writings*, ed. D. Masson, 12 vols. (Edinburgh: Adam and Charles Black, 1889), 3:225, 8:165. I have chosen to work with the generally preferred 1821 version because the tendencies I am concerned with are somewhat less obvious in the 1856 version, as if the older De Quincey were bent on obscuring them.

2. Emmanuel Levinas, *Humanisme de l'autre homme* (Paris: Fata Morgana, 1972), 11. Hereafter cited parenthetically in the text. Translations of Levinas, as of all other French texts cited, are mine unless otherwise stated.

3. See Georges Gusdorf's "Conditions and Limits of Autobiography" in *Autobiography: Essays Theoretical and Critical*, ed. J. Olney (Princeton: Princeton University Press, 1980), 28–48. For an early discussion of performativity in autobiography with a chapter on De Quincey, see Elizabeth Bruss, *Autobiographical Acts: The Changing Situation of a Literary Genre* (Baltimore: The Johns Hopkins University Press, 1976). See also Paul de Man's penetrating analysis of Rousseau's excuses in *Allegories of Reading* (New Haven: Yale University Press, 1979), 278–301.

4. Emmanuel Levinas, *Autrement qu'être ou au-delà de l'essence* (Paris: Livre de poche, 2001), 278. Hereafter cited in the text.

5. Levinas, *Humanisme*, 60. See Jacques Derrida, "En ce moment, me voici," in *Psyché* (Paris: Galilée, 1987), 159–202, especially 187, where he identifies the performative as not of the present.

6. From *Blackwood's Edinburgh Magazine* 57 (February 1845): 273. Quoted in J. Hillis Miller's *The Disappearance of God: Five Nineteenth-Century Writers* (Cambridge, MA: Harvard University Press, 1975), 40. For an excellent description of digression in De Quincey, see Miller, 39–49.

7. De Quincey, *Collected Writings*, 9:54.

8. In contradistinction to Rousseau, whose sensibility he spurns, De Quincey spends his time explaining his lack of pathos: "My thoughts on subjects connected with the chief interests of man daily, nay hourly, descend a thousand fathoms 'too deep for tears' . . . the sternness of my habits of thought present an antagonism to the feelings which prompt tears." From the readily available De Quincey, *Confessions of an English Opium-Eater* (1821), ed. G. Lindop (Oxford: Oxford University Press, 1985), 23. Hereafter cited parenthetically in the text.

9. Jean-Jacques Rousseau, *Confessions*, in *Oeuvres complètes*, vol. I (Paris: Éditions Gallimard, 1959), 5.

10. The often-cited passages where De Quincey declines to paint himself into his picture of happiness, or where he has a signal difficulty in persuading money lenders that his face is to be attached to his name, are further examples of a subject in crisis.

11. In this, the 1821 *Confessions* differ from De Quincey's other autobiographical works, including *Suspiria de Profundis* and, more especially, the *Autobiographical Sketches*.

12. Éric Dayre espies an unexpected connection between De Quincey and Maurice Blanchot's *Thomas l'obscur*, with its hero Thomas and its heroine Anne, on a somewhat similar basis. For Dayre, Ann is "an"—a prefix marking privation. See his *Les Proses du temps: Thomas De Quincey et la philosophie kantienne* (Paris: Éditions Honoré Champion, 2000), 426.

13. We should note, too, the importance for De Quincey of the hieroglyph, a writing as estranged from living language as possible. See De Quincey, "The English Mail Coach," in *Collected Writings*, 13, 270–320.

14. The possible is another name in Levinas for experience. See *Alterité et transcendance* (Paris: Fata Morgana, 1995), 44.

15. See Jacques Derrida's *Adieu: A Emmanuel Levinas* (Paris: Galilée, 1997).

16. See Charles Baudelaire, *Le Peintre de la vie moderne*, op. cit., *OC* II, 717.

17. See John Barrell, *The Infection of Thomas De Quincey: A Psychopathology of Imperialism* (New Haven: Yale University Press, 1991). This approach inevitably tends toward the reduction of the work to a document or case study, and places undue importance on the incidents that De Quincey has claimed are the mere pretext for digressions. For Barrell, the narrative is necessarily causal, and the deficiency is in the individual subject De Quincey, not in the structure of the subject itself.

18. See Jacques Derrida, "Violence et métaphysique" in *L'Écriture et la différence* (Paris: Éditions du Seuil, 1967), 139 for a discussion of Levinas's limiting of negativity to a determinate negativity.

19. See the *Autobiographical Sketches*, "My Brother Pink," as also the chapters on Richard, in *Collected Writings*, I.

20. Émile Benveniste, *Vocabulaire des institutions indo-européennes* (Paris: Éditions de Minuit, 1969), 93–4.

21. Levinas also says, "Woman is the condition of the receptive, of the interiority of the House and of habitation" (*TeI* 128).

22. Derrida, *Adieu*, 76.

23. The cottage itself is "in a sequestered part of Merionethshire," in a village "remote from the highroad" (*OE* 14).

24. The passage speaks of the problem in terms of respect: in all other areas, the I is "treated with respect" by the family; here, with the question of the women of the family, it is he who must respect.

25. Jacques Derrida and Anne Fourmantelle, *De l'hospitalité* (Paris: Calmann-Lévy, 1997), 51. All further references will appear in the text.

26. Throughout De Quincey's writings occur passages where he frames language to stand out as mentioned, and thus as an instance of language proffered in pledge. One striking case in the *Confessions* concerns De Quincey's eschewing of a harrowing description "of my malady and my struggles with it" in favor of asking his readers to accept his postulation "that, at the time I began taking opium daily, I could not have done otherwise" (53). In "Sir William Hamilton," the point of one passage is to *mention* a word before *using* it, which gives it the value of a token given in pledge or, as we say, in earnest:

> But now, reader, do not worry me any more with questions or calls for explanation. *When* I do not know, nor *how*, but not the less I feel a mesmeric impression that you have been bothering me with magnetic passes: but for which interruptions, we should have been by this time a long way on our journey. I am now going to begin. You will see a full stop or period a very few inches farther on, lurking immediately under the word earnest on the off side; and, from and after that full stop, you are to consider me as having shaken off all troublesome companions, and as having once for all entered upon business in earnest. (*Complete Writings*, 5:308)

With the second appearance of the word "earnest" and the period that contains it, De Quincey seals his promise to begin. The passage pledges, instead of merely explaining something. His Welshified English, which starts with language as cited, as instance of language, is not a language of commerce but of pledging.

27. The scene is rife with implications for De Quincey's relations with the Wordsworths and with Romanticism. Those differences were much greater than disputes over the apple orchard that De Quincey had uprooted, over his addiction, his marriage to a member of the servant class, and so forth, for they concerned the status Romanticism accorded nature itself. De Quincey exhibits

a number of traits that would allow us to group him with the sort of Modernism linked to Baudelaire rather than with mainstream Romanticism. For treatment of De Quincey and Romanticism, see Thomas McFarland's *Romantic Cruxes: the English Essayists and the Spirit of the Age* (Oxford: Clarendon Press, 1987); and Margaret Russett, *De Quincey's Romanticism: Canonical Minority and the Forms of Transmission* (Cambridge: Cambridge University Press, 1997). V. A. De Luca's *Thomas De Quincey: The Prose of Vision* (Toronto: University of Toronto Press, 1980) sets De Quincey firmly in a Wordsworthian perspective. Alina Clej, however, finds De Quincey to be a modernist in *A Genealogy of the Modern Self: Thomas De Quincey and the Intoxication of Writing* (Stanford: Stanford University Press, 1995).

28. Immanuel Kant, *Perpetual Peace and other Essays on Politics, History and Morals*, trans. T. Humphrey (Cambridge: Hackett, 1983), 118.

29. Not coincidentally, his gift of opium does too. Its effects are to cause space to "[swell] . . . and [be] amplified to an extent of unutterable infinity" and to bring about a "vast expansion of time" (*OE* 68–9). Several works deal with De Quincey's opium use in terms of its effect on his imagination, and thus in terms of its exorbitant side. See M. H. Abrams: *The Milk of Paradise: The Effect of Opium Vision on the Works of De Quincey, Crabbe, Francis Thompson and Coleridge* (Cambridge: Cambridge University Press, 1934); Althea Hayter, *Opium and the Romantic Imagination* (London: Faber, 1968); and, for a view directly concerned with opium as outside the circuit of exchange and thus of conditional hospitality, see Joshua Wilner's *Feeding on Infinity: Readings in the Romantic Rhetoric of Internalization* (Baltimore: The Johns Hopkins University Press, 2000). See also Charles Rzepka's *Sacramental Commodities: Gift, Text and the Sublime in De Quincey* (Amherst, MA: University of Massachusetts Press, 1995).

30. I am understanding what De Quincey calls "casual hospitality" as the equivalent of Benveniste's conditioned and conditional "laws of hospitality" and equating Derrida's "law of absolute hospitality" with De Quincey's "laws of hospitality."

31. Thomas Doubleday, "On the Source of the Picturesque and the Beautiful," *Blackwood's Edinburgh Magazine* 14 (September 1823): 251. The article was mistakenly attributed to De Quincey in an earlier version of this essay. I am grateful to Laure Cinquin for pointing out the error.

32. Doubleday, "On the Source," *Blackwood's*, 251.

33. Doubleday, "On the Source," *Blackwood's*, 253.

34. In the 1856 version, De Quincey fills out the conjecture that the Malay was "on his road to a seaport—viz., Whitehaven, Workington, etc., about forty miles distant," with a footnote commenting learnedly on a "slender current of interchange" between seaports, and on the usual route taken through the Lake Country by the Queen's messenger, circa 1579, none of which details

help us much toward an explanation of the mysterious envoy or De Quincey's identification of him as a Malay (*Complete Writings*, 3:402–3).

35. We may conjecture that events around the time De Quincey wrote the *Confessions* may have contributed to his calling his visitor a "Malay." In 1786, the East India Company acquired Penang Island; in 1795, the British captured Malacca; by 1819, a first British settlement had been established in Singapore; and in 1824, an Anglo-Dutch treaty solidified British presence in the area. The Malay in England on some unknown business is a reverse image of the British, gone on business to Malaysia. Perhaps the guilt or fear of the denizen of an imperializing nation drives the supposition.

Identifying the visitor as phantasmatically Oriental and understanding that, in De Quincey, the Orient is defined as a region where reigns a disorder at once threatening and, in its primeval power, productive, could well lead us to conclude with Barrell that

> [t]he oriental is for De Quincey a name for that very power, that process of endless multiplication whereby the strategy of self-consolidation, of the recuperation or domestication of the other, always involves the simultaneous constitution of a new threat, or a new version of the old, in the space evacuated by the first. The Orient is the place of a malign, a luxuriant or virulent productivity, a breeding-ground of images of the inhuman, or of the no less terrifyingly half-human, which cannot be exterminated except at the cost of exterminating one's self, and which cannot be kept back beyond the various Maginot lines, from the Vosges to the Tigris, that De Quincey attempts to defend against the "horrid enemy from Asia." (Barrell, 19)

Where I would part company with Barrell, however, is on the value to be placed on such conjectures, which he takes to be unproblematic. As shall be shown in a minute, the text is uncertain as to the basis of its representation in experience, so that any conjecture about why De Quincey called his visitor a Malay has first and foremost to be read against the backdrop of that uncertainty, which affects the national experience of imperialism as well as De Quincey's own.

36. The more awkward 1856 edition does not resolve the problem. It reads: "In a cottage kitchen, but not looking so much like *that* as a rustic hall of entrance, being pannelled on the wall with dark wood, that from age and rubbing resembled oak, stood the Malay." De Quincey, *Collected Writings*, 3:403. The fact that the Malay's clothes are "relieved upon the dark panelling" (56) contributes to the impression of a frieze or mural. De Quincey's formulations several times call attention to the fact that a frame provides figures or themes. See *OE* 5, where a scenery is said to "people" a dream, and *OE* 19, where "wall-fruit" refers as much to a London mansion as to fruit.

37. On the opium trade, see the informative study by Virginia Berridge and Griffith Edwards, *Opium and the People: Opiate Use in Nineteenth-Century England* (London: St. Martin's Press, 1981).

38. The original French reads *"Viens-tu du ciel profond, ou sors-tu de l'abîme?"* (Baudelaire, "Hymne à la beauté," in *Oeuvres complètes*, I, 24).

39. Levinas says this about the sincerity of such a speech act: "No Said equals the sincerity of Saying, is adequate to this veracity before the truth, to the veracity of the approach, of proximity, beyond presence. Sincerity is then a Saying without a Said, apparently a 'speaking to say nothing,' a sign that I make to Another of this giving of the sign, simple like 'good day,' but, ipso facto, pure transparency of avowal, recognition of debt" (*AE* 225).

40. The Malay passage might be profitably compared with Rousseau's accusation of Marion, which in Paul de Man's analysis is a radical, unmotivated fiction, characterized by "the absence of any link between utterance and referent" that gets taken up by the context "misinterpreted into a determination." See "Excuses" op. cit., *Allegories*, 292–3. One difference to be accounted for would be Rousseau's excessive acknowledgment of guilt and De Quincey's ironic (?) disavowal of it: "Guilt, therefore, I do not acknowledge" (2).

41. See Derrida, "Violence," op. cit., 149 for a discussion of the Levinasian face as nonfigural.

42. Jacques Derrida comments in *L'Animal que donc je suis* (Paris: Galilée, 2006) that Levinasian ethics does not make room for the animal, 125–6. See also "Violence et métaphysique" in *L'Écriture et la différence* (Paris: Éditions du Seuil, 1967), 139 and passim for an early text in which Derrida notes the limitations that Levinas puts on the other.

CHAPTER 5. EATING WITH THE OTHER IN *LES PARADIS ARTIFICIELS*

1. *Les Paradis artificiels*, (79; *OC* I, 444). I have quoted the English translation provided by Stacy Diamond, sometimes with slight modification (*Artificial Paradises* [New York: Citadel Press, 1996]) and have continued to provide references to the French version from Baudelaire's *Oeuvres complètes* cited throughout. All references will henceforth appear in the text.

For a discussion of Baudelaire's interest in the *Rêveries*, see Virginia Swain's *Grotesque Figures: Baudelaire, Rousseau, and the Aesthetics of Modernity* (Baltimore: The Johns Hopkins University Press, 2004). See also Cynthia Chase's "Paragon, Parergon: Baudelaire translates Rousseau," *Diacritics* 11 (1981); and Jean Starobinski's "From the Solitary Walker to the *Flâneur*: Baudelaire's Caricature of Rousseau," in *Approaches to Teaching Rousseau's 'Confessions' and 'Rêveries of a Solitary Walker,'* eds. J. O'Neal and O. Mostefai (New York: Modern Language Association, 2003), 115–20. See also his "Rousseau, Baudelaire, Huysmans (les pains d'épices, le gateau, et l'immonde tartine)," in *Baudelaire, Mallarmé, Valéry: New Essays In Honour of Lloyd Austin*, ed. M. Bowie et al.

(Cambridge: Cambridge University Press, 1982), 128–41. In one passage in *Artificial Paradises*, Baudelaire lauds De Quincey in terms that apply to Rousseau, as "a somber and solitary walker, plunged into the moving wave of the multitudes" (*AP* 30; *OC* I, 400). Baudelaire places the dreams fugues of the English *Confessions* and the *Suspiria* very squarely under the rubric of hieroglyphic dreams, melancholic in tenor (see, for instance, *AP* 138, 147–8, 154, 158; *OC* I, 497, 505–6, 512, 516), and whose indecipherable character indicates a supernatural force (*AP* 38–9; *OC* I, 408–9).

2. "'Il faut bien manger,' ou le calcul du sujet," in *Cahiers Confrontation*, 20 (winter 1989), 91–114. Translated by P. Connor and A. Ronell as "'Eating Well,' or the Calculation of the Subject: An Interview with Jacques Derrida," in *Who Comes After the Subject?*, eds. E. Cadava, P. Connor, and J.-L. Nancy (New York and London: Routledge, 1991), 115.

3. The three substances Baudelaire discusses in the text will each be associated with a different aesthetic: wine, the great producer of sympathies, is a symbol-maker; hashish, with its introduction of punctual difference and the exception, is ironic in character; opium finds resemblances over the points of a narrative between things characterized by self-difference and is an allegorist. Joshua Wilner has already discussed the function of wine in *Feeding on Infinity: Readings in the Romantic Rhetoric of Internalization* (Baltimore: The Johns Hopkins University Press, 2000), so it will not be a topic for us here.

4. This is how Michel Butor interprets them in a fine reading of the text aiming to explain artistic principles to the readers of Baudelaire's time by way of the analogy of drugs. See "Les Paradis artificiels," in *Essais sur les modernes* (Paris: Éditions de Minuit, 1960), 7–15. Also Claire Lyu's discussion in "'High' Poetics: Baudelaire's *Le Poème du haschisch*," *Modern Language Notes*, 109 (Sept. 1994), 698–740.

5. Baudelaire is a very partial reader who proceeds as a military strategist in a campaign, in any given situation beginning with a decisive separation of allies from enemies. By making him our lens, we give up the chance of doing full justice to Rousseau and De Quincey in this chapter.

6. Any of several sources might have led Baudelaire in this direction. He may have been influenced by the legend of the Old Man of the Mountains, which featured a chief who incited his followers, the assassins, to murder by feeding them hashish. The ensuing fantasies were advertised as a foretaste of the heaven that would be their guaranteed reward. The legend, which traveled to Europe with Marco Polo, was much quoted in nineteenth-century texts on drugs. Perhaps the habits of the group that met at intervals to eat hashish together in the apartment of Boissard de Boisdenier under the eye of the alienist Dr. Moreau de Tours, drew Baudelaire's attention to the ritualized aspect. See J. Moreau's *Du hachisch et de l'aliénation mentale: études psychologiques* (Paris:

Fortin, Masson, 1845), translated as *Hashish and mental illness* by Gordon J. Barnett (New York: Raven Press, 1973). A chapter called "Agape" in Théophile Gautier's tale "Le Club des hashischins," a tale that structures its narrative of a hashish fantasy around an invitation to a dinner party, might also have impressed him. See the notes *Les Paradis* (*OC* I, 1359–60, 1374–75) for Claude Pichois's succinct account of Baudelaire's sources.

7. A few examples: "I was brought back to myself" (*AP* 50; *OC* I, 419); I shall never seek (the hours of my folly) again" (*AP* 53; *OC* I, 421); "I shall never forget the tortures" (*AP* 46; *OC* I, 415).

8. Baudelaire has earlier evoked Rousseau by terming the ideal hashish eater "what the eighteenth century called the 'sensitive man'" (*AP* 62; *OC* I, 429) [*l'homme sensible*].

9. See Voltaire's letter of thanks to Rousseau for sending him the *Second Discourse*. It begins "I have received, sir, your new book against human kind. . . . No one has ever used so much wit to make us so stupid (*bêtes*). One wants to go on four feet when one reads your work . . . come drink with me the milk of our cows and browse on our grass." 30 August, 1755, *Correspondance*, vol. IV, ed. T. Besterman (Paris: Éditions Gallimard, 1978), 539. My translation.

10. For a discussion of the oral phase, see Sigmund Freud, *Three Essays in the Theory of Sexuality* (New York: Harper, 1962), 45–51, 64. Discussing what he calls oral or "cannibalistic pregenital sexual organization," Freud notes that in that phase, "sexual activity has not yet been separated from the ingestion of food," even as he notices the fundamental ambivalence of eating in the oral phase through the pathological form of thumb-sucking, a "sexual activity, detached from the nutritive activity, (that) has substituted for the extraneous object one situated in the subject's own body" (64).

11. Jean Laplanche and J.-B. Pontalis, trans. D. Nicholson-Smith, *The Language of Psychoanalysis* (London: The Hogarth Press and the Institute of Psychoanalysis, 1973), 212.

12. The transformation of the other lost into an object of desire is the story of Maman in a nutshell. Substitute for the dead mother, she is converted into a present object of lust for the young hero. Note, however, that the pretext that Rousseau uses to cause Mme de Warens to expel the piece of meat involves elements resistant to internalization: "I see a hair on it" (*OC* I, 108). Hair is an inorganic, dead thing expelled in the process of incorporation, pushed out through the bodily orifices. To follow this out would require a different sort of analysis of Rousseau than the one we are making in line with Baudelaire.

13. See Jean Starobinski's discussion in "Le Dîner de Turin," *L'Oeil vivant II* (Paris: Éditions Gallimard, 1970), 98–154.

14. See the *Rêveries* where Rousseau claims to have learned how to "nourish (my heart) from its own substance" (*OC* I, 1002).

15. Derrida says something similar: "The moral question is thus not, nor has it ever been: should one eat or not eat, eat this and not that, the living or the nonliving, man or animal, but since *one must* eat in any case and since it is and tastes good to eat, and since there's no other definition of the good [*du bien*], how for goodness sake should one *eat well?*" ("Eating Well" 115) [*bien manger*].

16. Augustine, *Confessions*, trans. R. S. Pine-Coffin (Middlesex and New York: Penguin, 1961), 220.

17. Important implications of the difference between interiorizing memory and the memory of signs are pursued in Paul de Man's "Sign and Symbol in Hegel's Aesthetics," in *Aesthetic Ideology*, ed. A. Warminski (Minneapolis: University of Minnesota Press, 1996), 91–104; Walter Benjamin's "On Some Motifs in Baudelaire," in *Illuminations*, trans. H. Zohn, first Schocken paperback edition (New York: Schocken, 1969), 155–200; and Cynthia Chase's "Getting Versed: Reading Hegel with Baudelaire," in *Decomposing Figures: Rhetorical Readings in the Romantic Tradition* (Baltimore: The Johns Hopkins University Press, 1986), 113–140.

18. "Doesn't that (that is, what I'm doing) remind you of (my forefather) Jean-Jacques?" would be one way to read the line *"cela ne vous fait-il pas vous souvenir de Jean-Jacques,"* making the deictic *cela* refer past the hashish eater's words to Baudelaire's authorial act of supplying them.

19. Readers can verify for themselves on the last page of Rousseau's *Confessions* (*OC* I, 656) that Baudelaire is right to have had some doubts about the literality of his translation.

20. Edgar Allan Poe, *Essays and Reviews* (New York: Library of America, 1984), 1426.

21. For an account of time in Baudelaire, see Jacques Derrida's *Donner le Temps: La Fausse monnaie* (Paris: Galilée, 1991) and Elissa Marder's *Dead Time: Temporal Disorders in the Wake of Modernity (Baudelaire and Flaubert)* (Stanford: Stanford University Press, 2001).

22. Alan Astro, "Allegory of Translation in Baudelaire's *Un Mangeur d'opium,*" *Nineteenth-Century French Studies*, 18, no. 1–2 (Fall-Winter 1989–1990), 165–171.

23. Various suggestions have been made. For some, De Quincey was led by a desire to sell his book to advertise his habit in the modishly exotic, Turkish form. John Barrell has recently claimed that it is an instance of self-inoculation against the fearful Orient, with De Quincey claiming "a recognizably Turkish identity—a kinship qualified, however, and hopefully made safe, by the adjective 'English,'" *The Infection of Thomas De Quincey: A Psychopathology of Imperialism* (New Haven: Yale University Press, 1991), 17.

24. Hunger is not an experience of the action of appetite, signaling the subject's power to dominate the objective world. Instead, it is an example of

the hero's suffering from the burden of his animal condition; or it sets him immediately in the situation of the suppliant outsider, reliant on the kindness of strangers and in need of supplements. His quest is not for objects to satisfy desire but rather for opportunities in which any internalization at all might take place. See, for instance, the time in Wales where, "I subsisted either on blackberries, hips, haws, etc., or on the casual hospitalities which I now and then received, in return for such little services as I had an opportunity of rendering" (*OE* 17).

25. cf. Benjamin's "On Some Motifs in Baudelaire," op. cit. *Illuminations*; Naomi Schor, *Reading in Detail: Aesthetics and the Feminine* (New York: Methuen, 1987); Paul de Man's "Excuses," in *Allegories of Reading* (New Haven: Yale University Press, 1983).

26. Taking in food without full benefit of normal processes is a motif in De Quincey. In "De Quincey's Crazy Body," (*Publications of the Modern Language Association* 114, no. 3 [May 1999], 346–58), Paul Youngquist quotes an early letter in which De Quincey explains to his mother that his school is disastrous to his health partly because of "the short time one has to eat one's dinner in: I have rarely time to push it down, and as to chewing it, that is out of the question" (350).

27. Nicolas Abraham and Maria Torok, *The Shell and the Kernel*, trans. N. Rand (Chicago: University of Chicago Press, 1994). In some cases, I have modified the translations slightly so as to clarify my point. All further references will appear in the text.

28. This discussion casts a new light on the problem of hospitality in De Quincey considered in the last chapter. Conditional hospitality can be linked to incorporation as can Barrell's discussion of De Quincey as exemplary nineteenth-century English imperialist. If the *Confessions* has to be considered in terms of introjection, however, as this chapter claims, then the orientalizing fantasy that props up English national narcissism is being analyzed by De Quincey as such, in the name of absolute hospitality.

29. J. Hillis Miller, *The Disappearance of God: Five Nineteenth-Century Writers* (Cambridge, MA: Harvard University Press, 1975).

30. The natural explanation demystifies her delusion—the sound has a plausible source in the rats. However, that demystification only explains the determinate form in which the absent interlocutors are revealed. It does not affect the larger question of the girl's premonition of *le côté surnaturel de la vie*, her sense of being in commerce with invisible forces. It calls the determinate form a "fantasy" but does not ask about the possibility that the fantasy might be true at another level: that level that Abraham refers to as the level of the conditions permitting language and fantasy.

31. See Torok's discussion of a dream of the feast, where the foods on the table represent objects yet to be introjected (*Shell* 114).

32. In a few places, Baudelaire invokes eating in the sense of incorporation, but that normalcy is misleading. Either eating is the overstuffing Baudelaire associates with consumer economy, with "all of history and mythology put to the service of gluttony" (*OC* I, 318), or it is a process of self-loss involving demystification. Barbara Johnson follows one such debunking in "Le gâteau," where the soul's nobility proves to be "modeled on the fundamental act of ingesting the outside which is constitutive of the repressed body." *Défigurations du langage poétique* (Paris: Flammarion, 1979), 79. My translation.

33. Benjamin, *The Origins of German Tragic Drama*, trans. J. Osborne (London: NLB, 1977), 177–8. All further references will appear in the text.

34. Hence Baudelaire's otherwise incomprehensible tone of triumphant exultation whenever he can give a body over to allegorization, as he does in "Une charogne:" ("Tell the vermin that will eat you with kisses / That I have kept the form and the divine essence / Of my decomposed loves" [*OC* I, 32]); or in "Le mort joyeux:" ("O worms, black, eyeless and earless companions, / Look at the free and joyous dead man coming to you . . . / Travel without remorse through my ruin" (*OC* I, 70).

35. Benjamin, "The Task of the Translator," in *Illuminations*, op. cit., 75.

36. For an account of the genesis and publication of the text, see Claude Pichois's discussion in *Baudelaire* (*OC* I, 1363–7). To Pichois, Baudelaire's translation makes De Quincey's text French: "he cuts, he recomposes, he writes a French book—and a classical one" (*OC* I, 1364). Emphasizing Baudelaire's success at claiming the book for the French republic of letters, Pichois calls the book one of those "great naturalizations" (*OC* I, 1364). Pichois is right to say that there is an adaptation to French taste going on. However, as we shall show, Baudelaire has conceived both his cuts and his elongations in a way that contests this characterization. In the view exposed in this chapter, if Baudelaire must first naturalize De Quincey—make his Englishness French—it is the better to get into French De Quincey's "Asiatic manner" (*OC* I, 1364).

37. Émile Benveniste. *Problèmes de linguistique générale* vol. I (Paris: Éditions Gallimard, 1966), 241. My translation.

38. De Quincey provided continuations in the form of appendices and the 1856 rewriting of the 1821 *Confessions*; as for the appendix that was the *Suspiria*, had De Quincey's death not intervened, says Baudelaire, it "was to have been curiously expanded" (*AP* 159; *OC* I, 517) [*devait s'étendre et s'agrandir singulièrement*].

39. Michèle Staüble-Lipman Wulf has provided a convenient edition of *Un Mangeur* for readers interested in making such a comparison. See her edition, appearing in *Études baudelairiennes*, vols. VI–VII (Neuchâtel: A la Baconnière, 1976).

40. See especially *AP* 79; *OC* I, 444.

41. De Quincey boasts of the English victory at Waterloo in *The English Mail-Coach*.

42. Baudelaire calls the text an amalgam several times, among others in the short introduction he gave in presenting *Les Paradis* to an uncomprehending public in Belgium (*OC* I, 519). Baudelaire states he does not know how much he has introduced of himself into the original, and cannot "recognize the share that comes from me" (*reconnaître la part qui vient de moi*). The claim made here is that it is not simply a matter of mixing the bones of one author with those of another, but of economizing the means so that it can be made to serve incompatible ends.

43. Baudelaire specifically links De Quincey's torments on opium to those of a man who cannot forget about the process of digestion (*AP* 134; *OC* I, 493).

44. The "bodily spasm," summarizes De Quincey's multiple leg movements and his repetitive awakenings: It also provides a figural equivalent for Baudelairian prolepsis.

45. The passage from *Fusées* situates the problem of the end of the world in terms of a radical loss of "vital energy, echo of the first ages" (*OC* I, 665) and relates it to a question that is not only rhetorical but contains a burning moral question having world historical implications. He asks: "What does it matter to me where all those consciences are going?" (*OC* I, 667) [*Que m'importe où vont ces consciences?*]. The question can be read as a reformulation of "*il faut bien manger.*"

46. The *Suspiria de Profundis* makes a modest book in De Quincey's hands, and a shortish chapter in Baudelaire's. For Baudelaire, the *Suspiria* show merely that the *Opium Confessions* require the interpretation constituted of dreams; whereas for De Quincey, the dreams are the payoff, the sublime and prophetic landscapes the *Confessions* announce. See, apropos of making more strenuous cuts in the *Suspiria* to make up for his procedures in the *Confessions*, Baudelaire's letter to Calonne, December 14, 1859: "The only way for us to agree, I think, is through the engagement I make to catch up by the brevity of the *Suspiria*" (*Correspondance* I, op. cit.) 630.

47. See the section called "Le Génie enfant," where Baudelaire states that the importance of anecdotes from an artist's childhood "has never been sufficiently acknowledged" (*AP* 138; *OC* I, 497). "Often, in thinking about works of art—not in their easily grasped material sense nor in the obvious hieroglyphics of their contours nor yet in the evident sense of their subjects, but rather in the soul with which they are endowed, in the atmospheric impressions they render, in the light or the spiritual shade they thrown upon our souls—I have been struck by something like a vision of their author's childhood" (*AP* 138; *OC* I, 497–8).

48. For a discussion of *Les Paradis* as a transitional work between the aesthetics of Baudelaire's verse poetry and that of the prose poems, see Robert Guiette, "Des *Paradis artificiels* aux *Petits poèmes en prose*," in *Études baudelairiennes, Hommage à W. T. Bandy*, vol. III (Neuchâtel: A la Baconnière, 1973), 178–84.

49. "'Il faut bien manger,'" op. cit., 114. My translation.

CHAPTER 6. SECRETS CAN BE MURDER: HOW TO WRITE
THE SECRET IN *DE PROFUNDIS*

1. Oscar Wilde to Alfred Douglas, June 2, 1897, cited in *The Complete Letters of Oscar Wilde*, eds. M. Holland and R. Hart-Davis (London: Fourth Estate, 2000), 602. All further references will appear in the text.

2. D. A. Miller. *The Novel and the Police* (Berkeley and Los Angeles: University of California Press, 1988), 195.

3. Eve Kosovsky Sedgwick's *The Epistemology of the Closet* (Berkeley: University of California Press, 1990) is to some extent a metonym for numerous essays and books that have considered Wilde in the context of Queer Theory and deserve a reading in their own right. The reader is referred, for starters, to Jonathan Dollimore's *Sexual Dissidence: Augustine to Wilde, Freud to Foucault* (Oxford: Oxford University Press, 1991); Christopher Craft's *Another Kind of Love: Male Homosexual Desire in English Discourse, 1850–1920* (Berkeley: University of California Press, 1994); William A. Cohen's *Sex Scandal* (Durham, NC: Duke University Press, 1996); and Jeff Nunokawa's *Tame Passions of Wilde: The Styles of Manageable Desire* (Princeton: Princeton University Press, 2003).

4. See Sedgwick's *Epistemology*, op. cit., 11. In her discussion of the deconstruction of normative cultural definitions, Sedgwick is not optimistic that it leads necessarily to liberation. She quarrels with Barthes on precisely that point in her introductory essay (10–11). All further references will appear in the text.

5. There was at least one shining exception: Richard Ellmann. See his biography of Wilde (*Wilde* [New York: Alfred A. Knopf, 1988]), which remains standard despite some contested facts, as also his assorted articles. In particular, the reader is referred to "The Critic as Artist as Wilde," an introduction to *The Artist as Critic: Critical Writings of Oscar Wilde*, ed. R. Ellmann (New York: Random House, 1969).

6. Michel Foucault's *Histoire de la sexualité: La Volonté de savoir*, vol. I (Paris: Éditions Gallimard, 1976). It is widely recognized that Foucault's discussion of the repressive hypothesis in the first chapters in some respects contradicts the theory of a progressive enlightenment. Sedgwick's suspicion that narratives celebrating modernity are no more liberated is in line with Foucault.

7. On this point, see Oscar Wilde, *The Decay of Lying*, in *The Artist as Critic: Critical Writings of Oscar Wilde*, ed. R. Ellmann (Chicago: University of Chicago Press, 1969).

8. Oscar Wilde, *The Picture of Dorian Gray* (New York: W. W. Norton, 1988), 49. All further references will appear in the text.

9. See also EC 19–22 for a discussion of the use of homosexual panic as a legal defense.

10. See for instance, Paul de Man, in "Roland Barthes and the Limits of Structuralism," in *Romanticism and Contemporary Criticism* (Baltimore: The Johns Hopkins University Press, 1993), especially 171–2.

11. When James calls Wilde "unspeakable" after the opening night of *Lady Windermere's Fan*, he seems indeed to be referring to the closet structure and what he calls the "blue" carnation (see Jeff Nunokawa and Amy Sickels, *Oscar Wilde* [Philadelphia: Chelsea House Publishers, 2005], 63). But the secret of the fictional character Marcher is left indeterminate, and the point is that it remains unspeakable as such for the other: in this case, May Bartram, who witnesses Marcher's life.

12. It is true that Sedgwick speaks of religion, but it is in terms of "kitsch," of a suspect sentimentality that gets incarnated by the male body. Following Auden, she finds the religious side of Wilde arch and painful, and so fails to take up a dissymmetrical secret that is not to be considered along the axis of the visible and epistemology. That secret may indeed, as Derrida states, entail an *"histoire des hommes,"* but it is not necessarily a story of homosexual love. Rather, as Derrida tells it in speaking of Abraham and Isaac, it is a story of murderous fathers and their sons. The address to the brother is through an account of that ruptured relation of filiation. See *Donner la mort* (Paris: Galilée, 1999), 149. I quote from David Wills' translation, *The Gift of Death* (Chicago: University of Chicago Press, 1995). The English version, which was published before the French, does not contain Derrida's brief discussion of the story among men in the first essay or the second essay on Abraham's sacrifice. All further references will be found in the text.

13. Oscar Wilde, *De Profundis* (New York: Modern Library, 2000), 60. All further references will appear in the text. There is some disagreement over whether Wilde's discussions take Christ as Redeemer and rely on a metaphysical system or are rather this-worldly, and are concerned with the redemptions of art. See G. Wilson Knight's "Christ and Wilde," readily available in *Oscar Wilde*, ed. H. Bloom (Philadelphia: Chelsea House, 1985), 35–44; John Albert's "The Christ of Oscar Wilde," in *Critical Essays on Oscar Wilde*, ed. R. Gagnier (New York: Macmillan, 1991), 241–257; Guy Willoughby's *Art and Christhood: the Aesthetics of Oscar Wilde* (Rutherford, NJ: Fairleigh Dickinson University Press, 1993).

14. The story of the letter's writing and reception is interesting. During most of his imprisonment, Wilde was allowed few books; access to writing materials was only for specific—largely legal—purposes. All materials and any writing were taken away for inspection at the end of the day. By the time Wilde was composing *De Profundis*, the more liberal Governor Nelson still required that he turn in all writing at the end of each day, but allowed him to keep writing materials and gave him access to his notes and manuscript on succeeding days. Wilde wanted to send the letter to Robert Ross, later his literary executor, with the idea that the latter would send a copy to Douglas. But Wilde's letter did not pass inspection by the Home Office, which saved it for him to take out of prison when his time was up. See Ellmann's *Wilde*, 510–16.

15. The claim was made in one of the several works of self-justification Douglas later wrote, *The Autobiography of Lord Alfred Douglas* (London: Martin Secker, 1929), 132.

16. Richard Ellmann, preface to *De Profundis*, xiii.

17. For Wilde, as a general rule our lives are not our own: "'Nothing is more rare in any man,' says Emerson, 'than an act of his own.' It is quite true. Most people are other people. Their thoughts are someone else's opinions, their life a mimicry, their passions a quotation" (*DP* 76). Because Christ's acts are those of one who has made exemplary the rule that one's life is not one's own, he is the "supreme Individualist." As Wilde shows at greater length in *The Soul of Man under Socialism*, most are false individualists, led astray by private property to "[confuse] a man with what he possesses." In *The Complete Works of Oscar Wilde*, ed. J. B. Foreman (London: Collins, 1966), 1088. See also, *DP* 75–6.

18. Lady Queensberry wants to engage Wilde "not to ask you so often to dinner, not to give you any money, to 'gradually drop you'," not "to let you know that she was writing to me," "not to send the lawyer's letter to your father warning him to desist" (*DP* 99). In general, she aims at a sort of dehiscence in dialogue, a gradual dropping away of energy that she hopes will culminate in silence. Nunokawa considers the wearing out of desire as part of a Wildean strategy of planned obsolescence for passion that keeps up with similar developments in capitalism. See his excellent *Tame Passions of Wilde*, especially 71–89.

19. The Marquess of Queensberry had a small celebrity as the sponsor of the set of rules of pugilism.

20. One such card left ostentatiously at Wilde's club incited his libel suit against the father, which suit was unsuccessful and landed Wilde in jail.

21. Bosie's father is the "proper representative of Puritanism in its most aggressive and most characteristic form" (*DP* 99), "such was the irony of

things that your father would live to be the hero of a Sunday-school tract: that you would rank with the infant Samuel" (*DP* 44).

22. The text is thus divided between a Platonizing part where dialogue is central and being true to oneself and one's capacities is the center of the meditation, and an idiosyncratic Christianizing part where parable, and what gives "men an extended, a Titan personality" (*DP* 76) is the question.

23. There is a puzzle here. Why would God, who hears the silence of the mute, need Christ to trumpet it to him? Could it be that the trumpet is an ear trumpet, a prosthetic device for getting across to a deaf God that the mute are silent? Or is it to get across God's deafness to humans? The fact that Wilde's God is in need of Christ's prosthetic device is significant of a reticence on Wilde's part as to the transcendent divinity that orients the second part of this chapter.

24. With the prosthetic, we get one key to Wilde's long interest in murder. The murdered always require devices to be heard. According to Genesis, traces of Abel's blood "crieth unto (God) from the ground." The mousetrap play of *Hamlet* is the "most miraculous organ" with which murder, "though it have no tongue, will speak."

25. For instance, if one were to ask about the subjectivity Wilde's Christ—man of exception—has produced by his recommendation, "Let him of you who has never sinned be the first to throw the stone at her," it would be hard to say whether the community of believers was to: come up with protocols to find the right executioner; line up to throw the first stone; give up stoning adulteresses altogether given the impossibility of finding a qualified executioner; eschew the death penalty altogether as a sin. Christ does what has to be done and produces a new saying, and that text is then instrumentalized as it is interpreted. For better or for worse, Wilde's Christ teaches not just that one could alter the past, but indeed, that that is all one can do (*DP* 85).

26. Christ's reencrypting gift is evident even in the sentence just quoted where Wilde describes Christ as the idyllic unity of sorrow and beauty. For the sentence also provides a definition of what an idyll really is: that is, the poetic program that works itself out in all the moments of Christ's life—its charms and betrayals, its "coronation-ceremony of sorrow" and death, the clothes gambled for, "the body swathed in Egyptian linen with costly spices and perfumes" and laid "in a rich man's tomb" (*DP* 74). Such a reading is entirely consistent with Wilde's insistence on Christ's ability to charm, and it certainly makes the claim that sorrow and beauty are one stronger if we have to consider that beauty may not only console for but also cause the violence.

27. Knight notes in "Christ and Wilde" that the parabolic style is key to understanding Wilde's fascination with the figure.

28. The quotation can seem to state an unequivocal fidelity to a Greek aesthetic program, at odds with the drift of our contention that in *De Profundis*, Wilde has extended this program beyond its recognizable limits to become something else. A look at the longer quotation would, however, confirm the point that Wilde makes classical aesthetics exceed itself. There, Wilde congratulates himself in having made the blots, errata, and corrections that would ordinarily be sacrificed for the right word into "an absolute expression of my thought" and to have found a way to express the requirement that language "be tuned, like a violin" (*DP* 105). The notion that one must include an account of the tuning of language in an autobiography says that texts do not express the thoughts of humans so much the thought of the prosthesis. If it can still be thought of as a Greek aesthetics, it is as the Greek of the dismembered Orpheus, whose head plays against the lyre in floating downstream.

29. The point is made partly by way of a shaping pun in which the theory that Wilde exerts "the *influence* of an older over a younger man" (*DP* 102, my emphasis) is pitted against Bosie's virulent *influenza* (*DP* 19).

30. A more light-hearted version of this plot can be found in "Lord Arthur's Crime," where the eponymous hero, a vapid society man, has his fortune told by a seer. The seer, who will turn out to have been a rival for the hand of Lord Arthur's sweetheart, tells him that he is fated to commit a murder, which murder Lord Arthur sets out dutifully to commit so as to be freed of his fate and to marry. When, after various misadventures, he succeeds, it is by chance the spurned rival—found standing on a bridge perhaps contemplating suicide—who falls victim. The story shows with remarkable clarity not only that a story can come back to execute its author as intentional structure and that a hero who decides to sacrifice his soul in the name of ordinary social obligations can bring this about, but also that the story itself can hesitate between a tragedy of the will and fate and a comedy of love and revenge.

31. Wilde defines the Philistine not as one who fails to understand art but the one "who upholds and aids the heavy, cumbrous, blind mechanical forces of Society, and who does not recognize the dynamic force when he meets it either in a man or a movement" (*DP* 92–3). The diagnosis is that Bosie is a creature administering social rules, his egoism a socially transmitted and conventional disease hostile to the dynamism of art.

32. In fact, he refers to it more than twice in the letter. See *DP* 91.

33. For instance, "I ceased to be Lord over myself. I was no longer the Captain of my Soul" (*DP* 58).

34. See the passage where Wilde traces the path that leads from his having sent a letter in the idyllic vein to Douglas by inexorable stages to prison (*DP* 25–6).

35. In one odd but logical formulation, Bosie's father fixation makes the two Queensberrys brothers: "the curious thing to me is that you should have tried to imitate your father in his chief characteristics. I cannot understand why he was to you an exemplar where he should have been a warning, except that whenever there is hatred between two people there is bond or brotherhood of some kind" (*DP* 94).

36. Wilde often addressed his friend Ada Leverson as "Sphinx" and entitled a story "The Sphinx without a Secret; An Etching."

Abraham, Nicolas, with Maria Torok. *L'Écorce et le noyau*. Paris: Aubier-Flammarion, 1978. *The Shell and the Kernel*. Translated by Nicholas Rand. Chicago: University of Chicago Press, 1994.

Abrams, M. H. *The Milk of Paradise: The Effect of Opium Vision on the Works of De Quincey, Crabbe, Francis Thompson and Coleridge*. Cambridge: Cambridge University Press, 1934.

Astro, Alan. "Allegory of Translation in Baudelaire's *Un Mangeur d'opium*." *Nineteenth-Century French Studies*, 18, no. 1–2 (Fall-Winter 1989–1990): 165–71.

Augustine, *Confessions*. Translated by R. S. Pine-Coffin. Middlesex and New York: Penguin, 1961.

Austin, J. L. *Philosophical Papers*. Oxford: Oxford University Press, 1970.

Balzac, Honoré de. *Traité de la vie élégante*. Clermont-Ferrand: Presses Universitaires Blaise Pascal, 2000.

Barbey d'Aurevilly, Jules. *Du Dandysme et de Georges Brummell*. Paris: Plein Chant, 1989.

Barrell, John. *The Infection of Thomas De Quincey: A Psychopathology of Imperialism*. New Haven: Yale University Press, 1991.

Bataille, Georges. *La Littérature et le mal*. Paris: Éditions Gallimard, 1957.

Baudelaire, Charles. *Artificial Paradises*. Translated by Stacy Diamond. New York: Citadel Press, 1996.

———. *Correspondance*. Edited by Claude Pichois and Jean Ziegler. Pléiade edition, 2 vols. Paris: Éditions Gallimard, 1973.

———. *Un Mangeur d'opium*. Edited by Michèle Stäuble-Lipman Wulf. In *Études baudelairiennes*, vols. VI–VII. Neuchâtel: À la Baconnière, 1976.

———. *Oeuvres complètes*. Pléiade edition, 2 vols. Edited by Claude Pichois. Paris: Éditions Gallimard, 1975.

———. *The Painter of Modern Life and Other Essays*. Translated by Jonathan Mayne. London: Phaidon Press, 1964.

Benjamin, Walter. *Illuminations*. Translated by Harry Zohn. New York: Schocken Books, 1973.

———. *The Origins of German Tragic Drama*. Translated by John Osborne. London: NLB, 1977.

Bennington, Geoffrey. *Dudding: Des noms de Rousseau*. Paris: Galilée, 1991.

Benveniste, Émile. *Problèmes de linguistique générale*. 2 vols. Paris: Éditions Gallimard, 1966.

———. *Vocabulaire des institutions indo-européennes*. Paris: Éditions de Minuit, 1969.

Berridge, Virginia and Griffith Edwards. *Opium and the People: Opiate Use in Nineteenth-Century England*. London: St. Martin's Press, 1981.

Blanchot, Maurice. "La Folie par excellence." In *Strindberg et Van Gogh*. By Karl Jaspers. Paris: Éditions de Minuit, 1953.

———. *Le Livre à venir*. Paris: Éditions Gallimard, 1959.

Blonde, Didier. *Baudelaire en passant*. Paris: Éditions Gallimard, 2003.

Bloom, Harold, ed. *Oscar Wilde*. Philadelphia: Chelsea House, 1985.

Brown, Wendy. "Freedom's Silences." In *Censorship and Silencing: Practices of Cultural Regulation*. Edited by Robert Post. Los Angeles: The Getty Institute, 1998: 313–27.

Bruss, Elizabeth. *Autobiographical Acts: The Changing Situation of a Literary Genre*. Baltimore: The Johns Hopkins University Press, 1976.

Butor, Michel. "Les Paradis artificiels." In *Essais sur les modernes*. Paris: Éditions de Minuit, 1960: 7–15.

Cairns, Douglas. *Aidōs: The Psychology and Ethics of Honour and Shame in Ancient Greek Literature*. Oxford: Clarendon Press, 1993.

Carassus, Émilien, ed. *Le Mythe du dandy*. Paris: Presses Universitaires de France, 1988.

Cassirer, Ernst. *The Question of Jean-Jacques Rousseau*. Translated by Peter Gay. New York: Columbia University Press, 1954.

Chase, Cynthia. *Decomposing Figures: Rhetorical Readings in the Romantic Tradition*. Baltimore: The Johns Hopkins University Press, 1986.

Clej, Alina. *A Genealogy of the Modern Self: Thomas De Quincey and the Intoxication of Writing*. Stanford: Stanford University Press, 1995.

Clogg, Richard. *A Concise History of Greece*. Cambridge: Cambridge University Press, 1992.

Coblence, Françoise. *Le Dandysme: Obligation d'incertitude*. Paris: Presses Universitaires de France, 1988.

Cohen, Thomas, et al., eds. *Material Events: Paul de Man and the Afterlife of Theory*. Minneapolis: University of Minnesota Press, 2001.

Cohen, William A. *Sex Scandal*. Durham, NC: Duke University Press, 1996.

Craft, Christopher. *Another Kind of Love: Male Homosexual Desire in English Discourse, 1850–1920*. Berkeley: University of California Press, 1994.

Dayre, Éric. *Les Proses du temps: Thomas De Quincey et la philosophie kantienne*. Paris: Éditions Honoré Champion, 2000.

De Luca, V. A. *Thomas De Quincey: The Prose of Vision*. Toronto: University of Toronto Press, 1980.

de Man, Paul. *Aesthetic Ideology*. Edited by Andrzej Warminski. Minneapolis: University of Minnesota Press, 1996.

———. *Allegories of Reading*. New Haven: Yale University Press, 1983.

———. *Blindness and Insight: Essays in the Rhetoric of Contemporary Criticism*, 2d ed. Minneapolis: University of Minnesota Press, 1983.

———. *The Resistance to Theory*. Minneapolis: University of Minnesota Press, 1986.

———. *The Rhetoric of Romanticism*. New York: Columbia University Press, 1984.

———. *Romanticism and Contemporary Criticism*. Baltimore: The Johns Hopkins University Press, 1993.

De Quincey, Thomas. *Collected Writings*. 12 vols. Edited by David Masson. Edinburgh: Adam and Charles Black, 1889.

———. *Confessions of an English Opium-Eater*. Edited by Grevel Lindop. Oxford: Oxford University Press, 1985.

Derrida, Jacques. *Adieu: À Emmanuel Levinas*. Paris: Galilée, 1997.

———. *L'Animal que donc je suis*. Paris: Galilée, 2006.

———. *La Carte postale: de Socrate à Freud et au-delà*. Paris: Aubier-Flammarion, 1980.

———. *Donner la mort*, Paris: Galilée, 1999. Translated by David Wills as *The Gift of Death*. Chicago: University of Chicago Press, 1995.

———. *Donner le temps: La Fausse monnaie*. Paris: Galilée, 1991.

———. *De la grammatologie*. Paris: Éditions de Minuit, 1967.

———. *L'Écriture et la différence*. Paris: Éditions du Seuil, 1967.

———. "Il faut bien manger, ou le calcul du sujet." *Cahiers Confrontation*, 20 (Winter 1989): 91–114. Translated by Peter Connor and Avital Ronell as " 'Eating Well,' or the Calculation of the Subject: An Interview with Jacques Derrida." In *Who Comes After the Subject?* Edited by Eduardo Cadava, Peter Connor, and Jean-Luc Nancy. New York and London: Routledge, 1991.

———. *Marges*. Paris: Éditions de Minuit, 1972.

———. *Le Monolinguisme de l'autre*. Paris: Galilée, 1996.

Derrida, Jacques, with Geoffrey Bennington. *Jacques Derrida*. Paris: Éditions du Seuil, 1991.

Derrida, Jacques, with Anne Fourmantelle. *De l'hospitalité*. Paris: Calmann-Lévy, 1997.

Dollimore, Jonathan. *Sexual Dissidence: Augustine to Wilde, Freud to Foucault*. Oxford: Oxford University Press, 1991.

Doubleday, Thomas. "On the Source of the Picturesque and the Beautiful." *Blackwood's Edinburgh Magazine* 14 (September 1823): 251–3.

Douglas, Lord Alfred. *The Autobiography of Lord Alfred Douglas*. London: Martin Secker, 1929.

Ellmann, Richard. "The Critic as Artist as Wilde." Introduction to *The Artist as Critic: Critical Writings of Oscar Wilde*. Edited by Richard Ellmann. New York: Random House, 1968.

———. *Wilde*. New York: Alfred A. Knopf, 1988.

Fondane, Benjamin. *Baudelaire et l'expérience du gouffre*. Paris: Éditions Complexe, 1994.

Foucault, Michel. *Dits et Écrits*: 1954–1988, vol. IV. Paris: Éditions Gallimard, 1994.

———. *Histoire de la sexualité: La Volonté de savoir*, vol. I. Paris: Éditions Gallimard, 1976.

———. *Moi, Pierre Rivière*. Paris: Éditions Gallimard, 1973.

Freud, Sigmund. *Three Essays in the Theory of Sexuality*. New York: Harper, 1962.

Frey, Hans-Jost. *Interruptions*. Translated by Georgia Albert. Albany: State University of New York Press, 1996.

Gagnier, Regina, ed. *Critical Essays on Oscar Wilde*. New York: Macmillan, 1991.

Genette, Gérard. *Figures III*. Paris: Éditions du Seuil, 1972.

Gouhier, Henri. *Les Méditations métaphysiques de Jean-Jacques Rousseau*. Paris: Vrin, 1970.

Guiette, Robert. "Des *Paradis artificiels* aux *Petits poèmes en prose*." In *Études baudelairiennes, Hommage à W. T. Bandy*, vol. III. Neuchâtel: À la Baconnière, 1973: 178–84.

Gusdorf, Georges. "Conditions and Limits of Autobiography." Translated by James Olney. In *Autobiography: Essays Theoretical and Critical*. Edited by James Olney. Princeton: Princeton University Press, 1980.

Hayter, Althea. *Opium and the Romantic Imagination*. London: Faber, 1968.

Hertz, Neil. *The End of the Line: Essays on Psychoanalysis and the Sublime*. New York: Columbia University Press, 1985.

Johnson, Barbara. *Défigurations du langage poétique*. Paris: Flammarion, 1979.

Kant, Immanuel. *Perpetual Peace and other Essays on Politics, History, and Morals*. Translated by Ted Humphrey. Cambridge: Hackett, 1983.

Kaplan, Alice. *French Lessons: A Memoir*. Chicago: University of Chicago Press, 1993.

Laplanche, Jean and J. B. Pontalis. *The Language of Psychoanalysis*. Translated by Donald Nicholson-Smith. London: The Hogarth Press and the Institute of Psychoanalysis, 1973.

Lejeune, Philippe. *Le Pacte autobiographique*. Paris: Éditions du Seuil, 1975.

———. "Le Peigne cassé." *Poétique*, 25 (1976): 1–29.

———. *Signes de vie: le pacte autobiographique 2*. Paris: Éditions du Seuil, 2005.

Lemaire, Michel. *Le Dandysme de Baudelaire à Mallarmé*. Paris: Klincksieck, 1978.

Levinas, Emmanuel. *Altérité et transcendance*. Paris: Fata Morgana, 1995. *Alterity and Transcendence*. Translated by Michael B. Smith. New York: Columbia University Press, 1999.

———. *Autrement qu'être ou au-delà de l'essence*. The Hague: Nijhoff, 1974. *Otherwise than Being*. Translated by Alphonso Lingis. Pittsburgh: Duquesne University Press, 1998.

———. *Humanisme de l'autre homme*. Paris: Fata Morgana, 1972. *Humanism of the Other*. Translated by Nidra Poller. Urbana, IL: University of Illinois Press, 2003.

———. *Totalité et infini*. The Hague: Nijhoff, 1961. *Totality and Infinity*. Translated by Alphonso Lingis. Pittsburgh: Duquesne University Press, 1969.

Lionnet, Françoise. *Autobiographical Voices: Race, Gender, Self-Portraiture*. Ithaca, NY: Cornell University Press, 1989.

Lyu, Claire. "'High' Poetics: Baudelaire's *Le Poème du haschisch*." *Modern Language Notes*, 109 (Sept. 1994): 698–740.

McFarland, Thomas. *Romantic Cruxes: the English Essayists and the Spirit of the Age*. Oxford: Clarendon Press, 1987.

Marder, Elissa. *Dead Time: Temporal Disorders in the Wake of Modernity (Baudelaire and Flaubert)*. Stanford: Stanford University Press, 2001.

Martin-Fugier, Anne. *La Vie élégante ou la formation du Tout-Paris 1815–1848*. Paris: Fayard, 1988.

Miller, D. A. *The Novel and the Police*. Berkeley and Los Angeles: University of California Press, 1988.

Miller, J. Hillis. *The Disappearance of God: Five Nineteenth-Century Writers*. Cambridge, MA: Harvard University Press, 1975.

Moreau, J. de Tours. *Du hachisch et de l'aliénation mentale: études psychologiques*. Paris: Fortin, Masson, 1845.

Nunokawa, Jeff. *Tame Passions of Wilde: The Styles of Manageable Desire*. Princeton: Princeton University Press, 2003.

Nunokawa, Jeff, with Amy Sickels. *Oscar Wilde*. Philadelphia: Chelsea House Publishers, 2005.

Pachet, Pierre. *Le Premier venu*. Paris: Éditions Denoël, 1976.

Pascal, Roy. *Design and Truth in Autobiography*. Cambridge, MA: Harvard University Press, 1960.

Pichois, Claude and Jean Ziegler. *Charles Baudelaire*. Paris: Fayard, 1996.

Poe, Edgar Allan. *Essays and Reviews*. Edited by Gary Richard Thompson. New York: Library of America, 1984.

Ricoeur, Paul. *Soi-même comme un autre*. Paris: Éditions du Seuil, 1990.

Rousseau, Jean-Jacques. *Correspondance générale*. vol. VI. Edited by Théophile Dufour. Paris: Armand Colin, 1926.

———. *Oeuvres complètes*. Pléiade edition. Edited by Marcel Raymond and Bernard Gagnebin. 5 vols. Paris: Éditions Gallimard, 1969–1995.

———. *The Reveries of the Solitary Walker*. Translated by Charles Butterworth. Indianapolis: Hackett Publishing Co., 1992.

Russett, Margaret. *De Quincey's Romanticism: Canonical Minority and the Forms of Transmission*. Cambridge: Cambridge University Press, 1997.

Rzepka, Charles. *Sacramental Commodities: Gift, Text and the Sublime in De Quincey*. Amherst: University of Massachusetts Press, 1995.

Sartre, Jean-Paul. *Baudelaire*. Introduction by Michel Leiris. Paris: Éditions Gallimard, 1947.

Schor, Naomi. *Reading in Detail: Aesthetics and the Feminine*. New York: Methuen, 1987.

Sedgwick, Eve Kosovsky. *The Epistemology of the Closet*. Berkeley: University of California Press, 1990.

Smith, Sidonie and Julia Watson, eds. *De/Colonizing the Subject: The Politics of Gender in Women's Autobiography*. Minneapolis: University of Minnesota, 1992.

Spivak, Gayatri. "Can the Subaltern Speak?" In *Marxism and the Interpretation of Culture*. Edited by Cary Nelson and Lawrence Grossberg. Urbana, IL: University of Illinois Press, 1988.

Starobinski, Jean. *La Relation critique*. Paris: Éditions Gallimard, 1970.

———. *La Transparence et l'obstacle*. Paris: Éditions Gallimard, 1971.

———. "Rousseau, Baudelaire, Huysmans (les pains d'épice, le gâteau et l'immonde tartine)." *Baudelaire, Mallarmé, Valéry, New Essays in Honour of Lloyd Austin*. Edited by Malcolm Bowie et al., Cambridge: Cambridge University Press, 1982: 185–200.

———. "Sur Rousseau et Baudelaire: Le dédommagement et l'irréparable." In *Le Lieu et la formule: Hommage à Marc Eigeldinger*. Edited by Yves Bonnefoy. Neuchâtel: À la Baconnière, 1978: 47–59.

Swain, Virginia. *Grotesque Figures: Baudelaire, Rousseau and the Aesthetics of Modernity*. Baltimore: The Johns Hopkins University Press, 2004.

Szondi, Peter. *Poésies et poétiques de la modernité*. Paris: Presses Universitaires de Lille, 1981.

Voltaire, François Marie Arouet. *Correspondance*. vol. IV. Edited by Théodore Besterman. Paris: Éditions Gallimard, 1978.

Warminski, Andrzej. *Readings in Interpretation: Hölderlin, Hegel, Heidegger*. Minneapolis: University of Minnesota Press, 1987.

Wilde, Oscar. *The Complete Works of Oscar Wilde*. Edited by J. B. Foreman. London: Collins, 1966.

———. *The Complete Letters*. Edited by Merlin Holland and Rupert Hart-Davis. London: Fourth Estate, 2000.

———. *De Profundis*. Edited and with an introduction by Richard Ellmann. New York: Modern Library, 2000.

Willoughby, Guy. *Art and Christhood: The Aesthetics of Oscar Wilde*. Rutherford, NJ: Fairleigh Dickinson University Press, 1993.

Wilner, Joshua. *Feeding on Infinity: Readings in the Romantic Rhetoric of Internalization*. Baltimore: The Johns Hopkins University Press, 2000.

Youngquist, Paul. "De Quincey's Crazy Body." *Publications of the Modern Language Association* 114, No. 3 (May 1999): 346–58.